MIKHAIL BAKHTIN AND
BIBLICAL SCHOLARSHIP

THE SOCIETY OF BIBLICAL LITERATURE
SEMEIA STUDIES

Series Editor
Danna Nolan Fewell

Number 38
MIKHAIL BAKHTIN AND
BIBLICAL SCHOLARSHIP
An Introduction

Barbara Green

MIKHAIL BAKHTIN AND BIBLICAL SCHOLARSHIP
An Introduction

Barbara Green

Society of Biblical Literature
Atlanta, Georgia

Mikhail Bakhtin and Biblical Scholarship:
An Introduction

Barbara Green

Library of Congress Cataloging-in-Publication Data

Green, Barbara, 1946–
    Mikhail Bakhtin and biblical scholarship : an introduction / Barbara Green.
        p. cm. — (The Society of Biblical Literature Semeia studies)
    Includes bibliographical references.
    ISBN 0-88414-020-2 (pbk. : alk. Paper)
        1. Bible—Study and teaching. 2. Bakhtin, M. M. (Mikhail Mikhaælovich), 1895–1975. I. Title. II. Semeia studies.

    BS600.2.G74 2000
    220.6'092—dc21   00-036572

08 07 06 05 04 03 02 01 00   5 4 3 2 1

Printed in the United States of America
on acid-free paper

TABLE OF CONTENTS

ABBREVIATIONS

INTRODUCTION

"Bakhtinian method is not modest: it will tell you how to teach, write, live, talk, think."

Caryl Emerson, First Hundred Years

Why Bakhtin?

The birth centennial of Mikhail Mikhailovich Bakhtin (1895–1975) has recently been celebrated, although his works have been known in the West only for the past twenty-five years or so—enough time for some appropriation of his thought by biblical scholars and for some hesitation about its value. As we are frequently reminded, biblical scholars tend to come late to trends in other disciplines, and the utilization of Bakhtin is no exception. And yet, given Bakhtin's patient and fruitful preoccupation with issues that deeply concern biblical scholars, his thought invites investigation.

Why This Book?

The origins of this book and the project behind it reflect well the slow-growing awareness of the potential of Bakhtin for biblical interpretation. Appreciation of the insight of Robert Polzin's volumes on the Deuteronomist (three so far: Polzin 1980, 1989, 1993) nudged me gently but persistently to venture into the study of Bakhtin. Yet it seemed too ancillary, too arcane, risked being another seemingly fruitless foray into the shrubbery of how literature means. But once I started reading not only books about Bakhtin but his own writings, I became increasingly convinced of their value. And though others have preceded me here, I found myself insufficiently guided both to do my own work and to assist students.[1] So my aim here is to present a study that will situate Bakhtin's potential for biblical studies as the century, which has been tumultuous for the field, turns.

---

[1] Three other biblical scholars who offer helpful explanation and analysis of Bakhtin while making use of him include Craig (1993, 1995), Newsom (1992, 1996b), and Pardes (1992 and forthcoming).

In chapter 1, I will summarize Bakhtin's life, stressing relevant parts; chapter 2 will set out his theory in what I hope will be sufficient but not overwhelming detail; in chapter 3 I will perform a particular text from 1 Samuel at some length and without needing to explain the mechanics constantly; and in chapter 4 I will present the work of four scholars working to some extent with Bakhtin in Hebrew Bible texts, commenting on their appropriation. A brief conclusion will end the study.

I am grateful to Robert Polzin for his patient help and encouragement, to David Shepherd of the Bakhtin Centre for his attentive and constructive critique, to the Society of Biblical Literature for assisting with a grant, and to Gregory Glover for his support. I am deeply indebted to Susan Carpenter for generous, helpful, and patient editing. Danna Nolan Fewell provided wonderful help in her role as series editor, as did Leigh Anderson of the Society of Biblical Literature and Bob Buller. Finally, I want to thank the two groups of students who formed Bakhtin Circles at the Graduate Theological Union in the spring semesters of 1998 and 1999. Studying Bakhtin with them, having their assistance with my project and helping them with their work, was the best learning and teaching experience I have had. It is to them that this work is dedicated: Karen Gale, Kendra Haloviak, Tim Robinson, Karen Wacome; Barbara Barkley, Cori Berg, Mark Bosco, Maria Bowen, Cornelia Cyss-Wittenstein, Uriah Kim, Susan Sutton, Jeanne Choy Tate; and Carrie Rehak, who participated inimitably in both.

A characteristic of our era, one very congenial with Bakhtin, is to prefer the particular to the abstract or anonymous. So I will preface my work with an explanation of why I have made a detour toward this eccentric Russian for my own study and teaching, not to suggest my situation as normative but as illustrative. It strikes me that the two most crucial issues currently facing biblical interpreters are those of subjectivity/alterity and representation.

To expand a bit, for I doubt the points need to be defended as significant (though of course they need to be unpacked): How do I myself now read, think about, act upon, and teach biblical texts in relation to the many and varied others who also have a claim on them? And how do I responsibly address the chasm that has developed between the historically representational narrative and its fictive character, given the impacted nature of those two realms (quickly referenced as historical and literary) and the standoff between them?

To put that pair of questions somewhat differently: It is my consistent experience that well-educated, generally sophisticated and faith-seeking individuals and groups (including scholars in other disciplines) often find that the Bible is not very sustaining. Upon reflection, or in a pinch, such readers discover (perhaps secretly and subconsciously, and I believe incorrectly) that they have outrun its capacity to nourish the imagination and the heart as well as the mind. The root of this perception of biblical inadequacy is a presumed naivete of its assertions, not so much now the scientific ones but the moral voices it presents. But does such a concern root exclusively in the text, or is it also a reading problem? How can we learn to approach the Bible with better strategies for understanding it and all else that is referenced there— God, the others, ourselves?[2] It is this cluster of issues that I hope to remediate partially here by situating Bakhtin's thought.

A final point in the matter of particularity: It matters to me tremendously that Bakhtin's aesthetics and ethics are interconvertible, that is, that his insights into literature are interwoven with his way of relating to others—friends or opponents.[3] I will offer some instances of the knit between theory and practice when summarizing Bakhtin's life but offer a hunch preliminarily. His primary biographers claim of Bakhtin that throughout his eighty years, which witnessed every major calamity of the Soviet regimes, he survived in no small part because he never met an interlocutor with whom he could not deal, presumably due to his capacity to listen respectfully and to avoid blaming others for choosing differently from himself (Clark and Holquist 1984, 254).

Another pair of scholars who write extensively on him point out that Bakhtin's *modus operandi*—writing and living—was not merely to confront the negative aggressively but to offer alternatives to it, to acknowledge some outsider angle while working to develop an implicated committed position (Emerson 1996, 109; cf.

---

[2] An excellent consideration of (mis)uses of biblical studies for ethics is presented by Cartwright. Newsom asserts: "I want to suggest that part of the problem is that the type of discourse which is natural to the theologian and which has been imported into biblical theology is not adequate for engaging the biblical text" (1996b, 291).

[3] For a distinct though related discussion of the question of the self-implication of a scholar and her work, see Schneiders (1998, 7–11).

Morson 1995, 51). Bakhtin gives every evidence of not only maintaining belief in God throughout the decades in which he lived—hostile though those were to the practice of religion—but in fact embedding the God-human relationship foundationally in his thought. Scholars, to be sure, disagree about the particulars of Bakhtin's faith, but few deny that it is central to him, however it worked and however little it may matter to some.[4] So Bakhtin is good company in which to explore issues involving self and others, cognition and value, ethics and aesthetics. He also insists upon the radical historicality and social nature of language and discourse—granted, not in ways sufficiently grounded for all of our contemporaries, but at least to some considerable extent. As a recovering formalist, I appreciate the corrective of his commitment to history. But he is at the same time a wonderful reader of texts, many texts, though of course primarily Russian novels, Dostoevsky in pride of place.

Finally, Bakhtin remained creatively optimistic about living and learning, a point that emerges repeatedly in the bits of information available about his life. In a characterization that recalls Mohandas Gandhi—as indeed much of Bakhtin's respect for the dialogic recalls Gandhian nonviolence—Emerson notes, "To live in a 'state of promise,' where we expect something productive of the world but are not determined by that product, might be said to sum up Bakhtin's vision of a healthy literary consciousness and healthy self" (1997, 16).

Some Caveats

Before adding flesh to those bare bones, some caveats are called for. In addition to the admonition to neophytes that Bakhtin is already something between a classic and a cliché (Emerson 1997, 3), a rather curmudgeonly expert chides those who claim Bakhtin as messiah.[5] Gary Saul Morson's main complaint is that ignorant enthusiasts make Bakhtin serve their own purposes in

---

[4] An expert like Emerson seems dubious about the centrality of religion for Bakhtin when she writes in 1990, but more convinced by the time she recommends Mihailovic's work in her centennial retrospective (1996, 168).

[5] Morson (1991) is a good example of a critique he makes frequently. Hirschkop (1989, 19) also warns about the dangers of misusing the spacious Bakhtinian thought.

violation of his positions patently to the contrary. So Bakhtin, Morson laments, is claimed as patron saint of structuralists, formalists, Marxists, New Critics, political activists, postmodernists, and deconstructionists, in each case not only inappropriately but grotesquely. What Morson demonstrates, besides his main point, is that the vastness and complexity of Bakhtin's thought makes it quite possible for the ingenuous to get him fundamentally wrong or to trivialize him. One does not need to read for long to be quite intimidated by the possibilities of serious miscuing.

A lack of competence in Russian is a serious obstacle (though few biblical scholars will commit to master yet another script, language, and culture), as is what will be for many an almost total ignorance of the layered contexts in which thinkers wrote in the Soviet decades.[6] Emerson (1997, 8–13) describes the flavor of what is called Aesopism, a sort of allegorical code by which Russians could signal their true intent without saying it bluntly. Those who have not been trained in or remained conversant with continental philosophy may founder. Such a convoluted matrix is liable to lead the unwary into a sort of fundamentalism.

More serious, perhaps, are the increasingly diverging analyses being brought forward by what has been characterized as the third generation of the Bakhtin wave: not now his students, nor those trained by his students, but a generation of critics who come from a more diverse and fractious readership.[7] Additionally, there are two distinctive sets of Bakhtin scholars, one produced in Russia, another trained in the West. Emerson characterizes one meeting of these two bodies as follows: "We outsiders, it seemed, were forever grasp-

---

[6] Todorov (1984, xii) complains about the quality of the translations (granted there may be better ones since he wrote) and does all of his own translations for his own book.

[7] Emerson (1988, 503) describes the state of Bakhtin studies, opining that the nature of the scholarly dialogue, the presence of a critical biography, the dedication of special issues of major journals to Bakhtin's thought, the increasing refinement of discussion of Bakhtin's ideas, the exposition of archival material, and the ever-widening appropriation and extension of Bakhtin all signal a mature discipline, even in so short a period of time. She points out (1995, 3) that scholars in diverse disciplines have found Bakhtin stimulating to their own thought and consciousness—fitting nicely with the dialogic spirit that he speaks.

ing a small amount of Bakhtin and then applying it to concerns within our own fields of expertise," a practice considered paltry compared to Russian appropriation of the man (1997, 33).

If Emerson feels like an outsider in some scholarly Bakhtin circles, what of the rest of us? Are we cluelessly leaping onto a bandwagon just as it is headed toward the boneyard? I have neither space nor competence to handle even summarily the critiques by those who raise serious questions about whether Bakhtin is sufficiently activist (e.g., Hirschkop), whether his critique of ideology is suitable (see Gardiner 1992); I am unable to say how adequate is the space he allows for subaltern liberation,[8] or how useful are his thoughts in cultural studies.[9] Of the critical refiners who are extending and challenging Bakhtin as they push his insight into new realms, the most useful for my purposes are the feminist critics, some of whose points will be picked up below.

Even for one determined to spend significant time on the Bakhtin corpus (primary and secondary), obstacles remain formidable, disincentives prominent. Bakhtin's own works, though engaging, are tough to handle. Tzvetan Todorov, understating, graciously characterizes them as not prepared for publication, the pieces not well articulated among themselves (1984, xi–xii). Though Bakhtin spent his life filling notebooks with his thoughts, preserving them for posterity was not much in his mind. Portions are undated and untitled, in many instances difficult to decipher, nibbled as they are by animals or corroded by the harsh elements. Nor have the writings emerged in chronological order.[10] And in any case, Bakhtin tended to revisit the same territory while pursuing various questions

---

[8] Hitchcock (1991, 1993) sets up the problematic of Bakhtin's dialogics and reads feminist and international subaltern narratives in terms of it.

[9] Caryl Emerson (1996) raises and responds to a number of issues from her point of view, as well as referring readers to other viewpoints. See Haynes (1995) and Stam (1989) for art and film, respectively.

[10] There are various ways to list and reference Bakhtin's writings. The bibliography included with this book offers perhaps the simplest listing of material, with English titles and publication dates of those English editions. See Morson and Emerson (1990, xvii–xx) for an alternate approach. Every reader will need to recall that scholars will be referring to Bakhtin's work in whatever way seems best to them and without feeling the need to provide the key for every other way it can be done.

rather than to edit past writings. He liked to pose an issue and consider it from a variety of angles, each of which added a useful facet. In an essay offering advice to scholars about making virtue of Bakhtin's stylistic features, Emerson notes helpfully that Bakhtin's pieces are not essays; she reflects that some of the most provocative parts of his writing are the tiny fragments, that his "longer worked-out pieces are baggy monsters of form," and that even the published portions are like "ripped-out segments of one vast philosophical project" (1983, 25–26; see also her preface to *PDP*, xxxv). Perhaps Katerina Clark and Michael Holquist (1984, 3–6) offer both caution and encouragement when they challenge that it is easier to domesticate Bakhtin's rather jargon-clotted language than it is to be genuinely attentive to the deeper currents of his thought.

It is neither practical nor necessary for "secondary scholars" to organize Bakhtin. Indeed, though such a statement can both seem and be irresponsible, the complete systematizing of his thought is neither possible nor desirable. Any biblical scholar wishing to use Bakhtin responsibly will have to resign herself or himself to many patient and careful rereadings, of both Bakhtin's own writings and the most germane secondary scholarship as well, with any feeling of smug competence receding against the far horizon.[11] It can be

---

[11] The most fundamental and fraught of the questions among Bakhtin experts concerns the so-called disputed texts. There are three books that certain experts think emerged from the circle of Bakhtin colleagues rather than from the man himself and so cannot be considered as representing his thought closely, or must be consulted with caution. Many commentators touch on this topic, to ground their work in one way or another. See Perlina (1983) and Steinglass (1998) for two summary presentations of the factors. Clark and Holquist (1984, ch. 6) think the works can be considered Bakhtin's; Morson and Emerson think not (1990, ch. 3). Bocharov (1994, 1012–18) presents a conversation with Bakhtin on the point. This issue provides a good example of others like it, where Bakhtin-for-Bible scholars may never have the competence to come to a really good decision but will simply need to declare the stance that seems best, quite obviously relying on others. More time will not help much. It is my choice to utilize the two disputed texts that are germane to my purposes without making a distinction between Bakhtin and his collaborators. I could well be wrong, but I do not choose to divert my other interests learning how to sort it. The issue ultimately debouches into questions of what authoring entails—a matter near to the heart of all Bakhtin theory.

reassuring to find oneself understanding better as one finds an old topic discussed afresh, but it does not make for fast study. The reward will be endless fresh insights.

So, again, my point here is not to offer an authoritative constellation of topics or even a detailed and nuanced discussion, which would in any case be inadequate and likely not helpful for the diverse projects to which Bakhtin's thought may be put. Rather, this book offers a map of a life work of a man, roughly drawn with some parts detailed better than others when they seem potentially most relevant to biblical studies—at least to mine. The notes refer readers to sources where the topics are more painstakingly discussed. None of us consulting him and them will soon run out of places to look.

Clark and Holquist's biography of Bakhtin is probably the best place to start reading, since it both presents the man chronologically and also occasionally stops to cluster syntheses of his thought as it formed over a lifetime.[12] Morson and Emerson provide an excellent counterpoint, since their own book is organized to present Bakhtin's ideas more synchronically—as they ultimately shaped up—though with chronological markers as well. The scholarship of David Shepherd, tending as it does toward the more social and embedded facets of Bakhtin, also presents aspects of thought not included by the others. Late in my investigation I

Other similar issues: Did Bakhtin's work genuinely develop, or was he mainly formulating fresh insights in response to the same agenda? What sort of *Zeitgeist* influence was philosophical (and practical) Marxism likely to have had on Bakhtin, such that even though he denies he was ever an enthusiast, still his thought will participate in some of its fundamental assumptions? Does Bakhtin read Dostoevsky well? How is his Rabelais work to be conceived in relation to the rest of his thought and writing? Does Bakhtin really think the natural sciences and humanities are as fundamentally different as he sometimes asserts (a similar question is posed about prose and poetry). And there are many others. Falconer (1997a, 26) opines that there remains lack of consensus about even basic issues of the man's thought.

[12] Since the book appeared and was praised as necessary and helpful, other archival material has also come to light that instructs us to be at least slightly critical of the near-hagiographical cast Bakhtin acquires as he emerges from the pages of Clark and Holquist. At least several of my students would disagree heartily that the biography is a good entry to Bakhtin.

found a highly practical introduction to Bakhtin by Sue Vice, who presents the key concepts with clear, contemporary examples.[13]

These six preeminent scholars more than any others usefully introduce Bakhtin, not in the sort of sketch that is provided here but in many of his multiple contexts. If the present book is the examination of some particular interesting flowers, Clark and Holquist, Emerson and Morson, Shepherd, and Vice take us on lengthy tours of the garden itself. And at least for me, the reading of Bakhtin's writings is more likely to be helpful as a result of their analyses. Having begun with the question of why we might benefit from considering the thought of Bakhtin, I will review his life, his ideas, and finally some appropriations developing from his insights.

---

[13] Vice (1997b, 1–2) laments the lack of scholarship suitable for serious nonspecialists, describing it, in effect, as too much or too little. She also identifies her main objective, which is to use Bakhtin theory in reading, not to make it an end in itself. Her book was immensely helpful to my work.

1.
Who Is Bakhtin?

"What did you do with your life? What did you do?"

Czeslaw Milosz, "Capri"

Introduction

A heterodox collection of pithy summations of Bakhtin can be mounted: his fellow-countryman Todorov (1984, ix) classifies Bakhtin as "the most important Soviet thinker in the human sciences and the greatest theoretician of literature in the twentieth century," while commentator Robert Crawford (1994, 9) calls him "*the* critic of the 1990s." Clark and Holquist (1984, 5) and Emerson (1997, 23) all use hearing imagery for him: he is characterized as having a third ear, or perfect pitch. Alexandar Mihailovic, a scholar most comfortable with Bakhtin's theological and spiritual aspects, classifies him as an "almost mythic sage" (1997, 1). Though some call him a thought-mongerer (e.g., Venclova 1998, 32), those with best access to the material agree that Bakhtin saw himself, ultimately, as a philosopher, a thinker.[1] Emerson's strong sense of him is as survivor (1997, 3, 70, 123). Clark and Holquist (1984, 212) posit, "On the basis of [the] unifying theory of language, Bakhtin rethought a wide variety of topics that had previously been conceived as belonging to separate disciplines." Morson and Emerson's way of putting it is that he produced, over his lifetime, a "radical revision of knowledge" (1990, 61).

There are several summaries of Bakhtin's life (mostly drawing on the information provided by Clark and Holquist—which is the case for mine), but it is important to present a brief sketch here, not to encourage a cult of personality but rather to ground Bakhtin's thought in the particularities of how he lived. I will organ-

---

[1] Clark and Holquist 1984, 3, 11; Mihailovic 1997, 12. Shepherd cautions that any characterization eroding the sense of Bakhtin as a theorist is not helpful (1996, 145).

ize the information into four periods: birth and schooling; young adulthood to exile; exile to discovery; discovery to death.[2]

Birth and Schooling (1895–1918)

Bakhtin was born on November 4, 16, or 17 of 1895, the exact date blurred by a slippage between two calendar systems and later obfuscated by his own use of different birthdates. His early years were lived in Orel (south of Moscow); his parents were "impoverished aristocratic," cultured and liberal, valuing education and arts (Todorov 1984, 3). Key to his early life was his relationship with his brother Nikolai, two years older, a beloved companion with a contrasting character balance from Mikhail. Their parents had five children: two boys followed by three girls.

In his early years, Bakhtin benefited from the influence of a German-speaking governess and the opportunity to live in several polyglot cities: Vilnius, Odessa (where he also learned a good deal about Judaism), Petrograd. At the age of sixteen Mikhail contracted osteomyelitis in his leg, a condition that would spread to the other leg by 1932, render him increasingly disabled and eventuate in amputation of one leg in 1938. Bakhtin attended university first at Odessa and then at Petrograd between 1914–1918, where he specialized in the classics, particularly Hellenism.[3] As the dates suggest, he was caught up into the "atmosphere of immense intellectual and political intensity" (Holquist 1990, 2) as well as the chaos of the revolution after 1917.

Young Adulthood to Exile (1918–1930)

As a young adult, Bakhtin lived first in Nevel (birth city of Marc Chagall) and later in Vitebsk from 1918–1924, where he met

---

[2] As indicated, Clark and Holquist present their *Mikhail Bakhtin* in chronological order. My summary comes from their work, amplified briefly as indicated in the few notes by information supplied later by Holquist (1990), by Todorov (1984), or by Emerson (1997) with its Russian sources. See also Hirschkop (1998a).

[3] David Shepherd (private communication) suggests that some of the biographical information presented for Mikhail more properly belongs to his brother; for example, it is unlikely that Mikhail ever matriculated at the university or acquired the degree in classics awarded in the popular version of his life. Hirschkop (1999, ch. 3) provides a substantially revised summary.

his wife, Elena Aleksandrovna Okolovich, of whom relatively little is known directly (but whose vital importance to Bakhtin can be reconstructed). Circles of intellectual and cultural discussion formed—if not around him, surely including him. Here he linked up with the two scholars under whose names some of the disputed Bakhtin texts were published: Valentin Voloshinov and Pavel Medvedev. The preoccupation of these men and women was the central set of problems clustered under neo-Kantianism: how the mind relates to the world, how the outside factors are processed by the mind.[4] But their interests also included art, music, literature, philosophy, religions, and science, which gave the voracious Bakhtin access to the sweep of new thinking in many areas in the context of shared appreciation and pursuit of "variety, difference, free inquiry, dialogue and debate. They believed in being free of conventional norms and the traditional bounds of a given discipline and in pursuing a life of the mind that was as rich and lively as possible" (Clark and Holquist 1984, 116). Emerson and Morson, who organize at least part of their book around Bakhtin's developing mind and literary corpus, make this early period the first of four major phases of his intellectual odyssey. Of the materials eventually published from this 1918–1924 period, critics locate his first published essay (eight paragraphs in length), later included in *AA* and also *TPA*.[5]

---

[4] Holquist summarizes the relevant matters as follows (1990, 3–7): From the 1870s on, "everyone" took up one or another stance on issues linked to how the mind relates to the world. Some had held (e.g., Leibniz) that the mind seizes and shapes sense data, others (e.g., Locke) that it passively receives them. Kant insisted that the process is dialogical, synthetic. The mind has concepts with which it understands, and the sense data is necessary to activate such concepts; both are necessary and function together. The Marburg school, which influenced Bakhtin, stressed the more metaphysical end of the process while remaining committed to be sure that its philosophy was in synchrony with new insights from the physical sciences. Bakhtin eventually pushed back from the Marburg school's quest for an all-embracing unity but remained committed to facets of the neo-Kantian questions throughout his life, albeit distinctively.

[5] It is important to keep in mind that the groupings of the portions of *TPA* and *DI* are the result of editorial choices (by particular English editors) and bear no necessary relationship to the chronological ordering of Bakhtin's writings.

Though one contemporary of Bakhtin suggests that what most characterized the experience of the group was "an ethic of politically committed spectatorship" (Mihailovic 1997, 90), Clark and Holquist (1984, 37) characterize this postwar and postrevolution phase, at least for some intellectuals, as a time of "desperate gaiety," though they remark as well that Bakhtin was out of step with his era in a number of ways. He was neither so enthusiastic about Marxism nor so zealous an avant-garde nonconformist as some. He struggled to survive physically and to establish himself as a professional intellectual, doing neither with much secure success. He and Elena returned to Petrograd around 1924.

However, the Vitebsk years were the period when Bakhtin began to work out the set of issues that would sustain his whole intellectual-ethical life: the problem of the self and the others and ways of sorting the relations between or among them.[6] His biographers sum up this phase:

> Thus all the work that can be associated with his name during this period—while continuing to extend his attacks on the transcendental ego, continuing further to underline the need always to take others and otherness into account, and continuing to emphasize plurality and variety—also lent itself to the new conditions as arguments against the increasing homogenization of cultural and political life in the Soviet Union that would culminate in the long night of Stalinism. (Holquist 1990, 8–9)

The period from 1925 until Bakhtin's arrest in 1929–1930 was characterized by his dialogue with all manner of formalist or "theoreticist" thinking. Consequently his circle moved closer to the study of language and responded to the linguistic structuralism represented by Saussure, to Russian formalism, to Marxist analysis,

---

6 Clark and Holquist (1984) account for part of the confusion about charting Bakhtin's ideas in an orderly way as they explain his procedure of keeping notebooks—some undated and untitled—in which he pursued the same topics, sorting out his reflections over time. It is possible to see the effects of the process, for example, as one reads from *AA* into *PDP*. The issues addressed are in many cases similar, but Bakhtin has made significant progress in clarifying his ideas for a reader. But, except insofar as we have dated books or essays, it is not as easy as might be desirable to track his thought.

and to Freudian systematic thought.[7] He debated with these major syntheses certain shared questions and concerns: How does a work reflect and express its social matrix? What does authorship entail? What does criticism undertake, and what can it accomplish? How is art both related to and also other than life "outside the book"? What is the role of the unwilled in human expression? But in every case he disagreed fundamentally with his interlocutors, abhorring the artificial abstraction and the system-ness of what seemed to exclude the particular and socio-historical.

More specifically, Bakhtin disagreed with the language formalists about the basic unit of communication (an abstract system or literary unit [the sentence] for them, a historically rooted speech occasion [the utterance] for him). Though appreciating the Russian formalist scrutiny of the text, he faulted their resistance to considering features outside of the formal and material, those expressing the values of the authoring process. He also sorted the history of literature in a way fundamentally different than did his formalist contemporaries, in a way that we might now say is less essentialist.[8] His writings also suggest that he appraised formalist analyses as undervaluing the listener, overvaluing the speaker, and rendering communication too mechanical (Lähteenmäki 1998, 76).

---

[7] A substantial amount of Bakhtin's writings and of the consequent writing about him is sorted in these particular issues, which though crucial to his thought, need to be summarized succinctly and their main relevance extracted. Morson clarifies: "Theoretism names the widespread tendency to assume that the world is adequately and in principle exhaustively describable by a set of norms and rules" (1995, 61). As to dates, Todorov (1984, 33–34) identifies Bakthin's *FMC* in 1927 and his *MPL* in 1928, the year of the emergence of his work, *FMLS* (part 3). See Bakthin's *SGOLE* (169) for a final comment. Vice (1997b, 11) perceptively notes that part of the difference between Bakhtin and some of these interlocutors is traceable to different interests.

[8] Recalling that Bakhtin revisits topics throughout his writing, for a sampling on this topic refer to Bakhtin's "The Problem of Content, Material and Form in Verbal Art" (in *AA*, 257–325), as well as to *MPL*, part 2, chs. 2–3. Clark and Holquist (1984, ch. 8) comment, as do Morson and Emerson (1990, 78–82 and elsewhere intermittently). Holquist (1990, 42–47) sums up the conflict between Bakhtin and Saussure, as does Danow (1991, chs. 5–6), who discusses Bakhtin and the Prague and Russian Formalist schools. Hirschkop (1989, 20–21) notes some affinities between Bakhtin-users and formalism.

The subject of Bakhtin and Marxism is almost too complex to summarize. But it is fair to say at a general level that Bakhtin opposed his master optic—dialogism—to dialectics and maintained the importance of freedom, choice, and space to struggle against or to resist the monologization of speech or the imposition of other forms. Clark and Holquist conclude their summary of Bakhtin's capacity to link stylistics and politics by suggesting that reported speech (one's quotation of another's speech) is the test case for a society. They refer to words he wrote in the year of his arrest:

> It has to do, in other words, with the relative degrees of freedom granted by speakers to those other speakers whose words they appropriated into their own. How people characteristically treat the speech of others does not merely reflect literary stylistics or rules of grammar and punctuation that apply when quoting but reveals attitudes about the circulation of alien words typical of whole cultures. The way discourse is ordered in a given society is the most sensitive and comprehensive register of how all its other ideological practices are ordered, including its religion, education, state organization, and police. Cultures can be classified as open or closed according to the way in which they handle reported speech. (1984, 236–37)

He opposed as well official language in its homogenized form that dominated public life, with official rhetoric and myths taking over literature and literary scholarship. He decried language becoming automatic, authoritative, or mechanical. Much in his works engaged such dogma in subtle dialogue. He was fond of using catch phrases of Stalinism but placing them into fresh contexts that undermined the official ideology.[9]

---

[9] For much more nuance about Bakhtin-Voloshinov and Marxism, refer to Bakhtin, *MPL;* to Coates (1998, ch. 4); and to Clark and Holquist (1984, ch. 10). Morson and Emerson discuss the topic virtually throughout their work. Bakhtin's student Bocharov (1994, 1016) summarizes his recollections of conversations he held with Bakhtin on many occasions in the last fifteen or so years of his life. Bocharov reconstructs: "But I am not a Marxist. . . . No, never. I took an interest in it, as in much else— Freudianism, even spiritualism. But I was never a Marxist to any degree whatsoever." But see below for a record of the arrest inquiry, which puts the matter a little differently.

Bakhtin critiqued Freud for being over-theoretical, for failing to take adequate account of the historical, hence over-privileging the material/physical; he also found Freud insufficiently nuanced about reflexivity and neither alert to the dialogical possibilities within his own "talking cure" nor appropriately indebted to them. Bakhtin resliced Freud's conscious/unconscious into two aspects of awareness: What Freud labeled the unconscious Bakhtin called unofficial consciousness—more inner, unfinalized, and authentic to the individual; to Freud's conscious Bakhtin equated official consciousness, which he saw more likely to be finalized, to be the authorities' speech, to be what must be said publicly. Hence he made a more political category—and a more historical Russian explanation—for factors such as censorship and repression, features that Freud grounded more psychically.[10] Bakhtin also disapproved of anything utopian or apocalypticist that discouraged personal or social responsibility. He resists categorization as either an absolutist or a relativist, since he relied neither on a categorical imperative nor on subjectivism. Neither was Bakhtin what Mihailovic terms an ideological zealot (see further Emerson 1997, 154–56; Morson 1995).

The second half of the 1920s was for Bakhtin a period of fateful involvement with religious societies. Clark and Holquist characterize Bakhtin as a believer in the Russian Orthodox tradition throughout his life, which they maintain against the fact that he eventually (for more reasons than one) ceased being a "churchman" or political adherent of the church. What seems established from their discussion is that he saw resonance between theology and his larger system of thought, studied Eastern religions and philosophical theology, and was linked with several of the religious societies (e.g. the Brotherhood of St. Seraphim) that had enjoyed some freedom but were about to be crushed (Clark and

---

[10] The ongoing conversation between Bakhtin and the psychological is vast. Bakhtin's own analysis (with Voloshinov) is found in *FMC,* and secondary discussion occurs in Clark and Holquist (1984, ch. 7) and Morson and Emerson (1990, ch. 5). A number of scholars pursue the Bakhtin-Kristeva connections: see Bové (1983), Cavanagh (1993), and Mary O'Connor (1993) for more detail. Morson (1986, 83) opines that Todorov's discussion of Bakhtin and Freud is the best part of his book. Pyper (1996, ch. 3) explores Bakhtin-Voloshinov and Vygotsky's ideas on the formation of consciousness in children.

Holquist 1984, ch. 5; for an expanded discussion, see Mihailovic 1997). They also point out, sensibly, that Bakhtin's "distaste for dogma and organization" would have put a brake on his zeal for belonging to "the church" per se. What seems to emerge is a man who took religion seriously and deeply and was able to do without (as became necessary) or transcend church structures, which (according to Emerson) he saw carried considerable theoreticist tendencies as well (Emerson 1990, 121–22).

In this "preexilic" period, Bakhtin's work on the novels of Dostoevsky was first published (an early version of *PDP*). This is the work for which he is perhaps still best known to most. The book gave him the opportunity to work out a number of his favorite philosophical issues in terms of literature.[11] To characterize it briefly: Bakhtin credited Dostoevsky with having invented, or discovered, but in any case brought to highest instance a particular way of writing, which is called polyphonic (a term to be explored below). Far from being simply a clever technique, Bakhtin claimed, the particular way in which Dostoevsky was able to expose and explore crucial human concerns amid the levels of character speech (reducing greatly the influence and control by the author or narrator) represented a major advance in human consciousness. Dostoevsky demonstrated alternatives to Hegelian dialectics, which subsumed interlocutors; to formalistic divorce of content and form; and to psychologism, which sought to ground subjectivity substantially in causal factors. The two editions of the book (in 1929 and 1963), Clark and Holquist point out, saved Bakhtin's life twice: first when a favorable review helped modulate his exile sentence, and later during the postwar period when the rediscovery of the books saved his life's work from obscurity.

But in 1929 Bakhtin was arrested (in a general roundup) for crimes against the state, apparently for something smacking of conspiracy and linked with religion, intellectualism, and the corruption of youth. The exact charge is not specified in the biography, though in later work Holquist (1990, 9) clarifies that

---

[11] Morson and Emerson (1990, 234) characterize its literary/philosophical aspects in terms of the toggling rabbit and duck image. There is no small secondary scholarship on Bakhtin's claims regarding Dostoevsky. Those interested may consult Bezeczky (1994, 324–41).

it was part of a "sweep of intellectuals associated with the underground church."[12]

Bakhtin was interrogated, tried, and sentenced to ten years on the Solovetsky Islands. He protested that he would not survive in his condition. For reasons linked both to his health and the intervention of influential friends (and presumably the timely publication and positive reception of his Dostoevsky book), his sentence was commuted to six years at Kustanai in Kazakhstan, where he was promised that the weather was "severe but healthy." The temperature averaged between minus 18 and plus 19 degrees, with wind so fierce that locals had to grasp cables when outside to avoid being blown away.[13] The Bakhtins lived first at Saransk and then at Savelovo, where they continued to reside even when his sentence was up in 1934.

Exile to Discovery (1930–mid-1960s)

Clark and Holquist (1984, 254; see also Emerson 1997, 3, 70, 123) present Bakhtin as a survivor: "Conditions were no doubt hard, but Bakhtin was a survivor. Despite his impracticality, he somehow managed to get through even the most adverse circumstances. His ability to survive was due in part to his equanimity, his sense of humor, and his capacity for accepting gracefully any interlocutor." They cite as well his ability to attract friends always willing to help him avoid the very worst that might have happened.[14]

Bakhtin was also nondoctrinaire in some surprising ways. For example, though it is difficult to imagine that he had any use for Stalin's five-year plans—either in their obvious systematic dysfunction or in their practical inability to provide food—he accepted a job as an instructor in bookkeeping techniques (and

---

[12] In the introduction to *AA* (xxxix), Holquist says that the reason is now known to be association with a society whose aim was to synthesize Marxism and Christianity. See Bocharov (1994, 1021) regarding Bakhtin's refusal to be vindictive.

[13] Apropos of the commuted sentence, Clark and Holquist (1984, 253–56) summarize that some 15 million lives were lost there during this period.

[14] Mihailovic also stresses this characteristic when commenting on Bakhtin's minimization of kenotic self-sacrifice (1997, 8, 75, 119, 141–42). Note as well Bakhtin's reflections on the value of laughter as an antidote to violence in "From Notes Made," *SGOLE* (134–35).

even wrote an article) to assist those struggling with the quotas, skills Clark and Holquist (1984, 256–57) suggest he learned from his bank-employed father. They characterize him as both lucky and circumspect while fulfilling the role of a model Soviet departmental head, careful to fall within the style and language required in that day. But there was nonetheless some kind of a "big scrape"—Bakhtin's expression—that necessitated a move (1984, 260). Yet Bakhtin did not think ill of those who adapted to Stalinism, and he himself tried to be diplomatic in responding to even the most extreme rhetoric of the era. One scholar summarized that Bakhtin avoided collaborating with the state and abstained from challenging it; he ignored the system while refusing to be part of its power structure.[15] As a last resort he would always say, "That is very interesting" (Clark and Holquist 1984, 325–26).

That his sentence ended in the mid-1930s was not so decisive as it might seem, since to be rearrested was not uncommon in the frequent purges of the era; nor was it easy for someone with Bakhtin's political record to be hired to teach. Nonetheless, Bakhtin did instruct and lecture occasionally and was eventually permitted to teach the German and Russian languages. But he was more often unemployed, a condition that left him with time for writing—two book-length manuscripts and five long essays in this period. He refers to other scholars and to books, though perhaps from memory rather than from actual texts. So this period of his life, which included the war years, gave rise to his work on novels and on time: the writings that appear (in English) as *DI*. It is during this phase as well that he worked up the manuscript on Rabelais and the carnival genre. He also wrote and filed in Moscow a major work on eighteenth-century literature and social realism and then used the draft manuscript for cigarette paper (starting from the end and smoking backwards). Unfortunately the building in which the publisher was located was destroyed during

---

15 Venclova (1998, 26). Bocharov includes among his conversations (1994, 1012–20) Bakhtin remembering compromises and misrepresentations he made at various moments in his life, acknowledged and regretted. Vice (1997b, 194) includes in a note (n. 15) a conversation between Bocharov and Bakhtin, where Bakhtin is blunt that he and others avoided perishing by betrayal.

the war and only the portions on Goethe avoided the rolling fingers of the chain-smoking Bakhtin.[16]

It is difficult to characterize the Rabelais/carnival work summarily. It seems at first—and always to a number of scholars—anomalous. For those who see great similarities between Bakhtin and Dostoevsky, Bakhtin's coherence with Rabelais seems ludicrous. But what Bakhtin well understood and valued in Rabelais was his sense of the rich interplay between apparently odd elements and his flair for mingling types of discourse. Bakhtin finds in Rabelais and in the carnival leaky borders a hilarious, irreverent celebration of all that was pompous, authoritarian, official, repressed, and silenced. Clark and Holquist note that such a work as the Rabelais, "written in the Soviet Union in the late 1930s and early 1940s makes so much of freedom and the unofficial/official distinction, it cannot fail to be in part a comment on its times"[17] and a very brave one at that, with its counter-ideology.[18]

Though Bakhtin wrote up the Rabelais study in hopes of being awarded a doctorate, it was not a simple matter. Once the war ended, Bakhtin moved back to Saransk (near Moscow) and filed the dissertation, but the defense and publication of the book stretched out for several more years. Indeed, the political climate changed just prior to his dissertation defense, making *verboten* any approval of things folk and primitive (such as the outrageous carnival that Rabelais and Bakhtin so enjoyed) and *de rigueur* the sort of "hurrah politics" that celebrated postwar Stalinism (which was lacking completely in the dissertation). Indeed, the Gorky Institute

---

[16] Shepherd (private communication) indicates that the story is apocryphal, but the note by Bocharov (1994, 1022) indicates that he heard it from Bakhtin himself, who commented appreciatively on the thinness of the paper.

[17] Clark and Holquist 1984, 305. In addition to *RW*, Bakhtin summarizes carnival and its menippean antecedents in *PDP* (122–37). For discussion of the work on Rabelais and carnival, see Clark and Holquist (1984, ch. 14), Morson and Emerson (1990, ch. 10), and Mihailovic (1997, chs. 5–6). Since I do not plan to say more about it, key though it is, readers are encouraged to explore this huge topic as they have need.

[18] For a representative but succinct characterization of Bakhtin and Rabelais—and the carnivalesque—see Vice (1997b, ch. 4) and her excellent references; also Coates (1998, ch. 7) and Ryklin (1993).

itself plunged into official disfavor at the same period when Bakhtin was hoping to be awarded a doctorate from it. So in addition to the years the work itself consumed (from 1940 on), the defense was first scheduled for 1946, then deferred to 1947, with the results not announced until 1951; finally a candidate's degree was granted in 1952.

Discovery to Death (mid-1960s–1975)

In the 1960s Bakhtin became more closely involved with social language theory and also began to re-edit and integrate various of his writings. His health continued to deteriorate in the grim circumstances of postwar Soviet society. But it was in the 1960s that his work (on Dostoevsky) was discovered by students—including Bocharov, who found the man well (they had assumed him dead, as indeed he might well have been). They moved his ideas closer to the mainstream of Russian thought, some even by publication. Bakhtin was also praised publicly by the esteemed Russian formalist Roman Jakobson (Venclova 1998, 27). The Dostoevsky work was revised and put forth again in this period. And Bakhtin seems finally to have found conditions—even in Moscow—under which he could teach and write, though few would likely consider them ideal.

His wife Elena died in 1971, to his deep distress. He started some new projects in the 1970s (on Gogol and Dostoevsky) and kept writing until the year before he died.[19] Emerson cites a series of occasions at this time where Bakhtin was interviewed on tape. Her narrative suggests that Bakhtin was no longer at his sharpest and had trouble recalling everything he was after, though he was conscious of that fact (see 1997, 31–33). Clark and Holquist (1984, 347) relate that while dying, Bakhtin asked someone to retell the story of Boccaccio's wily folk hero, Ser Ciappelletto: Having (mis)spent a life in crime and debauchery, he managed—thanks to a skillfully double-voiced confession to a priest who did not know him—to become most undeservedly remembered as Saint Ciappelletto. Bakhtin had always enjoyed the narrative and his

---

[19] Holquist states, in the preface to *AA* (xlv): "In the last five years of his life, Bakhtin began to fill his notebooks with sketches for articles on the question of author and hero, self and other, and the relation of art to life. He returned, in other words, to the same subjects that had engaged him in these [found in *AA*] from his youth."

desire to hear and relish it on his deathbed is suggestive. Bakhtin's death came on March 7, 1975 (of emphysema). His last words, taken down by the nurse in attendance, are richly enigmatic: "I go to thee." Reference wonderfully, suggestively ambiguous.[20]

Bakhtin, Postmodernism, and the Bible

Two other chronological points call for brief comment before shifting to a presentation of Bakhtin's thought: Bakhtin and the vast and multiple postmodernism, and Bakhtin's own view of the Bible. Barry Rutland helps situate the relationship between postmodernism and Bakhtin, reminding readers that the Russian worked prior to the flowering of the postmodern, though sharing common antecedents and constraints with it. He surely did his theorizing without specific reference to deconstructionist thought. But most Western readers in fact will likely consider Bakhtin's works against that backdrop.

Rutland's sense is that Bakhtin is both continuous and discontinuous with much of contemporary (anti-)philosophy, not easily contained within it, but coming to some of its insights by a different route (1990, 122–29). Some specifics: Bakhtin loved the humanistic tradition, surely including the classics of its literary canon. He enjoyed reconsidering endlessly how they had been shaped and had grown; and yet though he clearly esteemed some texts above others, he did not apply anachronistic standards to earlier pieces. His keen interest in the processes of authoring with their inextricable connections to consciousness was far removed from the "death of the author" phase of literary criticism (though Bakhtin did not conflate the historical author with the authoring artist).

His ideas have little affinity with narratological formalism, notably with its abstract implied reader.[21] He did not employ or seem to need the strategies of suspicion, since his dialogical and polyphonic ways of approaching the text offered adequate pathways for resisting the control of meaning, provided loopholes to alternative perspectives. There is little in his thought that seems

---

[20] David Shepherd suggests (private communication) that the Russian is not so dramatic as Clark and Holquist suggest (or we may infer) and that "I am coming to you" is also quite accurate.

[21] See Bialostosky (1983) for a comparison of Bakhtin and the Chatman school of thought.

patient with texts talking to texts; Bakhtin liked to think of particular readers, historically situated, as juxtaposing texts. Ken Hirschkop (1990) labels Bakhtin's dialogism a sort of populist deconstruction, while at the same time insisting that the metaphysics that Derrida seeks to overturn remains functional in Bakhtin.

Bakhtin's central emphasis on human consciousness is also at odds with much of postmodern thought (Hirschkop 1989, 93–99; see also Zavala 1988). Fundamental for Bakhtin was the irreducible responsibility of the individual, both aesthetically and ethically; there is nothing that seems compatible with nihilism, with endless deferral of meaning, or with extreme relativism. Though Bakhtin may have been overly optimistic about the freedom of the individual to create, it is surely a point he affirmed repeatedly. And though he considered the social to be key, it did not in any way excuse the individual from anything (see further Morson 1991; also Gardiner 1992, ch. 4 on Bakhtin, Barthes, and Foucault; Lodge 1990, 4–7).

A similar contiguous disjunction characterizes Bakhtin's attitude toward the Bible. He did not discuss the Bible much, compared to the many other works he loved to comb repeatedly for their stimulations to his ideas. His scattered remarks suggest that his assumptions about Holy Writ, as he called it, were far from those held today by those who work with the text professionally. In fact, since at the end of this century Western biblical scholars are likely to think of the Bible in terms so different than did the Russian Orthodox Bakhtin, it is perhaps best that he did not say too much about it. He considered it *the* authoritative (as distinct from innerly persuasive) text and did not approach it as he did "novelistic" discourse. That biblical texts could themselves be part of other tissues of language Bakhtin saw, as Mihailovic (1997, 48, quoting *DI,* 69) testifies:

> This theological subtext of the divine word reaches the ne plus
> ultra of expression in Bakhtin's 1940 essay "From the Prehistory
> of Novelistic Discourse," where he adduces the Gospels and the
> church fathers as virtual archetypes of the refracted or double-
> voiced word: "The primary instance of appropriating another's
> discourse and language was the use made of the authoritative
> and sanctified use [Russian word] of the Bible, the Gospels, the
> Apostles, the fathers and doctors of the church."

Bakhtin remarked that the New Testament is essentially dialogic, though it is not quite clear which text(s) his words reference.[22] That he imagined the biblical texts themselves as polyphonic is more doubtful; in fact, some of his criticism of linguistic critics as overly narrow can be turned toward his own views of biblical texts. Yet, as Carol Newsom (1996b, 293) urges, various questions over which historical critics have labored may be responsive to Bakhtin's strategies.[23] Bakhtin's ideas, as they are not only utilized but in fact stretched, make a contribution that he did not anticipate. Having situated the man amidst the intellectual and social contexts of the twentieth century, it is now possible to examine his thought in greater detail.

---

[22] Lodge (1990, 90–93). Walter Reed's study (1993) seems to fit in here as an investigation of how the multiple works of the canon can be read dialogically. Though useful and familiar to historical studies, it is a fairly minimal use of Bakhtin's thought.

[23] Newsom suggests (1996b, 297–98) that the ending of Job suits Bakhtin's theories even better than do the Dostoevsky novels, a view held by other literary scholars, mutatis mutandis. Prickett (1986, 210–13) is another scholar who insists upon the compatibility between Bakhtin's assumptions about the workings of heteronomous literature and the Bible, Bakhtin's own views of biblical authority notwithstanding. Lodge (1990, 97–98) affirms a similar point about monologism and polyphony.

2.
What Does Bakhtin Offer?

"An immersion in Bakhtin's thought will indeed transform the way one reads, but only after some time has elapsed, and in ways that are not predictable."

Michael Holquist, *Dialogism*

"Books about thinkers require a kind of unity that their thought might not possess."

Morson and Emerson, *Mikhail Bakhtin*

Introductory Contexts

Four questions for biblical scholars

Having now indicated angles from which at least one biblical scholar (myself) finds Bakhtin interesting, and having provided some context to his thought by reviewing his life, it is time to lay out his ideas in some detail. Prior to doing so, I will sketch the key challenges I think face those currently wishing to appropriate his strategies for biblical studies, points to which I will return at the conclusion of the chapter. I see four of them; others will arrange issues differently.

First, to what extent is it legitimate to appropriate his ideas so rooted in nineteenth-century Russian novels for ancient Hebrew prose? It is obvious that the Deuteronomist is not Dostoevsky.[1] With what shared assumptions—and with what subsequent moves clearly articulated—may Bakhtin's sense of intensely dialogic reality illumine earlier texts?

Second, given Bakhtin's insistence on the text as thoroughly historical and social, is there some space (perhaps in his theory of chronotope) to reangle the question of relevant historical data? The

---

[1] Lodge concedes (1990, 22–23) that Bakhtin's theories of the novel are suited for more than that particular genre. He adds (97–98) that Bakhtin came to doubt that literature as such is well-classified as fully monologic, thus opening up the notion of a continuum rather than categories.

field of Hebrew Bible studies in particular is faced with severe challenges to recovery of adequate, clear information for understanding well the referents of production and setting. The field is also experiencing the disintegration of consensus about whether substantial material (e.g., the Primary History) is to be placed early in its millennium or closer to the center—a difference of perhaps four hundred years. That is a big variance, and those asserting that there are virtually no early texts pose problems that demand rethinking of earlier positions. Additionally, despite or because of the difficulty of historical access, (Hebrew) biblical studies has been so dominated by historical reconstruction and genetic issues as to leave shriveled the questions of language that also interested Bakhtin. Is there a better way than either Bakhtin (who remained vague) or biblical historical critics (who are often too confidently obsessive) have modeled to weave together the represented world, the likely authorial world, and the specific historical and cultural presuppositions of readers?

Third, considering that Bakhtin situated the role of the author as simultaneously a reader, and in some ways as almost a peer of authored characters, one is led to ask, how can these insights be aligned with reception theories as they have developed in the last couple of decades? The understandings of author, narrator, and reader all need redefinition in view of Bakhtin's perhaps too naive sense of authoring.

Fourth, can Bakhtin's assertions about genre and its capacity to help us think elucidate interpretation? Might we ask, what is biblical narrative strategically, rather than what is it formally? How does *it* think? Assumptions about the theological character of the text have tended to cut it off from certain types of scrutiny. The various official groups whose text the Bible is (so the rich interpreting traditions of Judaism, branches of Orthodox and the denominations of Western Christianity) claim the text to be revealed, inspired, inerrant, and so forth, claims which if ontological rather than epistemological may continue to inhibit critical or analytical reading. Conversely, the difficulties posed by biblical theology projects often stunt critical conversations about its less orderly religious aspects. With these questions and perhaps others in mind, it is time to situate Bakhtin's ideas.

Four worldviews shaping Bakhtin

The best place to start to explain Bakhtin concisely is to locate his lifework in the main worldviews that gave rise to it and provided it structure for some time. I will sketch four such influences: philosophical, theological, scientific, and literary, again inviting those interested to follow notes to fuller discussion. First, critics agree that Bakhtin did his reflections in response to (if eventually in differentiation from) neo-Kantianism, which may be summarized briefly.[2] Kant's thought rose in reaction to the metaphysics of German scholasticism, which placed, in the minds of many, too great an emphasis on materialist factors of knowing. Kant's work— and that of the neo-Kantian thinkers that it generated—was taken up with the question of how the mind relates to the world. Kant stressed the mutuality of both partners, the synthetic process involved in knowing, thus avoiding two extremes. The mind does not receive sense data passively, nor is reality statically awaiting formation by the mind. Bakhtin's teachers and colleagues struggled during their lifetimes to redact and refract Kant's viewpoint in terms of their own insights. Bakhtin's primary debt to Kant seems to be on the question of how art relates to experience, i.e., how an author manages an aesthetic (specifically a literary) creation. Holquist (1990, 3–4) sums up: "Kant's breakthrough was to insist on the necessary intraction—the *dialogue* as Bakhtin would come to interpret it—between mind and world."

To anticipate the point that needs developing:

> Although the self/other distinction is a recurring preoccupation of many other post-Romantic systems of thought, Bakhtin is the only major figure to frame the problem in terms of authorship. He is distinguished not by his emphasis on the self/other dichotomy as such but rather by his emphasis on the essentially authorial techniques of dialogue and character formation which permit the poles of consciousness to interact while maintaining their fundamental difference from each other. (Clark and Holquist 1984, 80)[3]

---

[2] Michael Holquist summarizes the rudiments of neo-Kantianism at several places in his writings (see 1990, 2–6). An early essay (1984) treats the philosophical matrix. See also Emerson (1997, ch. 5) and Nielsen (1998) for the specific interface between Bakhtin's ethics and Kant's thought. Some readers will not need the digested form of the conversation that I found crucial for my own understanding.

[3] Makhlin (1997, 45–52) sums up Bakhtin's main project as the quest to overcome the ideological culture of nonparticipative autonomy—in being, art, thought, and so forth.

Human persons, their deeds and words, are not tightly bounded, sovereign monads but creatures with porous boundaries. Reality is utterly, fundamentally, relational.[4]

Alexandar Mihailovic develops a second, theological trajectory along which Bakhtin's thought traveled, a journey that those alert to its nuance will detect.[5] To an understanding of *logos* that is primarily Johannine, though indebted to the pre-Socratic and Stoic philosophical traditions as well, Bakhtin added the first seven church councils so formative for Orthodox tradition (Chalcedon in particular) filtered through the Russian intelligentsia of the late nineteenth century.[6] So concepts of trinity, divine creation, Jesus' incarnation, Eucharist—all of which he considered in terms of interpenetration (*perichoresis*) and interchange—are foundational for his insight that selves exist relationally: "Everywhere there is an *intersection, consonance, or interruption of rejoinders in the open dialogue by rejoinders in the heroes' internal dialogue. Everywhere a specific sum total of ideas, thoughts, and words is passed through several unmerged voices, sounding differently in each*" (Bakhtin *PDP*, 265, emphasis original).

The interpenetration of divine persons and of the human and divine elements permits neither isolated sovereignty nor abased self-annihilation. Bakhtin denied both that one participant stands alone and also that the other is swamped. His ethics are implied:

---

[4] For a good articulation of the places where Bakhtin meshes generally well with and occasionally diverges from the hermeneutical stream represented by Schleiermacher, Dilthey, Gadamer, and Ricoeur, refer to Gardiner (1992, ch. 3) and Scholz (1998, 149–54). Mihailovic (1997, 65–70 and elsewhere in his ch. 2) also explores in considerable detail the ways in which Bakhtin's ethics derive from and critique Kant's.

[5] Mihailovic (1997, 1–2) observes that many Bakhtin scholars are not interested in this question or even comfortable with the theological dimension, describing most as circling the topic of religion like a cat circling a bowl of hot milk. Indeed, it is absent from or minimized in a good deal of the secondary literature. Doubtless not all religious scholars would agree with Mihailovic, but command of the context is to be taken seriously. Anthony Ugolnik's work (1984, 1990) provides the specifically orthodox context as well. See also Coates (1998) for a Western Christian perspective.

[6] Mihailovic (1997, chs. 1–4) situates Bakhtin's *TPA* and his last writings in a larger theological context, visiting those sites of influence intermittently. For another and rather different discussion of Bakhtin and the Russian intelligentsia, refer to Morson (1995).

For Bakhtin, ethics presumes a physical setting, a fully illuminated purview of action and consciousness in which the subject participates. Bakhtin stresses above all that ethics belong to subjective experience yet are nonetheless reified and real, a position tantamount to an abolition of the dichotomy of subject and object.... The ethical dimension is generated during the act of reading as a result of the interaction between author and reader; it is the precipitant emerging after a reaction between two chemical compounds or the protective shell reflexively secreted by a fragile organism. (Mihailovic 1997, 53–54)

Finally, ethics demands a match of word and deed, requires embodiment and particularity with all of its messy, painful, and joyful challenge, calls for a signature on a customized life: "for him ethics are always generated from within and never imposed from above" (Mihailovic 1997, 54).

The scientific thinking of his day was a third major influence upon Bakhtin. He assumed the Darwinian sense of the vast and complex interrelatedness of the whole natural world, humans surely included, a set of webs discernible at every level of existence, exerting great impact on how life is lived.[7] The physics of human existence on which he counted and drew were indebted to Einstein's thought, which Bakhtin followed with great interest. The implications of one of Einstein's central tenets—that two bodies cannot occupy the same space simultaneously— contributed to Bakhtin's whole dialogical view of the self and other (Holquist 1990, 20–21). Even a detail so obvious as the slightly-differently angled eyes and ears that construct human seeing and hearing was of practical interest to him. Bakhtin frequently cited the significance of our living in a Galilean rather than a Copernican or Ptolemaic universe. The pattern is multiple centers, not simply one whose hub "we" inevitably inhabit.

A fourth and final influence to name here is literary, where some authors, such as Tolstoy, represented a sort of situated ethics that Bakhtin perceived to be neither quite systematized and absolute nor simply individualistic and relativized. For example, Bakhtin observed: "Both [Tolstoy characters Levin in *Anna Karenina* and Pierre in *War and Peace*] discover that they can

---

[7] See Holquist (1989, 23–26), which draws out the richness of the human body as a grand system.

make correct moral decisions without a general philosophy. Instead of a system, they come to rely on moral wisdom derived from living rightly moment to moment and attending carefully to the irreducible particularities of each case."[8] These four summaries are scarcely adequate to describe the depth of influence on Bakhtin, but they serve as reminders of the complex cultural world in which he moved.

An Architectonics[9] of Bakhtin's Thought

So, from within these four interlooped contextual circles, what question can I most usefully propose for Mikhail Bakhtin to answer?[10] I have chosen to organize under the question: How does an author create? Though set up to get to where I want to go, which is to read particular biblical texts, it is sufficiently comprehensive to enclose the key points, granted summarily; my hope

---

[8] Morson and Emerson (1990, 23–25) describe the Russian literary influence. Erdinast-Vulcan (1997, 254) offers substantiation for her contention that literary categories work better for the ethical issues Bakhtin is working with than do the traditional philosophical categories in which they are usually expressed. For a very strong statement about the near-impossibility of those ignorant of the Russian contexts ever understanding Bakhtin, see Makhlin (1997, 51).

[9] Bakhtin defines architectonics as "a focused and indispensable non-arbitrary distribution and linkage of concrete, singular parts and aspects into a finished whole, [something that is] possible only around a given human being as a hero" (translation by Morson and Emerson 1990, 70, quoting from *TPA*). They oppose architectonics to system.

[10] The chief and most comprehensive scholars on Bakhtin consider the question of how to organize his mammoth life's task for efficient review. Holquist and Clark, though projecting their seminal work chronologically, indicate that the master trope for Bakhtin is dialogism, a choice Holquist makes again in his later writing. Morson and Emerson (1990) preface their study with summaries of what they consider most fundamental: prosaics, unfinalizability, and dialogue (ch. 1), while Emerson's latest work (after reviewing issues that have arisen around dialogism, polyphony, and the particular interpretation of Dostoevsky) is organized in terms of outsidedness required for art and ethics. In each case, of course, the scholar is bringing an order to a vast system for particular reasons of his or her own, with none claiming to be definitive. For a different sense of drawing order from the heterogeneity, see Bonetskaia (1998, 83).

is to offer a rough map while allowing the notes to indicate access to primary and secondary sources for further nuance and argumentation. Bakhtin's neologisms are conspicuous, if irritating, and highlighting them at first reference provides access to key places where readers may search for fuller information. Any organization and description of the authoring process will inevitably be artificial and oversimplified, since the dynamic has been going on, presumably from the womb. Nevertheless, since it is a concept central to my particular sketch, I will first attempt a schema indicating how the three authorings (self, other, art) are managed and what character they have. Secondly, I will note briefly some implications for ethics, aesthetics, language, and reading.

How authoring works

Authoring is the key action of human existence.[11] I author my self; I am co-responsible for the shaping of others with whom I interact; and as an artist, I author a work of art—for present purposes, a literary hero, who will author others, and so forth. The authorings are related, overlapping, mutually constitutive.

First, a human being authors his or her own life. What I author will be myself, whatever else may characterize it as well. I start from a particular place, literally unique in time and space. Though my authoring is not in any sense an isolated or sovereign act, Bakhtin names *outsidedness* (*exotopy*) the major characteristic of my relationship with an other, the fulcrum by which I manage all authorings.[12] It is not to be equated with aloofness, neutrality, indifference, autonomy, or even security, given the fact that we share a huge web of kinds of things with others. But outsidedness marks me off from others in a fundamental way. "The non-identity of mind and world is the conceptual rock on which dialogism is founded and the source of all the other levels of non-occurring

---

[11] For more elaborated and nuanced discussions of this major set of theses, see Clark and Holquist (1984, ch. 3); Holquist (1990, ch. 2); Morson and Emerson (1990, chs. 5 [for the self], 6 [for the hero]); Danow (1991, ch. 4). Bakhtin talks about these matters throughout, but notably in his "Author and Hero," *AA*, and in *TPA*, 14–17. As Palmieri observes (1998, 44), Bakhtin's views on this key topic are scattered widely.

[12] Bakhtin's most efficient discussion of this concept may be read in "Author and Hero," *AA*, 15–22, but also in *PDP*, chs. 1–2.

identity that Bakhtin sees as shaping the world and our place in it," says Holquist (1990, 17–18).[13]

So an "I"—Bakhtin calls it *I-for-myself* (I as I look to my self from the inside—inchoate, fluid, and provisional)—moves into relationship with what he calls *I-for-the-other* (meaning how I look to an other) and *the-other-for-me* (which is how the other appears to me): Only in so doing does the unshaped "I" accept a view that helps me find any sort of edge or limit that is essential for my authoring.[14] I incline toward an other, live into his or her experience. I enter as deeply as I am able the space of the other—their particularity—perceive it to some extent with their eye or ear—and then return to my own space, remembering and marking—integrating—what I have experienced. The twofold trajectory of "empathizing"[15] and then returning makes my insight distinctive. Emerson suggests, "Bakhtin starts on quite an other ground: with the assumption (not, of course, original with him) that genuine knowledge and enhancement can only begin when my 'I' consults another 'I' and then returns to its own place, humbled and enhanced" (1997, 23). Friendly alterity, Clark and Holquist call it (1984, 70). I project myself only by undertaking this journey, allowing dialogue between my internally felt self (my image of myself) and the self-assessment that others hand me (including both how they size me up and how I see them). Bakhtin states:

> Self-consciousness, as the artistic dominant in the construction of the hero's image, is by itself sufficient to break down the monologic unity of an artistic world—but only on the condition that the hero, as self-consciousness, is really represented and not

---

[13] On p. 30 he calls outsidedness (my particular situatedness) the workshop where I do my authoring.

[14] See *PDP*, ch. 2. Erdinast-Vulcan (1997) also writes helpfully on this aspect of Bakhtin's work, commenting as well on the development of it. I am indebted to a student, Mark Bosco, for clarifying that, in the philosophical system from which Bakhtin speaks (German idealist aesthetic philosophy), spirit here can be equated with "I-for-myself" and soul for the self that I become thanks to the actions of the others as they temporarily stabilize me.

[15] Neither "empathizing" nor "sympathizing" quite catches the nuance of "sympathetic co-experience" that Bakhtin settles on ("Author and Hero," *AA*, 81–87); I will use "empathize" for that expression of his.

merely expressed, that is, does not fuse with the author, does not become the mouthpiece for his voice; only on the condition, consequently, that the work itself observes a distance between the hero and the author. (Bakhtin, *PDP*, 51)[16]

That is, though I cannot see my whole self, I start with some degree of self-consciousness and bring that into relation with another. In the process, I encounter an edge of what is not me but another, meeting that other but not vanishing into it. There is not a fusion but an engagement; I return from the encounter but am changed by it, have gained from it.

Second, simultaneously, I have a part in the authoring or constructing of others, particularly those with whom I have considerable or intimate contact. Just as I am constituted by what I experience in encountering others, so the same holds for them as regards me. In this sense, then, we are all authors and authored, repeatedly, endlessly.

To author in such a *dialogical* way is both to recognize the border between my self and an other and to sense that it is permeable, porous, repeatedly crossed in more ways than I can ever take in.[17] For Bakhtin, *dialogism* indicates double-voicedness, double-wordedness, both a general property of language and also a specific engagement of two voices in a single utterance (which will be identified below as polyphonic).[18] More than simple dialogue, dialogism conceives voices intensively engaged with each other, simultaneously listening and responding as well as influenced and shaped.[19] To author respectfully precludes, avoids

---

[16] See also Bonetskaia (1998) and Palmieri (1998).

[17] Many think that if there is one "big tent" word to sum up all of Bakhtin, it is "dialogical." All of his thought is permeated by awareness of this reality. The edges, surfaces, and depths of one reality slide constantly into relationships with those of other realities.

[18] Our transactions, including speech, are mutually constitutive for ourselves and each other. The pole opposite the dialogic is the *monologic* (*theoreticist*), that which tends to be finalized, transcribed, abstracted, systematically dialectical—all prizing and abstract control and order over the messiness of the actual.

[19] Vice (1997b, 45–46, 102). Pearce (1994, 2–6) explains the concept very clearly and creatively using the analogy of the telephone, which must

domination and control, neither requiring nor permitting the collapse of one into the other. To create in this way is to acknowledge the other with discipline, responsivity, and refinement, to negotiate rather than to bully.

Morson and Emerson note: "The essentially aesthetic act of creating such an image of another is most valuable when we seek not to merge or duplicate each other, but rather to supplement each other, to take full advantage of our special field of vision" (1990, 185).[20] Language that draws too extensively on spatial imagery of tidy sovereignty and borders misleads. An author is an engaged outsider. Hirschkop (1989, 20–21, 34) cautioning about the dangers of reducing Bakhtin's ideas to the too purely personal and literary, insists that dialogism is born of social interaction: "The social functions that discourse performs, and the practical effects it initiates, should be the object of our inquiry."

In addition, so third, to the dialogical authoring self and other human beings, an artist may choose to author what Bakhtin calls a (*polyphonic*) *hero*, preferring that word to the more general term "character."[21] This work of creation also arises out of life as lived.

---

be picked up for a conversation actually to occur. Then that conversation is shaped by both parties but can plausibly be fairly well understood by someone even listening only to one side of it.

[20] Feminists have been particularly critical of Bakhtin on this point, finding his optimism dangerously naive. Still, the possibility of respectful co-authoring is key to Bakhtin, to his own survival skills, and to the religious tradition from which he draws it (see Frank [1990] for further discussion of the theology; the feminist critique will be revisited toward the end of the chapter).

[21] Vice points out that the term "polyphonic"—referring in Bakhtin's usage to the copresence and participation of voices—is nearly as common as dialogic and closely related, implying that compositional elements are in constant conversation (1997b, 112–13). For a concise note on polyphony, refer to *PDP*, ch. 1, where Bakhtin contrasts the polyphonic novel with other kinds of writing. It may be helpful to suggest that polyphony is a particular subset of the generally dialogic, a special instance of authoring a hero who or which is more free of authorial control than is sometimes the case in authoring. Vice also tries to cut through potential confusion of categories by suggesting (50) that dialogism is a relational property, polyphony a literary form, and heteroglossia (see below) a description. Since "hero" is a technical term and ubiquitous in Bakhtinian writing and

In other words, I, authoring, can only bring into artistic dialogue the self I am working on; if I have minimal consciousness to bring, there will be not much dialogical authoring present. One scholar suggests, "Bakhtin projects this process, essentially, as the task of translating oneself from an inner language into the language of 'outward expressedness'"(Danow 1991, 69). Bakhtin insists that such a (polyphonic) hero an author creates is fundamentally a version of the self. An author, creating such a hero who is to some extent an alter ego, then by dialogue, engages and evaluates that being.[22]

Such a contention alters, though of course does not remove from discussion, the question of mimetic representation. No hero, in Bakhtin's sense of the word, can be explainable primarily in terms of historical referents. Bakhtin insists that neither can the etiology for such a character reduce to psychologism but is fundamentally linguistic and ethical. (And I would add that it is also spiritual, in the sense of lived experience of faith, a category that bridges a religious-secular binarism.)

As Bakhtin understands it, the process of authoring a polyphonic hero is carefully, intentionally chosen and requires skill. Morson and Emerson (1990, 232), taking great pains to make Bakhtin's thought clear here, confess that the notion of an author casting such a creature is counterintuitive.[23] In any case, the author projects from himself (Dostoevsky is always the prime exemplum for Bakhtin) not a conceptualized plot, not a psychological profile, but an idea or question for conversation. The polyphonic hero is constituted dialogically and by means of speech, since he or she

---

scholarship, and since I am headed toward a reading of the figure of Saul, I will use it, despite overtones of masculinity and hierarchy that it may carry in English. Shepherd advises (private communication) that the word emerges in English with slightly different overtones than in the Russian, where it is closer to "character."

[22] Palmieri (1998, 49–52). Pearce (1994, 96–99) warns about the inappropriateness of grafting Bakhtin's ideas about diverse subjectivity onto any interpretation that is universalistic or ahistorical. It is a good caution for those using him with biblical texts.

[23] Hirschkop (1998b, 27–29) cautions about excesses in Bakhtin's envisioning of this polyphonic authoring process, noting that all characters are authorial creations and so are not in any literal or extreme sense free of their authors; it is a point with which Pearce agrees (1994, 47).

will be a site of discourse—presumably one of several. That is, an author surrenders the more usual totalizing control and major finalization of such a character, delegates some omniscient authority, opting rather for something more horizontal. Discussion is what is enacted, not action:

> This transferral of words from one mouth to another, where the content remains the same although the tone and ultimate meaning are changed, is a fundamental device of Dostoevsky's. He forces his heroes to recognize themselves, their idea, their own words, their orientation, their gesture in another person, in whom all these phenomena change their integrated and ultimate meaning and take on a different sound, almost the sound of parody or ridicule. (Bakhtin, *PDP,* 217)[24]

The hero is the site of the working out of a (probably unresolvable) idea.[25] The idea will be discussed but not clearly resolved or managed according to any discernible formula.[26]

In such an authoring, there is no single center of consciousness—whether authorial or characteral—able to manage the agenda. The truth quality of what is being offered, Bakhtin maintained, demands multiple presentation: "As a result of such an ideological approach, what unfolds before Dostoevsky is not a world of objects, illuminated and ordered by his monologic thought, but a world of consciousnesses mutually illuminating one another, a world of yoked-together semantic human orientations" (*PDP,* 97). Characters become subjects as well as objects of authorial creativity.

---

[24] Morson (1986, 83) says that polyphonic authoring needs to be read as well as written polyphonically.

[25] For example, Bakhtin suggests that such an idea in *The Brothers Karamazov* is, "Everything is permitted if there is not immortality of the soul" (*PDP,* 89). On p. 203 of that work Bakhtin summarizes Dostoevsky's genius.

[26] Morson (1995, 61). Holquist comments (1990, 74) on Homeric heroes, which he, like Bakhtin, thinks are not (very) dialogic. But note the work of Nancy Felson-Rubin, which, using Bakhtin's strategies with a different understanding of the epic genre, seeks to reopen the question of how Homeric heroes can be construed. Falconer (1997b) also critiques Bakhtin's assertions about epic and demonstrates the usefulness of his ideas in terms of the classic epics of Homer and Milton.

An author may be surprised at what such a hero says. The authoring of a life goes on throughout my lifetime and is never able to be summed up or *finalized* while the subject lives (*PDP,* ch. 2). Morson and Emerson, struggling to expatiate Bakhtin's ideas on polyphonic creativity (which they think he did not define very explicitly), pose the main challenge as control: "In short, how does an author describe a hero as a whole without sacrificing the hero's capacity to develop in surprising ways?" (1990, 190). Briefly, the construction of such a hero is a matter of positioning discourse and awareness. Bakhtin's use of the term *ideology* seems paired with the hero's self-consciousness.[27] Self-consciousness and ideology (awareness of self and of the world) together mark the text, and they are in dialogue with but not the same as those of an author (or narrator). So all that an author ("the" author or an "authoring hero") brings to bear—from what is richly social and perhaps scarcely reflected upon in the creative process to what is intensely idiosyncratic is his or her projected ideology.

As is the case when one authors a self or an other, it is not in any sense a matter of aimlessness or a lack of viewpoint on the part of the author, any more than intentional nonviolence lived out is passive. To the contrary, it is decentered but not wandering.[28] The author's point of view comes into play in the choice of approaching insight dialogically rather than monologically and insofar as the author participates in the discourse with the hero: "Self-consciousness, as the artistic dominant in the structure of a

---

[27] For one discussion of ideology, see Bakhtin and Voloshinov, *MPL,* part 1, chs. 1, 3. Hugh Pyper summarizes: "By ideology ... Bakhtin means a more or less coherent system of values and interests which stake a claim in providing an interpretative key to the world" (1996, 68). Thus when Bakhtin uses the term *ideology,* he is referring more to a character's worldview than to his or her self-consciousness. On the other hand, as Lähteenmäki observes (1998, 89–91), consciousness is social as well as individual, is shared as well as "owned."

[28] Emerson (1988, 508) raises discussion and criticism of this much misunderstood point. Clark and Holquist try to compose a suitable definition, of ideology (1984, 224). On p. 205 they say: "We literally enact cultural values into our speech through the process of scripting our place and that of our listener into a social scenario." Their analogy: As any game "applies" its rules, so speech "applies" our values, which are not simply individual and private but also social.

character's image, presupposes a radically new authorial position with regard to the represented person" (Bakhtin, *PDP,* 57).

The author's "I" has a special place among the voices it inhabits, never reducible to some formula constructed by gender, class, race, though it will include these aspects among many others (Emerson 1988, 508–13). The author allows the hero to be whipped by discursive winds (including authorial) but avoids trumping the hero. The choice and capacity to maintain such a position (generally dialogic and perhaps specifically polyphonic) defines and delimits how the discourse will go but does not prearrange just what the outcome will be.

To create such a hero, again, involves outsidedness and also what Bakhtin calls *transgredience:* "the quality of being a potentially empathetic relationship (as both concerned 'insider' and of necessity 'outsider') to the other (as character and hero)" (Danow 1991, 70). Such an authoring, if extended by the artist, must be engaged also by the reader, to some extent at least. That is, polyphonic writing requires polyphonic reading.

Bakhtin's most sustained discussion of this vast topic of authoring and philosophical aesthetics occurs in *AA* and *TPA,* which explore in depth how an artist can create art—can express vital and living experience—without murdering it when form is imposed and experience objectified. Natal'ia Bonetskaia clarifies helpfully: Being is the act I do, with answerability a pole of it (1998, 91–92). As she describes it, an artist expresses her being and art partially exotopically, as responsibly and truthfully as she can from her distinctive position; being is an event that takes a form, has a moment of stability without being reified or even controlled by the author. It is the human spirit that takes form—not an art walled off from life—in a dialogical encounter between the artist and the hero created, and presumably between that hero and others (readers) who author as they encounter it.

To reprise authoring is to review what Bakhtin understands by the concentric circles of dialogism (with its wider diameter) and polyphony (narrower). The fundamental conviction is that all life—certainly human existence and language—is a matter of co-being, of relationship. Far from being individual units with tidy seams and impervious surfaces whose interactions are discrete, rather we live at our own edges, which are shared (and contested) with others. Our transactions, including speech, are mutually constitutive for ourselves and each other. Bakhtin also pointed out how dialogical are our daily lives, particularly in terms of conversations we run in our heads with "the others," whose responses to us and ours to them so shape our plans and action:

> The topic of a speaking person has enormous importance in everyday real life. In real life we hear speech about speakers and their discourse at every step. We can even go so far as to say that in real life people talk most of all about what others talk about—they transmit, recall, weigh and pass judgment on other peoples' words, opinions, assertions, information; people are upset by other peoples' words, or agree with them, contest them, refer to them, and so forth. . . . One must also consider the psychological importance in our lives of what others say about us, and the importance, for us, of understanding and interpreting these words of others ("living hermeneutics"). ("Discourse in the Novel," *DI,* 338)

A few other terms help clarify Bakhtin's process of authoring dialogically. I can see some facets of the others that they cannot see of themselves; I have a *surplus of vision* (or of seeing) in regard to an other, as of course any other has as well in relation to me.[29] I have a corresponding blindspot that I do not see, something that allows me to remain unfinalizable both to myself and to others. One cannot understand another totally, since while I still live, there is more to happen, more to consider; nor can I sum myself up even at a given moment, since part of me (the space behind me, as it were) remains out of my own purview. Related is Bakhtin's concept of *loophole,* the slit through which I can escape my own or others' efforts to trap me in some conclusive way.[30]

So the same authoring process constitutes both my self and an other, granted each in a different way. The minimum involved in authoring (whether in life or in art) is two consciousnesses. Emerson notes often in her writing that Bakhtin

---

[29] Bakhtin discusses the surplus of seeing in a number of places, as is true of most of his other concepts. Consult "Author and Hero," *AA,* 15–22 for a good start.

[30] A character can avoid the author's or another character's effort to trap him, as Bakhtin demonstrates with Dostoevsky heroes (*PDP,* 233). Presumably a reader can resist a narrator with some similar strategy.

has no interest in—and no special understanding of—a whole range of feelings that most of us live with all the time and that fill the modern and postmodern text: envy, nostalgia, regret, meaninglessness. In Bakhtin's universe those feelings cannot really exist, since they are predicated either on an impossible desire to escape one's own surplus and the responsibilities it generates, or on an invalid desire for mere replication of another's surplus. (Emerson 1990, 117)[31]

Morson and Emerson point out a further aspect of this respectful, dialogical, and sometimes polyphonic relationship between authors and others (which is also exemplified and described by practitioners of intentional nonviolence), where one can use one's own particular angle of insight effectively, anticipating with confident experience that another is capable of something new, can indeed walk down a path that she or he is already exploring to some extent but with only incipient awareness. Such an author invites the other along such a trajectory, encouraging such a new phase in a timely way, because of the exotopic angle.

Bakhtin's emphasis on authoring, central as it is in his works, invites a quick comment on the death of the author, described by Matthias Freise (see also Burkitt 1998). Freise notes (1997, 131–41) that Bakhtin's ideas are not particularly compatible with either the goals or results that formalists, structuralists, or deconstructionists activated when struggling to free text and reader from the author. Bakhtin's seeing skeins of relatedness and his insistence on human answerability and particularity are at cross-purposes with projects that reduce the author to a mere abstraction, the text to a pattern of devices, and the reader to simply a player of endless textual games. For Bakhtin, the position of the authors—all of them—structures the formal aspect of the work, the perceptual angles from which it will be constructed. The author is not equated with the person pushing the pen but represents the confluence of time, space, and other factors at the particular time the writing occurs.

A last elusive concept also described in Bakhtin's writing on dialogism is the partner Bakhtin calls the *third* or the *superad-*

---

[31] It seems fair to say as well, though, that our own lack of ability to see our total selves may give rise to some of those same dissatisfactions so prevalent among (modern and other) human beings.

dressee. Iris Zavala clarifies that, for Bakhtin, dialogics is actually tripartite, involving besides a self and an other, a presence or witness which she understands not as the ego or the unconscious, not the implied reader, not even the "thou" of Buber—but the person who understands and becomes a participant in the dialogue, although on a special level (1989, 51–57; see also Morson and Emerson 1990, 135–36).[32] Coates (1998, 159) describes "the superaddressee [as] the third party in every dialogue who offers 'absolutely just responsive understanding' to the speaker who fears being misconstrued by his or her immediate addressee." The third is a place from which the author can achieve ever-fuller understanding of the hero or other; the position provides a witness to assist the integrity of the author-hero communication. By standing over the author and the hero—not identified with either but related to both—the third helps effect the co-authoring, intensifies what the author sees of what he or she lacks and what the other can consummate from an exotopic angle. The moral strength of it, coupled with the sense of full understanding, makes clear the attraction between Bakhtin's Superaddressee or Third and God. The implications for such an understanding of God are vast and cannot even be sketched here. But what Bakhtin seems to allow is an understanding of God's presence and activity that is analogous to this process of authoring that is visible in linguistic activity (see Morson and Emerson 1990, 267).

Implications of authoring for ethics and aesthetics

The implications for ethics, aesthetics, and language are huge and worth some elaboration, partial though it will be.[33] First the ethical factors challenging an author can be considered: To no small

---

[32] Bakhtin comments on it briefly in "The Problem of the Text," *SGOLE,* 122–26. Holquist suggests (1990, 38–39) that Bakhtin's notebooks are his superaddressee. Perhaps so.

[33] Though obviously the topic runs the gamut of Bakhtin and his commentators, it is possible to refer to main sources: Emerson treats these matters (1997, chs. 3 and 5); Clark and Holquist's main spot is their ch. 3 (1984) explaining answerability; Holquist (1990) sets the essentials out in ch. 2 and then ramifies the implications for various usages. Though these points emerge in my arrangement as implications, that is not how they appear in Bakhtin's writing.

extent, my time/space—my particular life circumstances—are *given* to me in many aspects, but it is the human charge or destiny to *create* something of what I am given, a self and other elements as well (Morson 1995, 55; Holquist 1990, 22–23, 28–29).[34] To undertake that charge intentionally is to be *answerable,* or responsible.

One image Bakhtin offered for such integrity is the *signature:*

> Signing, then is the first step toward the truth of my situation. Only what is personalized can become available for clarification, wholeness and interaction. Thus, the most important thing about any act is: did I do it and do I accept responsibility for it, or do I behave as if someone else, or nobody in particular, did it? (Morson and Emerson 1990, 69–70)[35]

Emerson grounds this concept in Bakhtin's own life when she maintains that he steadfastly refused to see himself as—and to become—a victim; rather, he grasped the factors that were far less than ideal and made them the means of his survival:

> Russians researching their own past, for example, have been powerfully tempted to see residents of that prior oppressive regime either as martyrs or collaborators. Bakhtin was neither. He was a *survivor.* And in order to survive, both morally and physically (that is, in order to avoid causing harm to others and to avoid sacrificing himself to no purpose), he had mastered certain protective skills and evasive tactics. (Emerson 1997, 8)

So my particular condition of awareness of responsibility is what Bakhtin termed *addressivity.*[36] As a speaker I address my words to someone; my words have an addressed valence rather than generic and universal character. As a hearer I may agree to being addressed. But an individual can fail to work at or miss the sort of creative action Bakhtin had in mind in several ways. If to live answerably is to sign one's name to one's life, to avoid such

---

[34] Holquist uses "conceive" for create. I think they all mean that I transform what is given to what is dealt with creatively.

[35] Bakhtin discusses answerability most helpfully for our purposes in *TPA,* 42–65.

[36] Bakhtin's clearest statement on addressivity is in "The Problem of Speech Genres," *SGOLE,* 95–100.

an act was called by Bakhtin the seeking of an *alibi* or the evading of responsibility.[37] To avoid is itself a choice I may make. Bakhtin's other label for such avoidance is as vivid: "The *pretender* tries to live as the theorists of ethical 'norms' say we all should live, by simply performing or failing to perform abstract demands. The pretender lives 'representatively' and 'ritualistically'" (Morson and Emerson 1990, 31, drawing from *TPA*).[38]

As Bakhtin saw it, my life is not simply there, given, but must be authored; I must choose to live it as an event, must take some considerable responsibility for where I stand, for the quality of the life and work that I author. It matters how I do it, and the self I become makes a great deal of difference. We may not have much choice over whether we share a lot with others or not but retain considerable influence over how we manage that sharing. The point is to do it intentionally, with integrity. Such an ethics does not polarize large versus small, personal versus social factors but sees them as intrinsically related.

Sensitive to the ethical implications of Bakhtin's thought, David Patterson writes:

> The thing that distinguishes the dialogical relation, however, is that every word calls for a reply, so that the more I answer, the more I am responsible. The debt increases in the measure that it is paid; the distance and difference grow more pronounced with their acknowledgment. The response not only answers a call but itself calls for an answer; the affirmation is a confession, the revelation an indictment. (1991, 38)

The aesthetic link is most visible when Bakhtin discussed the author as artist (as detailed above), a process that he saw echoed in all authoring as an author recreates the logic of the other as a subject, giving it form from a position of outsidedness. The imposition of form, or perhaps better, the bringing of suitable form to

---

[37] Bakhtin finds useful examples of alibis and pretenders among Dostoevsky's heroes and other characters; see his discussions, for example, in *PDP*, ch. 5.

[38] Such false living may come from over-identifying with the image of oneself that one finds in the mirror rather than attending more courageously to what an "authored other" shows.

a particular medium, was a major question for Bakhtin (and the whole tradition around him). The greatest writers handle their hero as an "I," as a subject, though that is not easy to do. Emerson provides a suitable summary description of the aesthetic process:

> Once we have put in the necessary work to bestow a whole image on another personality . . . we find it first comfortable, and then compelling, to formulate words and actions in its "zone"; we welcome its responses; we begin to trust its integrity sufficiently to risk interacting intimately with it and investing ourselves in it. . . . And I know that another's personality has become a whole when, from my perspective, this personality ceases to need *only me*—only the questions I ask of it or the trajectory I impose on it—and declines to obey my fantasy without a murmur; in short, when it emerges as open and able to devise needs of its own. (1997, 222–23)

Bakhtin says, "For the hero the author is not 'he' and not 'I' but a fully valid 'thou,' that is, another and other autonomous 'I' ('thou art')" (*PDP,* 63).

The ethical and aesthetic factors play out most visibly in the characteristics of language that have gone into and emerge from such authoring processes, insights for which Bakhtin is best known and of greatest interest to literary theorists. He celebrated the impossibility of laying these aspects out in any definitive way; my purpose here is to highlight and interrelate them briefly. The overlap with much that has already been said should be evident.

The umbrella under which Bakhtin's positions on language all stand is the dialogic, which acknowledges the multiplicity and interconnectedness of voices at work simultaneously and at many levels in language, involves a way of hearing such languages consciously. So the point is not so much whether a unit (from a word to a novel) "is" monologic or polyphonic but where it may be best apprehended along the spectrum running from the more monologic to the more dialogic and polyphonic. The polyphonic character of a text is also a choice to be made or resisted by an author and a reader. To proceed efficiently here, we will start from small units and build toward larger ones. This array includes: words (and strings of words); forms of represented speech; utterance; heteroglossia; genre; chronotope.

Every linguistic expression, even if very brief, is composed of *words.*[39] Bakhtin wrote, "Each word tastes of the context and contexts in which it has lived its socially charged life; all words and forms are populated by intentions. Contextual overtones (generic, tendentious, individualistic) are inevitable in a word" ("Discourse in the Novel," *DI,* 293). Even single words—let alone tangles of them—are not unitary but have struggles for meaning raging underneath their ostensibly unified verbal skins. Every word *"is precisely the product of the reciprocal relationship between speaker and listener, addresser and addressee"* (Danow 1991, 36). Though we may think of words as most at home in dictionaries, in fact those tidy lives are arid and artificial. Words continue to inhabit all the contexts where they have been used, granted the impossibility of our coping with all of that richness.

Bakhtin warned against forgetting this characteristic of words in our desire to tame them:

> For the word is not a material thing but rather the eternally mobile, eternally fickle medium of dialogic interaction. It never gravitates to a single consciousness or a single voice. The life of the word is contained in its transfer from one mouth to another, from one context to another context, from one social collective to another, from one generation to another generation. In this process the word does not forget its own path and cannot completely free itself from the power of these concrete contexts into which it has entered. (*PDP,* 202)

He continued elsewhere: "Dostoevsky's basic artistic effects are achieved by passing one and the same word through various voices all counterposed to one another" (*PDP,* 256). Authors and heroes can choose to use (strings of) words that come from different contexts, with the reader also challenged to consider the range of contexts brought to bear.

The topic of *represented speech,* the intentional and specific use by one (author, narrator, character) of another's speech was of great interest to Bakhtin, both in literature and in life—so not simply abstractly but in particular languages at particular times. He

---

[39] Bakhtin talks about qualities of words often: "Discourse in the Novel," *DI; PDP,* ch. 5; *MPL,* part 1, ch. 1; "The Problem of Speech Genres," *SGOLE,* 60–61 sums up his thought on this point.

discussed it repeatedly, under the general topic called varieties of discourse, *double-voicedness,* or *reported speech;*[40] this large category may be understood as a particular intense and highly crafted use of literary language, drawing in and developing many other parts of his understanding of what an artist does and projecting a microcosm of what Bakhtin observes about speech elsewhere.

In short, reported speech is the language claimed to be that of another, so speech about speech, utterance crossing utterance. It will thus likely be part of a dialogue, in the basic sense of that term: a conversation in some way between two (or more) persons, though it can include many complexities beyond quotations. Someone takes over the speech or utterance of another; one borrows, and another lends—though perhaps unwillingly. Key is that there are now at the very least two centers to consider: the original utterance and the new use of it. In narrative, it will also be reported by someone, best called a narrator.[41]

---

[40] One compact summary may be found in *PDP,* 184–202 (actually, throughout ch. 5), also in *MPL,* 3.2; *DI,* essays 2 and 4; *PDP,* ch. 5; "The Problem of the Text," *SGOLE,* 110–17. Morson and Emerson (1990) offer their sense of a summary in ch. 4, Clark and Holquist (1984) most compactly on pp. 233–37. See Bagby for another viewpoint; it is he (1982, 36) who thinks that the discourse typologies are a microcosm of the rest of Bakhtin's ideas, a point that is attractive to me as well. Bakhtin discusses and modifies this key concept throughout his writing life.

[41] Since I have already discussed in some detail what Bakhtin understood by author and authoring, the clarification of his sense of narrator can be made fairly straightforward. As Vice summarizes (1997b, 4–5, 41, 67, 126–27, 146), Bakhtin was not utterly explicit or consistent on his relation between author and narrator. She concludes, and I agree, that it is most accurate to say that he did not make the error of equating "author" or narrator with the actual historical personage moving the pen across the page but saw the author as the artistic agency responsible for the formal effect of the text, which does not coincide completely with him or her. The narrator (and in Bakhtin's examples, the types of narrator vary so widely that it is questionable to be too reductive) is an authorial construct, part of the artistry of the text, a voice to be reckoned with; it is not found as an impersonal and reliable reporter but as one of the voices performing the text. Such an understanding does not violate Bakhtin but pushes his words toward a greater clarity and usefulness, standing now for us, as Vice notes, on several decades of narratological theory.

Since there are multiple facets engaged simultaneously with reported speech, each with its own effect but interlocked with others, I will discuss the topic in terms of four spectrums or scales: the questions of degree of narratorial intrusiveness, of participant identities, of clarity of boundaries between speakers, and finally Bakhtin's own scale of the degree of polyphony present.

The first scale to consider involves the narrator, usually (at least in biblical narrative) not a character. The issue to nuance here is the degree of intrusion of the narrator into the workings of the story and the consequent issue of reliability. If we imagine the scale extending from an extreme of narrative tags ("he said") all the way to the other extreme of narrator assertions so intermingled with character speech that they cannot be isolated, we can also posit some midpoints on the spectrum. How a narrator chooses to name a character (by title, proper name, patronymic); how much a narrator chooses to summarize character speech and what word choices are made in so doing; the angle from which the narrator reports dialogue, given that it can be done from the viewpoint of any participant but not all simultaneously; the choice to report the inner speech of some character(s) but not all—all these moves open space for scrutiny of textual dynamics.

It seems straightforward to accept a narrator tag at face value but possible to engage more resistingly and less complacently with certain other narratorial assertions. To assume narrator reliability, as though that voice were an unpositioned and nonediting voice, seems wholly inadequate (Bakhtin, "Discourse in the Novel," *DI,* 278).

A second charting to attempt or acknowledge involves the identity of the participants. Though there may usually be a non-character narrator, characters become narrators as well when they pick up the task of reporting each other's speech. So, simply to note some of the layered possibilities: the "borrowing who" may be a narrator, or a character; a character may borrow his or her own speech as well as that of another. The "lending who" is anyone from the second utterance of Adam onward, as Bakhtin was wont to say.

In order to comment on the quality of the reported speech, each center must be considered and then the relationship(s) between (or among) them. Here also can be placed the question of form of the reported matter: a clear excerpt from speech that the reader also witnessed; a reading from a newspaper or, perhaps, from a character's own journal or letter; the multiple attestation of an episode or event by several characters. All of these facets demand negotiation.

The third set of gradations concerns the clarity of edges between and among utterances.[42] Once again, it is fairly simple to proceed from what is less contested to what is more mixed—though how languages manage these edges varies considerably. In Bakhtin's terminology, if a narrator simply summarizes another absolutely, that category is not reported but *reporting speech*. But the line is not always clear between the two, as can be seen by a simple example:[43] She asked about his certainty. She asked if he was sure. She asked was he sure. She asked, "Are you sure?"

The slots most frequently suggested to render these distinctions include direct narratorial summary (she asked about his certainty), indirect summary (she asked if he was sure), narrator quasi-indirect speech (she asked was he sure), narrator quasi-direct speech (she asked, was he *sure*), narrator's positing of direct discourse (she asked, "Are you sure?")—with all that is implied in that vast category. The issue opened up once again is the source of reliability for the assertion: Is it unambiguously dependent on narrator, character? If the precise perceptual angle cannot be made clear, the reader's task will be correspondingly complex.

Fourth, and finally, we arrive at Bakhtin's own admittedly schematic and simplified chart, which includes most of the elements discussed here, though implicitly and rather jumbled in with each other.[44] What can now emerge more clearly from it is issues of "technical polyphony," how the voices of narrator and charac-

---

[42] Bakhtin and Voloshinov, *MPL*, 119–40; the discussion clarifies what sort of reporting context is placed around reported speech: how firm the fences are, or how permeable.

[43] Thibault (1984, 107). Different languages have different syntactic conventions to make these (and other) distinctions. As is obvious, the absence of quotation marks in a language makes the diagnosis more complex.

[44] Bakhtin, *PDP*, 199. His part 1, "Direct Speech of an Author/Narrator," aimed primarily at referents, has been problematized appropriately above. His part 2, "Represented Speech," is given two facets: the degree to which the language is personal to the character and the extent of social markers that it bears. Pearce (1994, 50–52) is quite clear about this aspect of Bakhtin.

ter(s) are distinct but intertwined, constantly and variedly inter-penetrating each other. Bakhtin's chief interest was his part 3, "Doubly-Oriented Speech," with its possible variations. Though it may seem that once we get to this most crucial part of his thought, the calibrations are too refined for biblical prose, the gain from noting his categories is still great.

Doubly-oriented speech is not angled toward a referent as toward the speech of another, hence its name. Bakhtin makes his way across a spectrum of types, using several roughly overlapping pairs of polarized terms to suggest tension or degree of polemic between or among users. First, speech that is consciously bor-rowed and reused may be worked "empathetically" with that of the "lending" dialogue partner (*unidirectional*), or moved toward more discrepant angles (*varidirectional*). The terms *linear* and *pictorial* suggest the same issue. *Stylized* speech is reaccented, but without the degree of tension that characterizes the *parodic,* used with more awareness and more hostility, whether it is simpler or blending closer to the *skaz* so beloved of the Russian theorists (see Morson and Emerson [1990, ch. 8] for a thorough discussion and many examples).

Reported speech may be *doubly-dialogized but passive*—some more overt and tending toward the more covert (which again will be unidirectional or varidirectional). Finally, there is the *genuine, active, double-voiced discourse* where the degree of dialogization is intense, resulting in microdialogues (familiar in the speech of certain characters in the works of Dostoevsky).

A reminder: In addition to this linguistic complexity, we can (theoretically) mine each unit for indicators of social situation and for idiosyncratic markers. So a character or speaker will articulate the matrix culture in some way and also have a particular and dis-tinctive linguistic fingerprint. As the speech is reported, it will be composed of elements that have come from other contexts. At this level, all speech is reported, since the components of any of it will all inevitably be well-used. But more specifically, the speech may be part of a conversation between two characters (or between the narrator and a character) where they sling each other's words back and forth; or the speech may also be filled with many possibilities of meaning from other sites (what might be termed "intertextual" borrowings from virtually anywhere). Finally, and perhaps addi-tionally, the reported speech may be heteroglossic, composed of a variety of kinds of language (e.g. social dialects), all communicating information that is significant.

It may be useful to attempt a simple English example. Stylized: "He said, 'She classifies herself as coloured.'" One can note in that particular reported direct discourse the presence of a technical term from bureaucracy, and in fact a trace of a British-based system, evidenced by the spelling. There is no hint that the two speakers are at odds here, though context might reveal that she was an albino, for example, in which case the borrower would be at odds with the lender. Parody: "He said, 'She is "coloured" all right—colored by the experience of being a white girl in the South.'" The male speaker is clearly at odds with the language of the female speaker whose speech he is using. An example of oral parody (*skaz*) might be: "He said, 'She colo(u)red.'" This quoted utterance may be a simple descriptive action or an import of black dialect, with its tendency to communicate without some of the final inflections of standard English.

And finally, a fourth kind of doubled reported discourse is the situation encountered when a speaker builds speech with a number of the above elements, making intensive use of dialogue with all the elements present even in trace as well as with absent but envisioned elements. Such speech is highly self-conscious and simultaneously alert to other presences at the site of discourse. The best example offered by Bakhtin is his excerpt from Dostoevsky's *Poor Folk* (*Letters of April 18 and June 12*). In this last type of reported speech, the character is drawn speaking with maximum independence from the authorial purposes. As the character uncaps an array of possibilities in his or her speech, the authorial control over the working of its construction (whether by character or reader) slips. The artistic skill needed for such authoring and reading is great. The ultimate point of all this analysis is that though there are many textual cues to pick up on, there is no sense in which "the meaning" will be able to be finalized. These enriched facets of artistry must be negotiated by responsible readers, who will choose among persuasive speech rather than relying on categories claiming to be externally authoritative.

But for Bakhtin, the key unit of language was not the phoneme, the sign, or even the word or the sentence but the *utterance*.[45] An

---

[45] For good discussion of utterance, see Bakhtin and Voloshinov, *MPL*, 99–109, *FMLS*, 120–28, "The Problem of Speech Genres," *SGOLE*, 67–72.

utterance may come in various sizes or genres, from a murmured "well" to *War and Peace*. (In fact, a novel comprises many diverse utterances as well as being one in itself.) What makes the utterance distinctive is that it is constructed already with a response anticipated; that is, it is both already a response to something and also framed so as to elicit a response—framed by one responding as well as anticipating a rejoinder of some kind. So an utterance is thoroughly dialogical.

Bakhtin also characterized the utterance as composed of both what was actually articulated and also what was tacitly assumed. To construct or construe an utterance requires an active grasping of contexts, demands an evaluation of what is going on, presumes some sort of aim or intention. Utterances in literature must be examined within the context of the work in which they appear— so a text is an interplay of utterances—but readers will also construe utterances from their own multiple contexts. Utterances, composed of words and texts, will bring to their new context a residue of their past adventures. The vast space for understanding is clear: If every utterance is in some way dialogic, and if words themselves are inherently disputatious (including intonation, a facet of language difficult to pick up off the printed page, since it is primarily audial), and insofar as textual heroes are constructed by loquacious viewpoints, then meaning is not monologically foreclosed.

Related to dialogism and polyphony but also distinct is Bakhtin's concept of *heteroglossia*.[46] Speech, Bakhtin noted, is diverse according to factors of class, profession, geography—omit-

---

Pyper stresses that it is its unrepeatability that most characterizes the utterance (1996, 63).

[46] Bakhtin discusses this much-loved concept of his in "Discourse in the Novel," *DI*. The most useful discussion and practical illustration in secondary literature, I found, is Vice's (1997b, ch. 1). She illustrates her contention that heteroglossia is one of the ways that novels are able to be polyphonic (or use hybridized speech). It seems one of Bakhtin's concepts less suited to biblical texts, whose Hebrew and Greek can on occasion be compared with other phases of themselves (e.g., New Testament Greek as distinct from classical), but I am not aware of places where a clear and sustained case can be made for class, gendered, or regional dialogue variation within a work.

ting one that many have added to his list: gender.[47] The polyphonic language in which Bakhtin was most interested was almost inevitably heteroglossic. Though a huge concept, it can be presented succinctly as the joyful recognition that in life or a literary work there are a number of social "language systems" in play at the same time, rubbing shoulders with each other, often in the mouth of the same speaker.

Bakhtin instanced a (theoretical) peasant who could speak a local patois to his fellows, would use religious jargon in church, another terminology when speaking to his lord, another to his animals, and so forth; and the master of the manor would use his own speech to talk to a peasant, who would understand that language though not use it—or would be pedantic if he did. Language in both life and literature embeds such texture.

Heteroglossia is related to the dialogic, since when we are listening (or speaking), we have the challenge of hearing these various languages in contention with each other, or construing the significance of the speech for the utterer in terms of the system from which he or she takes language.[48] This heteroglossic nature of speech remains strongly *centrifugal,* despite the efforts of some to systematize speech (render it *centripetal*) so that we can all be saying the same thing.[49]

As Bakhtin pointed out, we learn language from life, not from the dictionary, so we all speak a number of languages at once. In all these language occasions, an author can and will intend some particular meaning, and that meaning is to some extent made effective; but there is no way in which an author can—or should wish to—control all that is happening in a word, an utterance, the play

---

[47] Among those who work to remedy this deficiency of Bakhtin, see Bauer and McKinstry (1991), Hohne and Wussow (1994), Kehde (1991), and Vice (1997a).

[48] Lodge reangles the matter, asserting that heteroglossia is what is enacted at the site of a character—enacted and signed; both author and reader have many choices at such a site (1990, 67–75).

[49] For further elaboration of this linguistic tug of war, see Bakhtin, "Discourse in the Novel," *DI,* 271–73. Hirschkop insists consistently in his writings that the social aspects of language to which Bakhtin paid lip service but did not actually bring forth very deeply are of central importance and need to be exploited by those working with Bakhtin.

of reporting/reported discourse that compose a text. There is just too much to organize or tame. Hence the text will be unavoidably historical and social—drenched in social factors, not merely private and individual (Holquist 1990, 61).

Another way in which Bakhtin envisioned the shaping of discourse was by means of *genre*.[50] Genre is the overall shape of an utterance, the form it has taken to accomplish its purposes. In ordinary prosaic life, we all live amid a welter of genres, use our repertoire comfortably, and switch back and forth with little trouble; yet we can understand how an educated, literate person may be at least temporarily at a loss how to think in a genre that is new or unfamiliar (e.g., cocktail party chatter, a eulogy, an interview).

For genre is not simply a collection of devices or a particular arrangement of features into which an artist pours something she has already learned; genres are not whole, abstractable, or transcribable. Nor are they neat and tidy, but rather they inosculate—mix in with each other in surprising realms, embed themselves. There is vast genre heterogeneity at every level, in language and literature. For Bakhtin, genre was a particular way of working out issues of human consciousness, intimately connected with the project of meaning. He anthropomorphically but powerfully spoke of genres as having eyes and ears and memories. By such language he conveyed the sense that genres help us visualize and utilize things to which we may have limited insight (Morson and Emerson 1990, 284–85, 307 make some refinements of these points).

Though an author's selection is partly a matter of individual choice, genres are primarily and fundamentally social: we already shape our insights in accordance with the genres that are ready-to-hand in our social lives. They shape how we think, form our insight as we move within and among them; they do not simply contain what we happen to have thought already. If we disregard the way a genre thinks, we risk losing significant insight; genres

---

[50] For Bakhtin's most expansive work on genre and the various ways he traces the prenovelistic genres, consult "Epic and Novel," *DI;* he is more succinct and argumentative in *FMLS,* ch. 7, and briefer still when discussing Dostoevsky's originality in *PDP,* ch. 1. For some additional comment, consult Thomson (1984, 32–36). Pearce shows (1994, 73) how Bakhtin's latest writings made the addressee more prominent than had his earlier analysis.

can absorb some themes but not others. The artist learns how to think creatively within, to see reality through a genre.

The genres that most fascinated Bakhtin did not express insight philosophically or analytically but by developing specific examples; the polyphonic novel—his favorite genre—casts self-conscious heroes by altering authorial position. Genres are frameworks that fix the worldview of the ages from which they spring, collect and precipitate experience in some way, form residues and accretions and experience peculiar to an era or to some aspect within it. So the late nineteenth-century Russian novel works out in that genre something about capitalism that would not have been thinkable earlier; epics talk about their founding era in a particular way.

Related to genres both in terms of their socio-historical qualities and their capacity to shape is the *chronotope:* the interrelatedness of time and space (which can be artificially abstracted from each other).[51] Life and literature take place as constructed by time-space, and the influence of dominant chronotopes was one of the aspects under which Bakhtin reviewed the development that resulted in the novel. Comprising both what happens and how the happening is told, recognition of and collaboration with a chronotope open up a huge category of insight (the Paris salon will obviously embed and communicate a lot of culturally specific information about art, social

---

[51] Bakhtin's essay "Forms of Time and of the Chronotope in the Novel" (*DI*) reviews some good examples: the road (which helps generate the adventure novel), the castle (which makes Gothic romances feasible), the salon of nineteenth century. The chronotope is not "thin" but includes the various fixtures and props—that bring the setting to life and assist its communication and our understanding. That a chronotope can be considered at different levels of abstraction (e.g., the road) or from different angles (as above—authorial, readerly, and so forth), and that a chronotope can be a device, a motif, or a plot function need not distract from the main insight. Late in his writings Bakhtin commented on the difficulty of discussing all this relatedness in an orderly way; the chronotope, like his other major categories, draws the rest of the thread of his thought through that particular needle's eye. Holquist sums up (1990, ch. 5), as do Morson and Emerson (1990, ch. 9). Bakhtin's latest word comes in the short essay, "Novy Mir," in *SGOLE.* Some of the best development of this aspect of Bakhtin's work has been by feminist authors, who explore chronotopes that are distinctively feminine: e.g., Pearce (1990, ch. 5), which introduces a number of other examples, as does Vice (1997b, ch. 5).

values, class, gender, and so forth that would not have been thinkable in an earlier century, for multiple and various reasons). The best of the chronotopes, Bakhtin said, are very time and place specific. A chronotope is a kind of matrix; there will likely be main ones and subtypes in any given work, even perhaps congealed ones. The recognition of the facts of our groundedness in space and time is what made Bakhtin insist upon the chronotope. Clark and Holquist remind us, "We are constantly engaged in the activity of *re*-presenting the signals we get from our exterior environment, shaping these signals into patterns by means of particular chronotopes. Bakhtin argued that particular chronotopes are the defining or dominant features of persons, periods, and works of art" (1984, 279). They also observe of Bakhtin, "There is a sharp and categorical boundary line between the actual world as source of representation and the world represented.... The chronotope is a bridge, not a wall, between the two worlds" (1984, 279).

The chronotope raises to awareness the many questions implied in the notion of representing an action against a backdrop of time and space, which will include other specific cultural markers. To raise those particular artistic problems is not to solve them, especially when they are as problematic as they are with a good deal of the Hebrew Bible. But, as Morson and Emerson summarize, "It is as if each genre possesses a specific *field* that determines the *parameters* of events even though the field does not uniquely specify the particular events" (1990, 369–70). We can sometimes sense that certain chronotopes would be most unsuited to particular tasks of representation.[52] Outsidedness is key to our discerning the chronotopes.

How to Push Bakhtin

It remains, finally, to reconsider the four questions raised earlier about Bakhtin's usefulness for biblical studies in view of the

---

[52] For my purposes, the chronotope selected for representation is the founding moment of the monarchy. So it needs to bring into play the factors—economic, social, religious, political, macro to micro—that make the story tellable. As well, the chronotope of the composition is present: so perhaps a moment quite near the end of the experience of monarchy when a reflection upon it is possible, though perhaps one not able to be definitive in any sense at all.

points suggested in this chapter. This last step, however, is best preceded by the explicit recognition that the most fruitful use of Bakhtin involves not simply exegeting and explicating his work but developing it while simultaneously appropriating it—a project both compatible with all that Bakhtin represents and also undertaken by most Bakhtin scholars. The most helpful "takeover" of his thought, for my purposes at least, has been feminist analysis. The vast field of feminist studies includes both ethical and aesthetic angles; it sees art as both rising from and contributing to the quality of human lives. Virtually all feminist critique maintains a commitment to and record of working with language in actual as well as more theoretical circumstances; hence its lenses are valuable. The wide-ranging and deep-probing analyses expose both potentialities and weaknesses of Bakhtin's thought.

Ironically, Bakhtin had virtually no interest in gender and never mentioned it as a category of particularity; aside from an inevitable attention to bodies and social roles when working with Rabelais, he is virtually mute on the subject of gendered language, viewpoint, or culture. Nor does he seem to have been even incipiently feminist in his personal life. Consequently, it seems ludicrous to some that his writings be employed by feminists and outrageous to others that a(nother) male authority be used in feminist criticism. And yet, many insist, there is much of value.

If, as Adlam suggests, the rich diversity that is feminism can be linked by a common purpose to discern, critique, and aim to rectify the vast gender-based oppression present in culture, Bakhtin's work makes a number of contributions (Adlam 1997, 142–43). Leaving aside (as is my particular choice to do) the highly complex subfield of Bakhtin on Rabelais, the carnivalesque, and the grotesque body, his basic dialogic insight insists that a multiplicity of voices and intensive interjoinings from a variety of positions inevitably shape all linguistic reality (Vice 1997b, 162–76). All utterances are alloys, many times over. None is monologically correct or in control; the plurality decenters the patriarchal control from any one person or group, avoids the sovereign and authoritative, the dichotomous and binary, and does so without creating an essential feminine substitute. Bakhtin's insistence—flawed though it may have been in practice—that all construction is situational deprives the dominant angle from its claim to being natural and inevitable.

Bakhtin's sensitivity to the dialogical, heteroglossic construct-
edness of speech and to the irreducibly social and historical
contexts challenges all reductive meaning. All of his assumptions
about language and his work on distinctive chronotopes provide
multiple pathways of choice (and resistance) for those entering
any text. As Myriam Diaz-Diocaretz puts it: "[Bakhtin's theory]
proves that the monologic, self-proclaimed authoritative word of
patriarchy excluding women at different levels is not conclusive,
is not and can never be the last word" (1989, 131). There is simply no permanent, universal, natural, or inherent meaning in literary language. No one needs to or can claim a stance at the monologic rock of self-righteousness. Feminist thinking picks up more
explicitly on the not-articulated than did Bakhtin, who was more
alert to the multiplicity of the traces present, but the emphases are
compatible. Again Diaz-Diocaretz says: "A feminist critical vision
has to work precisely at the site where the speaking or writing
subject—in its dialogic nature—is grounded or from which it is
interacting, whether embedded with the patriarchal notions or
not" (1989, 135).

There is greater guardedness about the practical dynamics of
authoring and reading and their implications for intersubjectivity.
Feminist reactions to Bakhtin replicate feminist scholarship and
practice in general. Some will find androcentric texts and their production too dangerous to use; others will be more optimistic about
the creativity available to alert and sophisticated readers and urge
that once the heterogeneity is claimed—even valorized—then what
is different, diverse, hidden, excluded, and so forth can emerge
freshly (see Shumway [1994] for a sober evaluation of possibilities).
A key issue among feminist and postcolonialist readers is the like-
lihood of a benign encounter between uneven voices. That is,
Bakhtin's sense of authoring disregards power. Mary O'Connor
makes the point well: How can one (individual or) group really
relate to another without exploitation, dominance, or annihila-
tion—not so much in the abstract as given the obvious history of
the procedure and the uneven positions from which men and
women now start? She speaks for those leery of Bakhtin's coauthoring, which seems to have neglected to make explicit the fact
that the power relations in life and literature have been and remain
grossly uneven, an omission that makes likely the reinscribing of
the same negative patterns (Mary O'Connor 1993, 243–53).

A corresponding danger is that differences will be subsumed into the general. In a subject-to-subject encounter, where we inevitably see ourselves and the other inadequately (recall exotopy, surplus, and loophole), the risk of inviting another to co-create is perhaps too great. O'Connor points out that Bakhtin's unusual gendered imagery for this very transaction is itself pretty horrific (Bakhtin, "Author and Hero" in *AA*, 136, noted by Mary O'Connor 1993, 246). She poses: "Although Bakhtin takes us far, even in his early work, towards an analysis of the subject that includes its relation to other subjects, we must extrapolate and dialogically expand his theory to come to some theory of how gendered subjects can interrelate."[53] Mary Pollock, conceding that Bakhtin's ideas should further a male critique of the patriarchal, admits that it does not feel very possible from her experience as a feminist writer; the engagement will not be equal, especially if the "weaker" invites the "stronger" into her viewpoint rather than the inverse, or perhaps into some mutually shared space (1991, 231–40).

Again, one thinks of nonviolence, where a similar critique is made. To recognize, acknowledge, and in fact accept the interrelatedness of all life is inevitably to become part of exploitation, both as "givers" and "receivers." It will happen. If Bakhtin is correct about the inevitable and ubiquitous coauthoring that goes on constantly, then the abuses will have to be addressed, not the project itself abandoned. And the confrontation will need to be particular, not occur simply in the abstract. If Bakhtin's claims about answerability can hold firm and truthful, then the struggle for responsible dialogue seems worth the effort, at least to me.

So, recognizing that Bakhtin cannot have solved all our problems for us but may (with some help) have clarified some useful ways to proceed, what can be distilled at this time in terms of the four questions raised above?

First, to what extent can Bakhtin's "Dostoevsky insights" be brought to bear on Hebrew prose? Since Bakhtin came to the insight that it was the "novelness" of language (not just "novels"

---

[53] Mary O'Connor (1993, 257). Hitchcock (1991, 198–204) raises some of the same issues in terms of colonialist concerns. He senses that Bakhtin's understanding of dialogic authoring is too prone to takeover by the stronger. Not all outsidedness or exotopy is so benevolent as Bakhtin seems to assume.

per se) that was of significance to his thought, and since he himself criticized theorists who did not see deeply enough, there remains no barrier to investigating more hopefully than he did how biblical language can be worked dialogically, even polyphonically. Part of his interest was to set up long genealogies of how earlier texts were related to much later ones, studies that exposed many commonalities among linguistic expressions. So the charge that a "modern" criticism is inappropriate for an ancient text seems moot. The workings of biblical language are grist for the dialogic mill, with results needing to be evaluated on their own terms.

A second question involves the Bible's complex and impacted historical issues. Bakhtin maintained, without demonstrating very adequately, the need for historical context at every stage of reading.[54] In any case, historical studies have moved so far since he wrote that his methodology would need substantial repositioning even had it been more explicit. The historical problems for (Hebrew) biblical texts are caught between the hairs of a now too-inadequate quality and a too-vast quantity of data. Historical investigations must make both explicit and sophisticated their ways of reconstructing reference from ancient literary texts, freeing themselves from any naive presumption that things were necessarily or probably as described. My sense here is that Bakhtin's chronotope, the particularity of the time-space that anchors the productions, settings, narration, and reading of texts will be useful. To ask about time/space forces specificity. The chronotopes will be more provisional than dogmatic, will seek to suggest possible and plausible contexts—any number of them—rather than seeking to pinpoint facticity.

To situate the socio-historical context of sixth-to-fifth centuries communities in Judea and Babylon while exploring the heteroglossic facets of two different texts (e.g. Lam and Isa 40–55) seems a fruitful way to proceed, perhaps with literary and social-scientific practitioners collaborating rather than any trying to do the whole project alone. A freshly considered spate of materials around "the exile" suggest a fertile site for scholarly collaboration, including Bakhtin. The chronotopic sketches will remain provisional, since so

---

[54] His discussions of the viability of the carnivalesque in various eras seems the closest he comes in any extended way.

many details must remain unknown; but the posited situations—including those of readers—will be less abstract and more vivid, granted there may be a diversity of reconstructions offered.

As Clive Thomson puts it, the chronotope is a way to acknowledge that texts carry historical information in an indirect way, much of which may not be so easily divined from what they assert or even from general circumstances of production, but which must be questioned carefully for their information (1983, 15–16). Newsom gets at the same point when she asks how to read the history that we do not experience directly but only as ideology, especially when the referent is pretty wholly absent from the text—or seems absent to us, as may be the case of the non-exilic group and Second Isaiah (1992, 73–78). Bakhtin's calling attention to the multiple historical and social experiences already loaded into language at any site will inevitably alter the task of historical reconstruction. A dialogical project shared between those with more literary interests and those whose preferences are more genetically reconstructive seems promising.

A third question arises around the construction of meaning, whether by author(s), textual voices, or readers. It seems that, after Bakhtin, the question must be reconfigured, both in terms of what he said and also what he did not quite reach. As has been suggested, Bakhtin did not theorize so much about the reader as about the author. In fact, many have noted that his own reading of key texts was more to comment on their construction than to consider their effect. And yet he did read constantly in his investigations, thus demonstrating if not articulating much about what a reader does. His boldest statement about reading was that "the authors creating the text, the performers of the text (if they exist) and finally the *readers* who ... *recreate* and in so doing renew the *text—participate equally in the creation* of the represented world in the text" (emphasis added).[55]

---

[55] Bakhtin "Forms of Time and of the Chronotope in the Novel," *DI,* 253. He makes the comment while talking about the importance of correct perception of the chronotope by readers, but it seems the sentence has wider application as well, since a good deal of related artistry is hanging off the chronotope. The best situating of Bakhtin and reception theory are Shepherd (1986, 129–45; 1989), Halley (1989, 163–79), and A. White (1984). Bakhtin cautioned that a reader is liable to make—needs to

It strikes me, pondering Bakhtin's ideas, that authoring and reading proceed analogously with certain sports, since both actions proceed in a linked way but distinguishable manner. Consider a game, like (North American) football, where one side may control the ball and hence be playing offensively while the other side is playing defensively. The experiences of the two sides are different in a number of ways, but they are playing the same game, making moves in constant and manifold relation to each other, as in fact Bakhtin never tired of repeating.

So just as the author constructs the self inevitably while shaping a hero, so does the reader bring a self to the process—granted, at a series of removes from the author. It seems obvious that the author is not thinking of the many future real readers who will pick up the text; Bakhtin also makes explicit that neither does any real reader actually make contact with the real author. The author does not so much draw back from the text (disappear or die) as exert a kind of presence that has little to do with control. Active, answerable readers, construing from their own unique positions, will shape the true potential of a deep text, breathing it into something genuinely new. The authoring process is what a reader has access to vis-à-vis an artistically authored text, and how a reader performs a text is procedural too, rather than punctiliar, with multiple possibilities at every turn.

Morson and Emerson suggest in this context:

> Finally [readers] can take maximal advantage of the differences and of their outsidedness by an act of creative understanding that is truly dialogic in the best sense. Readers may make the differences [between the author's and their own chronotopes or contexts] occasions for exploring the potentials of the work in a way not available to its original authors and readers, and so

---

avoid—three sorts of errors: presuming a naive realism in the text (which we may fairly say is a major "mistake" in the study of the Hebrew Bible); presuming a naive biographism (mistaking the implied author for a flesh-and-blood person—also not absent from biblical study); and what he calls a naive reception, where the reader disregards the key cues from the chronotope (and presumably from other historical factors as well) and over-modernizes the text. In "From Notes Made," *SGOLE*, 144, he indicates that a reader can know "better" than an author. See Pyper (1996, chs. 2–3) for additional theorizing about reading.

become enriched by something truly in the work but needing their own special experience to provoke. (1990, 429)

Bakhtin's devotion to and skill at playing the many textual cues should dispel or discourage any reading that is arbitrary or irresponsible, and his example invites other interpreters to be explicit about their own strategies.

A large range of readers is called for: some will be more literary, some more broadly cultural—e.g., artistic; the bent of some will be more theoretical, while others will be more politically invested. New combinations are already in evidence, as feminist studies show. Links to the field of spirituality or ethics will seem less purely private or personal, insofar as they rise from dialogue with the embodied situations of other readers as well. The circle of persuasive readings will increase in quantity, quality, and diversity. Morson and Emerson sum up: "In short, artists create potentials for the future by exploiting the resources of the past" (1980, 288).[56]

Finally, the fourth challenge shared by Bakhtin and biblical studies: genre. If Bakhtin is helpful when he uses genre not as a virtual synonym for form but rather for a text's (i.e., author-reader's) way of thinking, it becomes clearer that genre considerations need more care. Bakhtin's own ruminations on the history of genres are probably more illustrative than practical to biblical scholars. But his practice of considering genre as historical and social as well as a matter of individual choice remains key.

For example, if Polzin is on target (which is not to say definitively and exclusively correct) in identifying the early chapters of 1 Samuel as parabolic—not because they resemble the form of Nathan's story to David in 2 Sam 11 but because of their way of working out issues, what implications will that have for readers who attend to the genre? If the story of Saul is a parable of the kingship as experienced, it will provide another angle on the question of viewpoint. Both Polzin and Pyper make use of the *mise en abyme,* a small genre that invites the reader (along with the author and characters) to reconstrue pieces of narrative in constant relation to others. But the clearest example, perhaps, is the carnival genre. It is not enough simply to assert that the features of Bakhtin's carnival are present in a book like Esther; Esther

---

[56] They discuss (1990, 284–90) this problem of "who owns meaning." Refer also to Holquist (1981, 163).

must be read explicitly and boldly as a carnival, even if such a strategy seems and generates effects unfamiliar.

Some of the past historical issues may broaden out a bit: not simply, is the Deuteronomistic History (hereafter DH) the product of a double redaction, clearly discernible in certain patterns and phrasings? But, how can the vast multiplicity of voices in that text be well heard? The thoroughly historical and social nature of literary language challenges, beyond a doubt, the categories that have attended the Bible: revelation, inspiration, and the like. Those insights are invaluable, as recently demonstrated by the work of Wilfrid Cantwell Smith (1993); those concepts do not replace or override the constructed sense of all texts but must work collaboratively with such claims. A similar warning pertains about abstract and timeless theological assertions that are generated off the Bible. The multiple voices on biblical site as well as the many pertinent circumstances must be acknowledged, a process that will slow cosmic pronouncements and call for some review.

So, why Bakhtin, who Bakhtin, what Bakhtin, how Bakhtin—the challenge to biblical scholars is clear. The next two chapters will test the suitability of the appropriation from several points of view.

3.
Saul Struggling to Stay: A Bakhtinian Reading of 1 Samuel 17:55–20:42

"[Saul's] character zone is filled with doubt and uncertainty. Surrounded by a dubious aura, Saul is the epitome of a questionable choice.... our introduction to him ... is one who ... continually asks questions."

Robert Polzin, *Samuel and the Deuteronomist*

"There is no single Bakhtin and we have ... to recognize this aspect of his theoretical texts by letting pertinent passages cross one another dialogically, as it were, in answer to questions put to them in our study."

Anthony Wall, "Characters in Bakhtin's Theory"

"Ultimately, dialogue means communication between simultaneous differences."

Clark and Holquist, *Mikhail Bakhtin*

Introductory Points

The aim of this chapter is to perform a responsible and compelling reading of a section of the Saul narrative using Bakhtin's category of reported speech, and thereby to lay forth some dynamics of how that category works in ancient Hebrew prose. Those strategies will center on the Deuteronomist's authoring of the figure of Saul, on my particular reading of that character, on the king's own construction of his life, and on ways in which other characters draw him.

The technicalities of method are laid out in the previous two chapters on Bakhtin and his thought, with additional sources referenced; explained here is only what is minimally necessary to show what I am doing. This chapter does not focus so much on methodology as on reading. It is one of an eventual set of essays, using facets of Bakhtin's theory to explicate the figure of Saul in the text of 1 Samuel. But since its aim is to show how Bakhtin's insights can be helpful, I have shifted from the more usual taut essay to a fuller (not to say baggier) exploration of textual units.

What drew me to bring Bakhtin's approach to this text was the highly transactional nature of Saul's language to and about himself and others and their correspondingly intermeshed way of speaking to and about him. That is, in the one hundred verses that I have chosen for focus (1 Sam 17:55–20:42) I have classified the discourse as follows:

A. Speech of Saul (which comprises all of his talk):
1. seven questions that invite an answer: 17:55, 58; 18:8; 19:17, 22; 20:27, 31
2. two cases of enhanced language (oath) in which standardized language is used: 19:6, 20:30
3. his quotation and interpretation of another: 18:8
4. his crafting direct discourse for others to say under his authority, so as to be persuasive: 18:22, 25
5. his quotation of himself, not totally truthful: 18:22, 25
6. his self-talk (three times), undoing what he has formerly said or making specious announcements: 18:11, 17, 21
7. his issuing of orders or commands (five times) that fail to happen: 17:56; 18:17, 21; 19:15; 20:31
8. speech given him (twice) by other characters: 20:3, 7
B. Speech to Saul:
1. He is almost always addressed with respectful, even guarded or evasive terminology—
2. by all but Michal: 19:14, 17.
3. Jonathan addresses assertions naively, not seeming to hear that they may arrive differently than he ostensibly intends them: 19:4–5; 20:28–29, 32;
4. "they" report information he seems to want to hear or know: 18:7, 20, 24; 19:19, 22.
5. Abner seems to evade response: 17:55, perhaps the servants as well.
6. David sounds self-deprecating to Saul in the three sentences he says: 17:58; 18:18, 23 (the third is to the servants presumably to report to Saul).
C. Speech about Saul, exchanged by the others, is ordered around how Saul is treating David and aimed toward securing a change in tactics:
1. of Jonathan: 19:2–3; 20:2, 3, 9, 11–15, 16, 18–23; 20:3, 42
2. of Michal: 19:11; of David: 20:1, 3, 5–8, 10
3. of others: 19:24

D. The only other language is Jonathan to the servant, speech actually addressed in code to David: 20:36–38.

E. Narrator speech will be examined and categorized below.

But my assumptions are the following: Bakhtin's theories render impossible, undesirable, and irrelevant the terminology that assumes narratorial reliability, omniscience, or sufficiency.[1] The author—or any narrating voice (whether a character or the extradiegetic voice of the usual biblical narrator)—provides a particular type of recitative mapping, showing skeins of optional pathways, more than any reading can ever utilize. Any narrator, and certainly the one under consideration, has a rich repertoire of moves and will be able to change pace; hence that language must be taken up responsively by a reader. The narrator of 1 Samuel resembles little that of 1 Chronicles or of Isaiah.

Since narrating and narrative are a form of representation, there is no reason to think of the narrator as inevitably "in the know" about realities outside the fictive. There is no dispensing of gobbets of fact, even and perhaps in particular about God. Whatever the Bible's authority is, traditionally understood in terms such as revelation, inspiration, canonicity, and the like, it does not reduce to or rest upon factual reporting.[2]

What distinguishes Bakhtin—as well as relating him to a number of other contemporary theorists—is his attention to the language of narration. It is the vast system of language options that makes texts signify: where the language has been used before, how it is shared among various participants, how readers may choose to exploit it. He presumes, prescribes, great attention to how phraseological representation is managed, by narrators and characters. But

---

[1] Polzin's work on 1 Sam, which is key to my own work and immensely fruitful in bringing Bakhtin to biblical study, continues to call the narrator omniscient (1989, 19–21), though he also assigns the narrator skills where that quality is placed on hold, as it were. Polzin's narrator is surely capable of reducing the broad angle and standing with a character to offer his or her viewpoint, with the result that we know little more of their consciousness than they do. Elsewhere the biblical narrator proceeds very differently.

[2] The best discussions I know of, at least within my own tradition (Roman Catholic), are those of Sandra Schneiders. For a compact summary see 1991, ch. 2, discussed at greater length in the second edition of her work, *The Revelatory Text: Interpreting the New Testament As Scripture* (1999).

far from limiting us, those factors liberate us as readers into the vast maze of connections, as everyone dialogues with everyone else. Bakhtin is not inattentive (at least theoretically) to issues of historical reality, but rather like a judge in a courtroom, he insists that we attend to how the information comes to us rather than assuming it makes no difference. E.g., courts value and use differently stipulation, hearsay, expert witnesses, lawyer remarks, instructions from the bench, and so forth. We are called to listen carefully to the said and unsaid demands that we not cross carelessly into realms of the historically realistic or the psychologically plausible. Our journey requires that we reach for data from those realms but not without labeling our moves carefully, explicitly. That is, when reading "like Bakhtin," we do not try to peer beneath the frame to see more of the picture but try to see well what is presented on the verbal canvas.

Bakhtin understood that language in general and surely human exchange were profoundly dialogic, literary language all the more so. Additionally, authors of most interest to him, creating or shaping "polyphonic heroes," proceed in respectful relationship with their characters, not "finalizing" them over their heads to readers but drawing them so that they evolve their own awareness, especially their self-consciousness, as much on their own as possible. My contention here is that the 1 Samuel narrator (referred to heuristically as the Deuteronomist) can be "pushed" or read to author Saul more polyphonically than is usually imagined. Of course Saul is no Raskolnikov, but the amount of construction of and by him makes him a good candidate for Bakhtin's strategies. Saul is more transparent than many, and more suggestible for others, readers included.

To reposition for immediate use the vast topic of how Bakhtin saw speech as polyphonic, one may think of its properties in concentric circles, each becoming more intense as the circumference shrinks. The sort of discourse most characteristic of polyphonic novels is more engaged with other speech rather than aiming to reference external data. What Bakhtin organizes is how speech crosses and engages other speech, what relationships can result as centers of consciousness intersect. Though in some ways narratorial speech differs from character language, in this rough schema we can utilize the same categories for both, since characters become narrators when they quote.

Bakhtin's schema, like that of Hebrew discourse linguist Cynthia Miller, shows speech organized across a spectrum. Miller's work on the relationship between reported speech and reporting contexts is rooted in discourse linguistics and compatible with Bakhtin, though much more content to classify forms as an end in itself than he was ever prone to do.[3]

Miller's most helpful points can be summarized, with particulars added as needed. First, the rough divide of direct or indirect discourse is not adequate to the subtlety and diversity of biblical Hebrew's syntax. She creates a spectrum that includes four slots (with many particular verbal constructions adding variations): direct discourse, free indirect (also know as quasi-direct and, for Bakhtin, concealed reported speech), indirect, reduced indirect (or semidirect [Miller 1, 42–48, 81–83, 129–33, 281–84]).[4] A challenge is to diagnose whose center of interest or focus governs in indirect discourse, since two (or more) will be involved (a project for which she supplies some criteria).[5]

Bakhtin moved beyond the formal classifying of the speech forms to ask questions about how the centers of consciousness are engaged when speech centers cross and speakers are borrowing from each other. Is the reported speech done sympathetically with the original intent (assuming that such can be known)? Or is it

---

[3] Miller (1996, 64); a clear chart indicates what her interest is and makes the overlap with Bakhtin's doubled speech evident, though each of them ramifies and complexifies in a different direction.

[4] Her summary of the categories of indirect speech is on p. 141.

[5] E.g., deictics are the most useful indicators of viewpoint (1996, 73); reported speech almost never uses sentence fragments, volitives, or exclamatory particles, though indirect may do so (75–80); the infinitive construct לֵאמֹר does not introduce direct discourse (75). Miller summarizes the functions of the expression הִנֵּי (behold), which is the most common way to indicate indirect speech and viewpoint, though not the only way and not its only function (85–90). That deictic marker does not require a verb of perception though may use one, and it may indicate the arrival of a new character onto a scene as well as a particular point of view. It may also represent the merger of character and narrator viewpoint, assert something a character cannot wholly have known. She also restricts the insights led off by הִנֵּי (behold) to perception not thought—a distinction I find too rigid. She also usefully advises that indirect speech may be suspected when things do not fit quite right for direct (81).

stylized to some extent, whether used in a more linear way (more aligned with the first user) or more pictorially (less aligned)?[6] Is the doubled speech more parodic (whether simple or a peculiar oral brand that is not discernible in Hebrew)? He found some reported speech to be doubled but passively so, the use of one speaker more hidden or more overt; and at least in Russian novels, his final and favorite category was genuine active, double-voiced discourse, the sort that Dostoevsky heroes engage in when they do microdialogues with others inside their very fraught and self-aware heads. The nuances are important here, not because the text of 1 Samuel will use them all, but because they instruct us to listen attentively for the ways in which one speaker makes use of the language of another.

As those who use and develop Bakhtin have said better than did he, the responsibilities for such a reader (i.e., one who aims to read polyphonically) are great. Though Bakhtin was not alert to the relevance of his theories for the ancient classics, I aim to show how useful they can be, particularly when we are dealing with the construction of God, a constant enterprise in the Bible.

The reader, in addition to being sensitive to the text, must be self-aware, willing to be answerable for her choices, and willing to make them creatively (Bach 1997, ch. 2). She will acknowledge and celebrate her personal and political situatedness, all that runs the gamut from private and idiosyncratic to public and social, allowing for what is conscious and less so. Reading protocols and choices affect the text, not in precisely the same way that writing choices do, but closely, analogously. The more a text has been crafted with all this dialogue and polyphony proffered, the more effectively it can be read with the same strategies brought to bear.

So why have I, reading, noticed such narrative features of the text, or why are they of interest to me? First, I am pondering my own experience of problems Bakhtin explores—both in myself and in others. In other words, I have noted a preoccupation with the self that inadequately accounts for the others, generating (and being generated by) a refusal of responsibility. The dynamic can be read at many levels: the tendency to blame others for what is partly my doing; the determination to strive simultaneously for

---

[6] Bakhtin also used the terms "objective" and "pseudo objective" for these choices made by one speaker using the words of another.

opposites; a resisting of insight that is scary or distasteful and the magnification and projection of it onto an other; the avoidance of confronting boldly what is most desired and most forbidden.

It strikes me that many of these issues live more in the realm of words than clunky deeds, which is to say that most of us do not take a gun and go into the post office but construct our opponents and ourselves more indirectly, more subtly—often verbally, whether in real discourse or in soliloquy, or if fortunate, in prayer. Nevertheless, the refusal of responsibility is constantly embodied, acted out by us as well at all levels, from our eating choices to our economic decisions in light of global poverty and homelessness, even to our reaction to the thousands of pieces of space garbage polluting the neighborhood of our solar system.

As the Saul narrative makes clear, there are no discrete spheres of private/public, small/large, domestic/professional. The same human malaise underlies all the choices any of us make regarding these spheres. Or, we may refuse to claim responsibility for them in any way that might reroute lives that are already going in some other direction—even if not necessarily a bad one.

I am also always searching for strategies of reading Scripture that offer alternatives to the ones available to most educated and committed readers, strategies that tend to be literal or allegorical in some basic sense. I think drawing Saul in a Bakhtinian fashion offers better approaches. I read with people thirsty for deeper ways of appropriating Scripture. I find the representation of speech to be a wonderful way to show texture and to move myself and others as far away from all the forms of fundamentalism that exist, including prooftexting, typologizing, allegorizing, mimetic fallacies, formalism, and so forth. The biblical figure—Saul here—becomes not a "role model" but a much more complex re-presentation or refraction played by a reader.

Stipulations made, my thesis can be offered: I have come to see and plan to sketch Saul struggling to maintain his status and to survive over against, as he seems to see it, the silence and strength of God and David (and others). Another way to put that is to sense Saul, in frantic dependence on others, sliding inexorably into isolation. Saul spends himself and splits himself on this apparently obdurate and disapproving rock of God-with-David. It is his destructive fragmenting of himself and his manipulation of multiple uncertainties while refusing to acknowledge what he is doing that are of interest to me.[7] Interpenetrated with others in a variety of ways he does not acknowledge, provoking things with little awareness or answerability, he is not well-centered in himself. Frantic, driven, off-balance, unraveling, he shows us a lot.

The plot action is primarily talk. The ethical and aesthetic problematic that the text works is the question of survival and status: How can Saul survive as king, as founder of a dynasty, as a human being in relation to God?[8] He tries and fails, failing for the most part because of how he tries; he contends against his own best interests. His talk is destructive of what he most wants; his talking may obviate his listening. He becomes both unwilling and unable to "sign his own life," to claim responsibility for his moral choices.

Does silence, the nonresponse of God, throw Saul off, throw him into his own talk? Is that the spirit that frets him: God's silent disapproval, having decided that Saul cannot continue to be king? Saul is fraying at the edges as he tries to reweave himself, and he is at constant cross-purposes with himself and others. Such is the authoring I want to explore. As I do so, I am conscious that, though I am reading speech, I am really reading myself to explain it; that is, I can observe the verbal dynamics of the text, but if I

---

[7] It is difficult to establish a base from which to do a small piece of narrative. In general, I would like to start with Polzin's positions as the default. His work on the Deuteronomist, 1 Samuel in particular (1989), is unlike any other. His very deft use of Bakhtin is so subtle and yet so tacit that it wants a lot of scrutiny. Among the foundational understanding that Polzin argues and that I need to presume are that both God and Saul have selected David; God's rationale may be hidden from us, but Saul's choice is hidden from himself, in that he does not see the confluence of divine and royal actions (152). Seeing, showing, looking and appearing are braided by the language of narrator and characters (157). The issue of God's powerful (dis)approval (the spirits sent) is not simple, like Saul or David either carrying an umbrella or no longer having it at the ready. "The heart of the matter is that even if the presence of David intermittently frees Saul from the evil spirit that will more and more come upon him, David, the new vessel of God's spirit (16:13) must finally overwhelm him." It is not clear whether the spirit leaves Saul once and for all (157–58).

[8] One of the root differences between two astute interpreters such as Polzin and Jobling is that Polzin (following Bakhtin) assumes that character consciousness is the driving element, whereas Jobling makes plot primary (1998, 6–7).

want to account for them, I must sign my reading, acknowledge my own aesthetic and ethical choices.

With these preliminary points presumed now, the plan of the chapter is as follows: I will demonstrate my thesis, and its component parts, by looking at three phases of constructing or authoring. In the first eight short and scenic segments (17:55–18:30), Saul is more active, but he loses initiative as the tide turns in four pieces (19:1–24); and by chapter 20, in a more complex and protracted episode (of fourteen units), he is acted upon and has become reactive.

Since I am starting *in medias res,* it remains for me to state the minimum of what I am assuming regarding Saul from what has already been narrated: Saul's origins are oddly shared with Samuel (a la Polzin; 1 Sam 1–3). We meet Saul on his first mission, which is a failure (ch. 9). Saul is simultaneously and repeatedly designated as king but also contested as such (chs. 9–12). He is fired twice—first from being a dynastic king (ch. 13), and then from being a (sitting) king (ch. 15), but he refuses to vacate his position. That refusal marks his determination to survive with status and with a son.[9] Finally, the quick moment of 17:38–39 offers us a *mise en abyme,*[10] a quick enacted moment of who Saul is, which will be explored and represented in many ways, always with new

---

[9] Assuming as I do that Polzin is correct to see Samuel's birth story as a succinct summary of the whole story of kingship, told in a more leisurely way in the story of Saul before it is given in the rest of the DH, the fact that Samuel is to abide forever (1:11, 22–23) adds complexity to Saul's firing.

[10] Dällenbach (1989) seems to be the major authority on this small genre, if that is what it is. To summarize a topic that needs, in his view, both precision and some scope for its occurrences: Dällenbach links the expression first to heraldry, where the design of a whole shield is found emblazoned in the middle of the shield (in the "abyss/*abyme*"), and then to the sort of refractions possible with mirrors. The *mise en abyme* is a structure or process by which the whole of a narrative is refracted in a moment of it, where some key moment is represented to a character (and reader) that is crucial for transformation. His examples help: a character receiving a message to read refracts the process by which a text is authored for (and by) a reader; or a character recapitulates a deed that the narrator is reciting foundationally in the story. My sense is that Saul's action in 17:38–39 mirrors the whole dynamic of his reign, possibly the whole self-destructiveness of monarchy. It is a hypothesis in need of considerable elaboration. See Pyper (1996, ch. 2) for additional helpful discussion of the concept. Polzin uses

effect: Saul himself clothes David in own his royal gear to do a job that Saul must but cannot do—and David refuses the clothing/arming gesture but accomplishes the deed.[11] It is Saul's part in which I am most interested, but David's response is part of the moment.

I also assume and suggest that DH presents the story of monarchy in Israel and Judah, toward or after the end of its existence in Judah. I am not much interested in the precise amount of facticity that is contained in the narrative; I assume the narrative reflects in many ways the era from which it comes and, to some extent, that which it aims to present for us. Consequently, it is a thoroughly historical work, but to assert that point does not get us terribly far into the question of factually accurate reporting of the past. What is said is more important than how closely it measures up to past events.

I also sense that the story of Saul is a miniature version of the monarchy itself.[12] So far as genre is concerned, I think DH may be read responsibly as a sustained, critical reflection on the cost of dynastic leadership. I also discern elements of a "succession narrative" in the ancient and classic sense of that genre, where Homer and

---

the expression "story within a story" (e.g., of ch. 17) to point to the same general thing (1989, 170 and 1993, 38).

[11] See Polzin (1989, 162–76) for intriguing insights about the Goliath episode. He chooses to take the dialogues (first between Saul and Abner and then between Saul and David) at the end of the combat very seriously as highly tuned narrative rather than to follow cues to redaction and textual corruption or confusion. That is: Saul's fresh seeing of David at the end of the scene where David kills the tall leader is a highly apt climax of the episode. That Saul repeatedly names the key issue as "whose son" and thereby holds up a mirror to the battle scene eventuates in Saul's "impressing" David into his own household rather than letting him return to his father. That is (my words now, rather than Polzin's), Saul once again clothes David as a royal as he did in 17:34–35 and as Jonathan does in the very next moment.

[12] A cardinal suggestion made of the priestly dynasty and subsequently explored by Polzin (1989, chs. 1–2). That is, a narrative that seems mimetically plausible may be generating a very different communication than its surface suggests. For a more explicit effort to relate these stories to the cultural circumstances that likely produced them, see Jobling (1998, 143–75), where he comments briefly but helpfully on the work of historians and social scientific theorists and researchers.

Hesiod and the Hittite poets, and later the Greek tragedians, narrate for us how ancient cultures are set by the process of superhuman sons contesting with fathers who (mostly unsuccessfully) resist them.

Part 1: Saul's Active Authoring: 17:55–18:30

The first part of Saul's story of struggling to stay as king consists of a series of five episodes where he takes initiatives, interspersed with narrative comment. The point here is to watch the talk and to observe the narrator comment.

i. *Whose son is David? Whose father is Saul?* (17:55–58)

It is my choice to start in the midst of the Goliath episode, near the end of its recital but actually at its climax, since this scene overlaps David's slaying of the Philistine. Saul questions three times whose son the young man is: He asks first Abner; then, through Abner, anyone who might know; finally he asks the young man himself. The repetition is insistent, the phrasing largely consistent. It is met first with a statement under oath that Abner does not know; secondly by no response to Saul's order to find out except to bring the boy from the battle; finally by David's reply that names Jesse of Bethlehem, Saul's servant, as David's father. Leaving aside the much-discussed mimetic issues—how can these two not know who David is, given the narrative's unfolding since chapter 16—we may ask, what lies behind Saul's question, behind Abner's refusal to take it on, and behind David's response?

Saul's asking in itself constructs his character (zone), his persistent interlinking with others (narrator included) that invites them to carry some of his responsibility for knowing. Perhaps Saul asks a leading question here, strategizing to take control of a situation that may be out of hand at the same time it is coming under firmer management. At a moment where the king has had to admit he cannot handle one large adversary, he is getting a grip on the ostensibly smaller competitor.

Some see the interrogative tone as dismissive (Polzin 1989, 174–75, cf. Edelman 1991, 133–34). Abner's enhanced refusal of the question is clear here;[13] he first denies knowledge and then disre-

---

[13] Fokkelman reminds us (1986, 191–92) that Abner will take the task of asking the young man's identity in 26:14. Is it risky for Abner at this point to know more about David than Saul admits to knowing?

gards the second question in favor of bringing the young man to speak for himself. David, who speaks to Saul directly only twice in these one hundred verses (and only four times in the entire story of their relationship!) responds here. If Saul's third question is more than a simple request for information but rather a control strategy, even an oblique offer of patronage, David meets it deftly.

But why should the question of sonship be an offer? Why should sonship be an offer? Why should a question be doing two jobs rather than simply requesting information?[14] Sonship is and continues to be *the* topic between these two: Who is David in relation to Saul? Whose son is David? Which son will succeed Saul? Whose son has gone to do the job that Saul has proved incapable of doing? Whose son has accomplished it? Not Saul's son Jonathan, in any recognizable way, but the son of Saul's servant Jesse of Bethlehem.

It is also important to take a moment to ponder all that Saul does not say at this moment of meeting the young man who has slain the Philistine, so that the one question, asked three times, provides the sole focus: Whose son? Since this agenda will develop between them, here we can see that Saul is drawing himself tentatively as father to David, who refuses to draw himself as son to Saul, to sketch Saul as his father. And in fact the conversation has already commenced before these two engage it here, at very least from our overhearing the rewards promised to any who will fight Goliath successfully (17:25–27). Perhaps it has been on the table facing Saul since the words of Samuel to him in 13:14 and 15:28, where first the king's dynasty and then he himself are removed from royal power.

What response does Saul invite from David? The young man spoke more carefully and deferentially earlier in the scene (17:32–37), calling himself the king's servant when he was trying out for the job of giant-slayer. Now, having killed the aggressor, he is less deferential, more confident—even defiant, in the assessment of some.

Saul's first three utterances have been loaded questions, and in one way or another, each has missed its destination. If Saul wants

---

[14] It was the consensus of the second Bakhtin Circle class with whom I shared this essay that I was too insistent upon the importance of this sonship motif. Perhaps so. In any case, their critique points out a real problem of any reader, myself here, authoring/reading in such a way that is both fairly clear and also remains open or unfinalizing.

to hear David's identity before the young man returns to the king, wants to get the information from anyone who may know it, and if he hopes to see David willing to be his son, he fails on each count. Those with whom he speaks deny, disregard, and then dismiss, perhaps disdain his overture; and David wraps Saul's three-ply question into a twist somewhat at odds with the questioner's intent.

The narrator's task here is to position carefully our angle: Saul's interest in the question of fathers and sons emerges as he sees the boy go out to meet the Philistine—an analepsis, since the deed (and its aftermath) has already been described at 17:48–51 (Fokkelman 1986, 190–91). The narrator rewinds the film, as it were, and positions us not this time with the boy and the giant, coming nearer each other as they did in vv. 41–50; but rather we stand now in the camp with the king and his lieutenant, watching the young man go forth and awaiting news, perhaps with an uncertain or divided heart. As David is slaying the Philistine, narratively speaking, Saul is inquiring about whose son he is. And when David is brought before the king, giant's head in the slayer's hand, the question is pressed again.

The narrator's job here, besides directing traffic by assigning tags, is to set the time of the threefold inquiry, which intersects with the trajectory of David's quest. And the narrator links the uttered question of Saul with earlier scenes that make the same question urgent.[15] Undeveloped here, except by a reader, is the question of what Saul wants of David, what he has in mind for them both.

ii. Narrative interlude: Jonathan makes David a king's son—or does he? (18:1–5)
A comparatively lengthy reporting block follows this key scene of Saul and David's first post-Goliath encounter. Since the plan here is to watch the drawing of Saul (which I am claiming is fairly polyphonic) to observe the narrator when there is no reported speech

---

[15] See Polzin (1989, 174–76) for suggestions of the relationship between this and the following scenes and the narratives of Jonathan in 1 Sam 14. Jobling has an excellent summary and discussion of the father-son-surrogate pattern in 1 Sam (1998, 112–16). He claims, no doubt correctly, to have been the first to publish on its significance. I have been working on it for some time under the expression "dynastic sons," which includes royal and priestly.

is important. As before, we are directed where to look: As Saul's
attention was caught previously by David's going forth to
encounter the Philistine and held until slayer and slain head are
before him, so here Jonathan's ear is caught by David's coming to
the end of his response to Saul's question.

And the narrator, standing next to Jonathan, reports, "When
[David] finished speaking to Saul, the self (נֶפֶשׁ) of Jonathan was
bound (קָשַׁר) with that of David, that Jonathan loved him as his
own self." Whose view is that, whose perception? It is typically
classified as an omniscient narrator insight or as a report from the
angle—the self (נֶפֶשׁ)— of Jonathan. But my contention is that by
subsequently describing two gestures by which Jonathan makes
David an equivalent of his self—and so Saul's son—and by the
manner of continued attention to their relationship as the narrative
develops, the view we are given is Saul's. With sonship on his
mind, and having heard his offer parried, Saul watches Jonathan
make David a brother. But to become a brother is not necessarily
to be a son; it is a matter of perceived relationship.

The next report is of an action of Saul's: The consequence of
the conflation of these two young men into one self is that Saul
does not permit David to return to his own father—that is, David
is constrained to remain with Jonathan and Jonathan's father.[16]
Jonathan next is described as making a pact with David (which we
shall witness intensified later, as we will the love of Jonathan for
David, a state reported here again) conferring upon him his own
royal accoutrements: robe and armor—sword, bow, and belt.

The narrator ties the covenant and the clothing to the bond
between the two sons, linking it as well to another scene for us:
As his father tried to do above (17:38), the son now clothes David

---

[16] Edelman (1991, 136) calls it house arrest. Polzin (1989, 175) points
out the custom of the king in 1 Sam 8:11–13, which includes the taking
of sons and daughters. Brueggemann (1990, 9) picks up on the conspira-
torial undertow of the verb קָשַׁר (bind, conspire), which binds the two
brothers as though against the father. McCarter (1980, 305) has a nice note
on the resonance between this scene and that in Gen 44:30–31, involving
as well a father and two sons. McCarter, with others, also notes that these
gestures of clothing and covenant are not purely personal but have political import as well, as these simple words like "love" and "good" are technical covenant terminology.

with his own attire;[17] and contrary to the scene with the king, David here does not refuse Jonathan's gift.

Saul, who presumably remembers—or of whom we remember—his own clothing of David with royal gear, watches his son perform the same gesture unrebuffed.[18] The actions of father and son are narratorially intertwined and placed here in anticipatory summary of some scenes that will be detailed as the story unfolds. (The narrator runs the tape forward in preview, so to speak.)

For narratorial summary ranges now far beyond the moment of its matrix, to tell us before we witness the detailing of it, first that wherever Saul sent David forth, he succeeded; and second, that Saul placed him over the men of war, an action pleasing in the sight of people and servants of Saul. Jonathan and Saul—David too—we are shown, place David in position as Saul's surrogate. Jonathan clothes him; Saul requisitions and then sends him; David succeeds; and people and servants appraise, approve this development.

The scene, again, is a narratorial preview of what we will watch shortly as the characters enact it. Its placement here is to underline, to confirm what is at issue: whose son David is, and at whose behest. By becoming one with Jonathan and by being kept away from Jesse and at Saul's tasks, David is made Saul's son. The narrator role here has been simply to underline and summarize, to gather into one place what we might otherwise miss: how David becomes Saul's son.

How can the narrator describe the invisible binding of selves? By the visible gift of clothing and the pact, accepted though unreciprocated as we see it to be so far. We are told as well as shown Jonathan's love, as are told of Saul's for David at 16:21, where Saul made him armor-bearer, as Jonathan has done here, giving him his armor to wear, a charge reversed in 17:38 when David put the king's weapons from him. So now David bears not Saul's but Jonathan's armor.

---

17 Fokkelman, ever the careful observer, notes that father and son each give David four items (1986, 199).

18 Fokkelman's presumption (1986, 199) that we are to envision David as wearing these garments once they have been given to him suggests an ongoing "speech act" in the story. Jobling (1998, 49, 93–99) considers the abdication by Jonathan to be significant for kingship in general.

By clothing David as himself, Jonathan makes David Saul's son, a position David refused from the father but accepts from the son. The sole narrative outcome of the slaying of Goliath is that David becomes Saul's son. It is a distinctive and key outcome of the slaying of the large enemy, a singular emphasis. The slippage among actions of the triangulated characters is visible. Saul pushes, Jonathan offers, David accepts what has been proffered.

iii. Women make David heir apparent—or do they? (18:6-9)

But after the analeptic and proleptic narrative notes in the preceding two scenes, we are returned to the fresh aftermath of the victory, to the homecoming of the heroes. As women greet the warriors in song, we hear the refrain—or what becomes a refrain in the David story.[19] The song unfolds rather classically according to parallelism's patterns: verb (has slain), subject (Saul), object (number or unit killed); no verb (original carried over) subject (David) object (number killed). What is the construction of the women's utterance? How are they authoring?

It has been construed by some commentators as intentionally insulting to the king, by others as not so.[20] In context, the song is at least plausibly nonpejorative to Saul; why assume first that women would derogate him as he returns from battle? Or perhaps the women, like Abner and the servants in scenes to come below,

---

[19] Michael O'Connor (1995) discusses the poem at some length and with comparative material. He is of the opinion that the direct object nouns refer to units rather than to numbers and that the terms of the comparison favor David over Saul, though he also concedes that it is difficult (if desirable) to get equal terms. He comes down, ultimately, on the undecidability of the valence on the weighting of the terms.

[20] A sampling indicates the issues considered: McCarter (1980, 312) thinks the women make an invidious comparison, causing Saul to become envious—a construction that looks more his than the narrator's; Edelman—who cites additional references (1991, 137)—thinks the attributions of credit are equal. Revell (1996, 112–13) suggests that though the women's omission of the king's title may be conventional, it may also imply a lack of respect for him; Klein (1983, 188) refers to Ps 91, where the same terms are used in parallel, without much hint of partisanship; Fokkelman as well (1986, 214) thinks the terms are not inevitably antithetical. "Myriad" is the next named integer after "thousand." The point, I think, is to look not for a universal but contextual intonation.

are cautious. The song is tactful and spacious in its generality—
since neither king nor boy slew hundreds or myriads; rather, one
of them—named second—slew one! In any case, the women's
verse succinctly takes up the recital of slaying from the narrator's
more elaborate telling of it in chapter 17.

The key point to notice here is the two utterances of Saul.
First, he rewrites the song, setting his version in parodic dialogue
with that of the women: "They gave to David myriads but to me
they gave thousands." Saul, not unreasonably, has displaced himself as subject of the verb "has slain," has placed himself second
instead of first. His version of events may be more closely accurate than the song we have just heard. But Saul, in one of his most
characteristic moves, makes the singing key—"They gave," he
emphasizes, subordinating the event to the recital of it—spinning
the women's spin.

Saul's song is a parody of the women's, reverses their likely or
at least plausible intent as he scrambles their recital. And, more
telling yet, he draws from their song—or from his own—or from
the (dis)harmonizing voices—one conclusion, rushing again proleptically far down the field to the end result: "What still [remains]
for him except the kingdom?" Saul's wording, though brief, implicitly blames the singers and the other subject of the song, far
though he has removed their words from their control. The utterance he dreads is his own, though he credits it to others.

Or, in case we think his conclusion is warranted (knowing the
story well), we may ask whose words come true? Is Saul parody-
ing the song, or exegeting it? Why may the women sing as Saul
suspects them to do? Who allowed David to be the giant-slayer?
Saul is angry at the messenger and the message while refusing to
see his own signature on it. We hear him rewrite the song, in his
head. There is no indication that either part of this speech is
shared aloud. His construction, hateful to him as it is, begins to
shape reality as it lives, not out in the open, but at least partially
from inside his own head, cut off from communication with others. Since he now begins to speak to himself, it becomes more difficult for him to reach others or they him.

If Saul's first three queries missed their goal of getting a son,
so are his fourth and fifth utterances poorly cast. He utters here
the thing he most hates and fears—himself failing to be king—
while disclaiming any responsibility for it. That combination brings

his construction closer to accomplishment, Saul hating it all the while.[21] His question about what else remains but the throne is also a development of the topic of sonship: The heir has every-thing but the throne, he says. Who gave the warrior the king's armor? Who made him a son? What do sons of kings anticipate, except the kingdom, eventually? Saul blames others for his own doing, refusing his own share and perhaps substantially misread-ing them.

The narrator's job is again simply to position Saul and sum-marize his angle of reaction to the song, prior to letting us hear the transcript: Saul is angry. As he returns from the Goliath inci-dent with David, as the towns of Israel are filled with the sound of rejoicing, Saul reacts hotly to the song as he construes it, blam-ing others for what they did not quite say; and the outcome is that Saul eyes David from now on—from this day of the Philistine killing on, which confirms the conversation above that Saul had not been watching very carefully until David left to meet the giant. Others' eyes, we have just been told, are appraising David as pos-itive; Saul embarks on a lonely journey to eye him as bad. Starting from his own sense of himself as king, Saul, having made David an heir, now struggles to eliminate him from that role. We may note as well that music is part of what has set Saul off here.

iv. Saul tries to kill his son but misses (18:10–11)

Saul's next speech is also to himself, a pattern that will attend him for a while and mark his indecision, conflict, and perhaps duplicity. It picks up the verb from the women's song, which he now employs in the first person: as the women sang, "Saul has slain ...," Saul now says to himself, "I will slay...," "*I* will slay.... I *will* slay"? And his self-selected target is not the thousands or myriads of the vic-tory song but the one, David, to be slain against the wall.[22]

Saul authors David as quarry, draws himself as hunter, a very warped portrait for all concerned. Saul's inner speech is the

---

[21] Fokkelman (1986, 210) notes that at a moment of rejoicing, Saul is angry.

[22] Later on in this story of kings and dynasties, the Deuteronomist will take to using the expression "any who piss against the wall" as an equiv-alent for the male heirs that the speaker vows not to leave alive (e.g., 1 Sam 25:22). So even an apparently gratuitous expression like "against the wall" carries a savor of the (non)survival of sons.

announcement of a resolution, a plan.[23] Planning, he draws himself as somewhat more competent than he actually is, starting on
a quest of a prey who will end up stalking him. His inner speech
sets a goal he will never accomplish and so comes to announce a
failure of his power. Saul will not strike David at the wall, not on
the first or second try. We may note that there is no character
response to Saul here: not from David, nor from anyone else. An
odd silence. Silence, the absence of inner or outer speech, attends the failure of the plan. Saul never apologizes, never explains, never
acknowledges, never reflects directly on his failure, at least in the
Deuteronomic authorial construction. Saul's spear becomes from
now on a weapon not so much turned against David as against his
own competency to wield it, since to throw and miss (as he will
do until David takes the spear from him at 26:12) diminishes him.
His self-talk deludes him, lets him down.

The narrator sets Saul's short and ineffectual speech, private
and hopefully lethal, against a backdrop of words we do not hear
reported, once again managing primarily the task of showing us
what sets the reported words into motion. It is the next day, presumably the one after Goliath's death has been effected and celebrated. Immediately, the narrator notes that Saul is raving, spear in
hand, in the presence of David, who is playing, lyre in hand, as
before (16:14–23). Now, however, things have changed.

The same scene pre- and post-David's doing Saul's job is actually very different. The narrative setting reinforces the impression
being built up that Saul has commandeered a son from his father.[24]
Additionally, having watched Saul react suspiciously to the joyful

---

[23] Miller notes a number of passages where, though the narrator uses
the word, "said," it is clear from the context that it has to be an inner
thought (1996, 85, 187–91, 290).

[24] The first sending of the boy, with a gift to accompany him, is followed up by a royal request that the boy remain permanently with the
king, a request evidently not granted, given 17:17. Source and redaction
criticism propose a different reading here, which is possible and has certainly been popular. But if fatherhood and sonship are the question at
issue between Saul and David as I am proposing here, and if my drawing of Saul as one who authors unwittingly and blindly his own failure of
kingship has merit, then the passages read differently.

song of the women, how may we anticipate or imagine he will react to the playing and singing of David? The narrator draws our eyes to the respective hands and what they hold, perhaps attunes our ears to the words of the two, one raging and one soothing? It seems at first that the narrator gives an explanation what the character cannot know, diagnoses Saul over his own head to the reader. But actually, such is not the case. For in 16:14–15 the servants of Saul have said very candidly to him that an evil spirit from God is tormenting him. So the narrator simply draws it as present at the scene on the morning after the return from battle.[25]

This narrative interlocking of two scenes (this present one where David's role as evil-spirit-from-God-banisher is anticipated and the earlier one [16:14–23] where Saul himself invites his servants to bring David to court, once they have suggested such a remedy) reinforces the point being drawn: Saul has made David his son, has made himself dependent on him, though he now regrets it in at least some (not necessarily linearly sequential) aspect.

The narrator adds the detail that Saul misses, twice. Saul fails as a warrior again, fails to strike, twice. We hear him announce one attempt; the narrator says David escaped twice. Or, alternatively, Saul misses again to arm David; David avoids accepting the weapon of the king, again. In any case, Saul's words once again (his fifth utterance) miss their effect. His quest for destroying his heir emerges into the open in deed if not yet in word, does not simply reside in his or the narrator's mind.

Does Saul take refuge in the alibi of the evil spirit, cloak his plan to pin David under his temporary and spirit-induced raving? The thought is suggested by what we will see David do when he arrives at the royal seat of Achish of Gath (where he feigns madness). But in any case, a final point has been put in place by the skillful narrative authoring: Saul's ultimate opponent is not just David but God. That the narrator is not drawing that point outside the reach of Saul is a point to be developed below.

v. Narrative interlude: appraisals of the king's son (18:12–16)

There follows another narrative block, quite similar to 18:1–5 in both form and impact: No character talk is reported but the result

---

[25] The spirit from God is introduced in 10:6, 10, at 11:6, and brought back at 16:13–14.

of character appraisal is specified, first by means of the narratorial positioning of our attention, then by summarizing what we have witnessed and will see unfold below. As before, the summary is achronous rather than strictly chronological. "Saul feared David greatly because YHWH was with him but had left [סור] Saul. And so Saul removed [סור] [David] from his presence and placed him as officer [שׂר]—of a 'hundred,' and he [David] went out and in before the people. But David was successful [שׂכל] in all his ways; and YHWH was with him. And Saul saw that David was very successful [שׂכל] and dreaded him. But all Israel and Judah loved David because he went out and in before them."

Whose perception is being communicated? Is it only an omniscient and finalizing narrator? I think not, since the narrative reports the basis of Saul's fear: God's change of position in regard to the king and the one he made his son. Saul's consequent removal of David gives rise to the success (שׂכל) of David, an effect of YHWH's presence with him. That insight is what Saul shrinks from and does not voice yet, while all Israel and Judah love David, who is doing military deeds among them. Can YHWH be with more than one of them, with more than one anointed ruler at a time? Though fired, Saul insists on seeing himself as king; and though he has been told he has been replaced, he refuses to vacate in favor of his successor.

Saul has had two communications from the prophet Samuel, as (un)reliable as that character can be shown to be, that God has appointed a man in place of Saul's heirs (13:13–14) and has rejected Saul from being king and has given the kingship to a man better (טוב) than himself (15:26, 28). The question of how many people know of the anointing of David is disputed among scholars, but Saul knows that someone other than himself, other than his lineage, has been chosen in his place. So already knowing it, and now sensing himself ditched by God in favor of David, Saul deflects his interloping opponent, whom he himself invited to interlope.

David's success at the task of being king (at 8:20 the king is to go out and come in before the people [Klein 1983, 188, but cf. Polzin 1993, ch. 5) serves as reminder of Saul's rejection, the very point he is struggling to avoid as he grasps his position in one hand while letting it slip through the other. Saul's action, prompted by what he dreads without verbally articulating it, hands David

successful (שׂכל) occasion to "go out and come in" before those
who then approve of him, i.e., find him good, better (שׂוב) in their
sight. The success clinches for Saul that God has abandoned him,
a piece of information recalling what he was told when first his
heirs and then himself were removed from legitimate rule. The narrator is making explicit what Saul has occasion to recognize and is
nascently, still wordlessly, reacting to.[26]

Secondly, the narrator underlines for us that Saul's reaction is
singular and isolating, since all Israel loves David; but the matter
is conflictual as well, since Saul loves him too, and indeed was
first to love him (16:21). This summary recalls the earlier one
where Saul cooperated in making David his son (18:1–5), ramifies
it by showing Saul watch David succeed at the task, adding now
the information that Saul sees the reason for David's success,
namely, God.

Saul's ultimate opponent in these stories, the opponent with
whom he most deeply contends, is God, or Saul's best understanding of the deity. The narrator reports Saul's perception that
God has turned from him. Is it also a fact? Rather a projection?
A fear? A grief? That God regretted making Saul king, wanted to
remove him from that position, Saul has been told. Saul's conclusion is that God has abandoned him, a conclusion the narrator shares with us without approving it. God has abandoned the
project of Saul's kingship and gone on to the next candidate.
Saul's inability to abandon his reign makes him an opponent in
the literal sense of the word: one who has set himself against
the project of God. Saul's energies, as we see as the story
unfolds not only in these hundred verses but to the end of the
book, center on hugging kingship to himself, a project that is
largely destructive.

---

[26] This may be a good place to recall the significance of overlap
between narrator and character speech, that is, the dialogized speech so
dear to Bakhtin. It seems unremarkable to classical Hebrew Bible criticism, so far as I know: since the narrator is crafting the characters, why
marvel when the narrator reuses the same words? But once we—reading—see the hero and the narrator sharing the same language to comment
on realities, then we can track it as careful representational technique that
allows, or draws, the character and narrator to be converging on insight,
in company with ourselves.

vi. Saul offers to make David son-in-law and then reneges
(18:17–19)

With David now ensconced as Saul's son, moving in fact ever closer to his inheritance, and with Saul fearful of David but not admitting such a thing aloud or to others, Saul undertakes his quest for David as his son-in-law. The same verbal pattern constructs this lateral paternal move of the king: Saul himself invites David to this position, presumably without seeing its ultimate effect. Saul's speech doubles now in a new way. He says one thing aloud, another to himself. In his first speech, Saul asks David to consider his[27] elder daughter Merab: "Her I will give you for a wife—only be a warrior for me and fight YHWH's wars." Saul's second utterance of the scene is not in the same mode but is rather likely speech to himself, as we have seen him do before. He adds, *sotto voce* (as it were—the narrator simply says "he said"), leaving us to construe that it has to be a different phase of communication: "It shall not be my hand against him but let it be the hand of the Philistines."[28]

The first direct speech seems clear enough and echoes what we heard at the battle in 17:25: the marriage to the daughter of the king comes with strings. What David must do to be son (-in-law) is fight for YHWH. Having begotten this child, her father continues to author her as simply his own. And Saul is now braiding outer with inner speech, letting those contend within him—never a simple thing. He is also splitting off the public linkage—marriage to the king's daughter as a reward for successful combat—to resplice it with his secret plan—marriage with the king's daughter as incentive for unsuccessful combat. Echoing in the discourse is the sense that David has already earned the prize, yet Saul indicates such service must continue if the commodity Merab is to be his.

Besides the doubled speech from Saul, we also now get David's first rejoinder here, and his second (and last) speech to

---

[27] The phrasing is an excellent example of the use of הִנֵּי (behold) to show Saul pointing out his daughter to David. The father sees her as his, a problem that will flower in the case of "his" other daughter Michal.

[28] Miller (1996, 294–95) supposes it may be a matter of a simultaneous construction or desire—all the more complicated grammatically and psychologically. As I shall develop in the next section, Saul's wish may as well be a prayer: let not my hand . . . but their hand.

Saul in this section under current scrutiny. David's reply to Saul's offer is a question: "Who am I, and who the [unit] of the clan of my father in Israel, that I should be son-in-law to the king?" The topic enjoined, once again, is whose son David is. He self-deprecates, perhaps; or he parries the offer, not based on being a fighter (which is the qualification Saul mentioned) but on the basis of his own sonship. David's rejoinder presses Saul in a place of sensitivity: Jesse's son is not worthy to marry King Saul's daughter. But David again recommits to his own lineage and away from Saul's. If it was courteously but discernibly defiant at 17:58, the more so here. But a self-deprecation is simultaneously dialogized, at war in some ways with the fact it purports to assert. Such a characterization invites a denial from a dialogue partner. So David is now speaking dually as well as is Saul.

Saul's silence as rejoinder to David's transactional comment is noteworthy here. It is not possible, I think, to get the full or unambiguous sense of what David invites by his assertion, but it is not difficult to see his remark as pregnant in some way. And is it rebuffed by Saul? Since his silence—his nonrebuttal—is followed by an evident acquiescence, that construction seems plausible. Saul does not override David's self-assessment but condones it, betrothing Merab to another. Efforts to explain Saul's motivation for the aborted first betrothal of a daughter to David seem misplaced.[29]

The narrator's positioning of this scene is characteristic of what we have been seeing: not to explain but to reflect the character constructions of themselves and each other. For the daughter Merab is, at the time of giving her to David, given to another for a wife. What has Saul heard from David? What did Saul invite from David? What is the import of the king's rumination? Who is playing with whom—besides both men with Merab? Why does Saul change his mind, if indeed he does change it? Was the offer sincere? Which offer? How was it received, returned? We are left with choices: Saul heard his offer declined or rejected—or perhaps invited carefully—and he acceded to David's "no" or rebuffed his "yes." The scene is reenacted at once.

---

[29] E.g., Edelman (1991, 140–42) supposes that David was not able to pay the brideprice in time. She concludes that the prospective son-in-law, not the father-in-law, broke the contract. It seems overread to me.

vii. Betrothal t(w)o (18:20–29)

This short unit, in so many ways like the preceding scene, provides (at least until we come to ch. 20), the most complex discourse in terms of character and the narrator dynamics. Speech becomes more doubled, doubled in a variety of ways. Since the content of the eight verses is fairly straightforward, the small unit offers a chance to show technique and underlying methodology in greater detail than has been the case heretofore. So, in addition to spending more time on the passage, I will also start with the narrator instead of the characters and not treat the passage in chronological order but select verses to demonstrate the ways in which Bakhtin's ideas have greatest exposure and exercise.

Narrator reporting speech

It is time to gather and organize in more detail the narrator operations characteristic of this and other scenes. I have shown, so far, that the narrator's strategy has been twofold: First the narrator directs our attention to the key places to look as we attend to the characters: at Saul's gaze (17:55, 57) as he speaks; at Jonathan's ears (18:1) as he divests himself of his heritage; at Saul's ears and eyes (18:8, 9); at the hands of Saul and David (18:10); at Saul's eyes (18:15); and at his split language (18:17–18). Second, the narrator stresses connections that remind us of how much information characters—Saul in particular, for present purposes—have access to and can be construed to be processing. Thus we are able to hear the subtext of royal fathers and sons played out among Saul, David, and Jonathan in every scene we have witnessed. We are also made privy to the intensity of the opposition Saul is mustering against his awareness that God has withdrawn support from Saul's kingship and offered it to a "better" (טוב) man, one able to "go in and come out," to win approval, be appraised as טוב (good) in the eyes of all.

That Saul has himself invited the better man to be part of his court—has made him a son—is something that Saul struggles to avoid acknowledging verbally, obvious though it may look from a reader's viewpoint. My point now is to show the narratorial moves in somewhat greater detail and to dispel any sense of omniscience or neutrality here. The narrator of this story makes constant choices about how to relate the tale.

A final preliminary point: Alice Bach has a useful strategy. She suggests readers flesh out in order to flush out the narrator, by

which she means the reader must actively and constantly engage
with the angle of telling (Bach 1997, ch. 2). The Saul narrator, as
has often been noted, handles Saul, Jonathan, and David very
unevenly. My best imagining for the persona behind the narrator
voice speaking would be Saul's analyst: critically and minutely
attentive, sympathetic to the man more fundamentally than to his
roles as father or king, relentless if gentle in pressuring Saul to
confront what he is both struggling and resisting to say and hence
acknowledge. I offer that hypothesis simply to make clear that it
is not at all suitable to the narrator's handling of David or
Jonathan. With what palette does such a narrator work when
drawing these rich characters?

To start with the simplest of narratorial choices: This narrator for
this scene uses tags, names, brief epithetic descriptors, summaries.[30]
(The most minimal tag—the verb alone with no proper name or
free-standing pronoun—is not exemplified in this passage.[31]) The
three main characters are called by their names: Saul is called just
that fourteen times, and only at the end of the scene does the narrator call him "the king" (18:20 [bis], 21 [bis], 22, 23, 24, 25 [bis], 27,
28 [bis], 29 [bis]). David is named twelve times with no descriptor
(18:20, 21, 23 [bis], 25, 26 [bis], 27 [bis], 28, 29 [bis]—though what
role he is to have [and so what descriptor] is the point of the scene).

Michal is named twice (18:20, 27) and both times given her
patronymic; had it not been used twice within eight verses, we
might suspect that, unlike Saul and David with whom we have
been working, she needs introduction. How she is referenced is a
choice: besides her name, she is marked as a king's daughter. It
identifies her factually and also ties her to her father as his possession to bestow—a relation that would certainly be key in the
cultural setting.

It is also useful to consider the impact of the absent descriptors, which we can do by supplying some and weighing the

---

[30] Revell (1996, ch. 7) summarizes and classifies conveniently the treatment of Saul in the DH material that pertains to him. His assumptions
about the consistency and strength of narrative convention may be different from mine, but his information provides a platform for discussion
of the narrative choices.

[31] A main interest of Miller is to weigh some distinctions among many
of these verbs.

impact of them: e.g., imagine "David, Saul's surrogate giant-Philistine fighter" or "David, formerly promised to Saul's elder daughter." To withhold a descriptor or an epithet is a weighted choice, one that we must not overlook.

Three other narratorial moves worth specifying involve more complex decisions made along the scale of intrusiveness. First, the whole scene is set off by a report for which no one takes, or can be given, absolute responsibility. Who reports to Saul Michal's love for David is not revealed, with the result that it cannot be carefully assessed; it is, temporarily, an unsubstantiated rumor even for us. The narrator reports the report, but its genesis remains unclear: Michal does not express it; Saul does not see it; the servants do not take responsibility for it; David does not claim it (18:20).[32]

The question is not simply one of facticity: Did Michal love David, yes or no? The question here is, whose angle is reported and with what cause, what effect? The narrator says literally, they told [it] to Saul; an unsubstantiated allegation is what gets this scene to move. Shortly it will be confirmed by a witness, but it does not start that way.

How do all involved (king, servants, intended bridegroom, prospective bride, and so forth) react to the report that the thing was valuable in Saul's eyes/appraisal? Why do they react, and with what effect? That it pleases Saul may be responsible for inviting a report of it (part of Saul's characterization is to move people around, which often invites the same manipulative tactic in return); that the preceding affiancing failed may spur the servants to prime another situation. Saul likes to get good information and not bad; people working for the powerful often like to bring pleasing information. And have we as readers believed the report or not? Why, or why not, and with what effect?

Even were we to accept the assertion as reliable narrative reporting, it leaves still a lot unsaid (why does she love him, what attracts her, and so forth).[33] But is it the perhaps fallible impres-

---

32 Miller, instancing 18:24 (which is similar to 18:20), calls the summary "semidirect speech" and clarifies it as a narrator intrusion of a different level from a paraphrase (1996, 281). Exum (1993, 43) considers it an expression of Michal's point of view, a conclusion that seems dubious.

33 I actually think this is a pretty omniscient and nonpolyphonic remark by a narrator who is not prone to such; but since I am aiming to show

sion of "them" that she loves him? Since we do not get to see it, simply are told it, our angle is much reduced. How do we decide?

Actually, I do not think there is sufficient space for making this a narrator report of someone else's viewpoint rather than his own, but it shows us the possibility and the implication (suppose it was *not* the case that Michal loved David?). The narrator here is drawing, with various crayons, Saul, Michal, the servants, and even David (and some absent characters as we will see below). Saul, once he learns of it, finds "it" valuable. But what is valuable: the love? Why? The report of the love from his servants? We read it one way, but even this "factual" report is spacious!

A second, more complex narrator strategy is to summarize what we might have heard verbatim: At 18:23, 24, and 26 we are shut out from the scene and handed instead an opaque expression.[34] What Saul's servants said to David, what the servants relayed back to Saul, and what response was brought back to David are all truncated for us into a deictic. Why, or more precisely, with what effect, does the narrator exclude scenes that might have been deliciously detailed?

One possibility is to imitate or replicate a court scene where rumors abound. Another is to minimize the sense that Saul is managing the scene; neither does David or Michal control it fully. Events have their own collaborative momentum, servants their own hidden purposes. The choice exposes a bit more clearly the range of possible narratorial options, since we can see ourselves closed out here. It may be part of the minimization of, in this case, the servants. It is not an even-handed choice—a classist bias, we might say—for whatever reason, to avoid drawing these "downstairs" characters very fully. The narrator may think it not important to suggest much, or the minimal sketch may draw the servants "wary." Hence the unsuitability of words like reliable, omniscient, determinate, and so forth; they are not wrong, just not sharpened to do the job at hand. It is Bakhtin's way to get us into "suspicion." Our narrator makes ideological choices, has to, does. We need to note some of them.

---

nuances in the alternatives to the assumption of omniscience, I am going to stress my alternate assumptions here, relying also on the fact that Saul himself becomes a holder of this viewpoint by the end of the scene.

[34] Miller calls this language, neither a verbatim nor a paraphrase, semi-direct speech (1996, 281).

We may, third, note a similar vagueness or lack of precision at
18:20 and 26, where Saul first and then David is reported as
appraising matters positively: "It pleased him" is said vaguely of
the report that Michal loved David. So many unexplored points.
And similarly toward the end of the scene, David's view of being
son-in-law to the king is positive: "When they [servants] told David
these things/words, the thing seemed good to him, to be son-in-
law to the king."

It looks like a narrative comment, but is it unambiguous?[35] Or
is it a narratorial report of their appraisal of the impact of their
words, which were about how (not) to be son-in-law? I think such
a case can be made, based on the fact that the servants may react
in terms of the job they have been assigned to do (get David to
be son-in-law), whereas David's frame of reference is more extensive and routinely held close to his chest. At very least, we are
given rather minimal information about what and why David
thinks the thing—whatever that means—good (יִישַׁר); it is the same
language used of a report of Saul in 18:20.

The narrator is setting their moves in dialogue; whether they
know it or not, we do.[36] Whose design, this betrothal? It looks less

---

[35] Alter suggests (1981, 118) that "the narrator tells us exactly what Saul
feels toward David—fear—and why he feels it—David's astonishing military success." The comment misleads, in the sense that "exactly" suggests
a singleness to Saul's feelings, which may be more complex and inde-
scribable. In an article discussing narrator and character reliability, Amit
suggests that the narrator and God are axiomatically reliable but everyone
else may be theoretically suspect (1992, 205). I think so clean a break over-
simplifies the situation and mixes theological categories with literary ones.
Or, to put it differently, I think asserting that God cannot be unreliable is
a mimetic fallacy. Fokkelman's rumination about Saul's "emotional satisfaction from the exercise of power" (1986, 233) is out of place in the sort
of speech-linked analysis I am attempting. If I understand Bakhtin correctly, it is the sort of psychologizing he did not appreciate. This verse represents what Polzin (after Bakhtin) calls concealed reported speech.

[36] An astute commentator like Savran, however, asserts the following
(1988, 77): "The narrator has complete control of his characters, deciding
what words they will speak, and when they will speak them, whether in nor-
mal direct discourse or in quoted direct speech. He determines not only what
will be spoken, but when it will be repeated, to whom, and under what circumstances." The Bakhtin assumptions would not make these matters so

like Saul's to me by the time I finish looking carefully, though I recognize that I have been faked out by the servants. What is odd here—unusual for DH—is that we cannot do the meticulous comparison of directions, execution, report, reaction that is sometimes so revealing.

Character reported speech

In this short section there are five bits of reported speech (18:21a–b, 22, 23, 24, 25), unusual, perhaps, in that none of them is a two-party conversation. Additionally, we see Saul adding to his repertoire: if twice above he would speak aloud and emend or counter silently to himself, now he makes those two moves and also speaks through intermediaries, designing speech for them to put into play.

The first direct discourse can be exemplified in two utterances of Saul: one to himself and one addressed to David. At 18:21a the narrator says: "Saul said, 'I will give her to him that she may/will be a snare[37] to him and that the hand of the Philistines may be against him.'" The matrix (as at 18:17) is introduced as "Saul said," but we can see that he is speaking of someone and not in any visible way to someone. I think we may take it as self-talk, especially since it is somewhat at variance with what he says aloud in the second half of the verse.[38]

---

wholly manageable by the narrator. In Bakhtinian terms, Saul's and David's character zones are intersecting as the language of their appraisals match.

[37] The range of possibilities for construing the snaring is vast. It is a very spacious and open-ended comment that will repay investigation of how it travels from other conversations. Exum observes (1992, 73, 84) that Saul is the one ensnared by Michal's love for David.

[38] This brace of Saulide speech raises a place where I diverge from Polzin. His comments here are too absolute for me: "The narrator lays bare Saul's mental and emotional life.... we find out exactly what was in his mind.... we are told everything about it." (1989, 177). I think rather that we get a small glance and are unable to "finalize" Saul here. Aside from Saul's deviousness, which I do not doubt, how can two clear positions, or our construction of them, begin to exhaust this complex moment? Polzin characterizes the narrator revelations of "Saul's inner life and evil intentions" and "Saul's perfidy ... here described in unambiguous terms" as too nearly didactic and propagandistic a reporting. I think the narrator's depiction more susceptible to nuance. Alter, too, construes the section quite differently from me (1981, 116–20).

Once we get to the second part of the verse, we have the narrator representing character speech.[39] The challenge now is to discern the degrees of objectification; put differently, to analyze whose viewpoint is being represented in the speech.[40] At 18:21b the narrator gives Saul direct discourse, the sort English puts in multiple quotation marks (which Hebrew does not do): "Saul said, 'You shall now (today) be my son-in-law.'"[41] We can see that the proposal is direct discourse, addressed to "you," though it receives no immediate response here, nor is it tagged as direct discourse in one of the ways Hebrew can do.[42] In a fuller investigation we might explore

[39] Scholars seem to agree that biblical narrative clearly prefers direct speech to alternatives (Alter 1981, 67; Miller 1996, 2), though Miller's system for sorting is more complex than Alter's. Miller's nuancing of the possibilities between direct and indirect discourse and her reminders that languages manage the gradations variously will repay more study. See Miller (1996, 61–89) for a good discussion. Savran's work is more explicit about texts he is discussing and less inclined toward statistical comments.

[40] Alter proposed in 1981 (116) a hierarchy of reliability that is useful to a point but is too tidy and unnuanced for present purposes and, in fact, for many purposes, valuable though it was to me for a long time.

[41] There is an odd word, "a second time," which may or may not be part of the quote; Fokkelman (1986, 242) links it to David's doubling of the brideprice when he brings it, though he reads it otherwise as well (236). McCarter's text criticism is useful here, perhaps, as he reminds readers that the Hebrew and Greek texts do not manage this scene in the same details. For implications of McCarter's observations, see his remarks (1980, 315–19). Pyper, not apropos of this passage but in pursuit of a more general point, offers alternatives to the strategic choices made by text critics (1996, 14–15); he plans, he says, to read less cautiously, even if he overreads. Too much caution may be as detrimental as too little. Miscall makes a different sort of point here, observing that the discussion of the two "betrothal scenes" between Saul and David cannot be well-considered apart from the words of promise uttered in 17:25. So this is actually a third reference, not simply a second one (1983, 84).

[42] Fokkelman (1986, 229) suggests that the tone of Saul's proposal—blunt and not warm (though on what basis, he does not divulge)—belies the content and serves to stress the inferior position of David, his nonequality with the king's family. And then, understandably in such a transaction, David responds as an inferior. I think rather that David's last words to Saul that allow much space for his own inferiority are his first words to Saul, offering to undertake to do the king's job. After that task is completed well, I think David's language changes increasingly toward superiority to Saul.

what is implied by "son-in-law," but, in a word, it is not succession. Saul, we will learn, has four sons; David as son-in-law is not a step closer to the throne for him, but perhaps (as is explored later in 2 Sam) a closer control on him by the king.[43] While we are looking at language, we can see Saul's self-obsession in this betrothal: it is not marriage of David to Michal but really to Saul.[44] Notable is a lack of response to the offer. Or rather, silence is the response.

The conversation that goes on between what Saul says to himself and what he says to David shows him perhaps as purposely divided (a clean lie) or alternatively as split and indecisive—but in any case, running two plans.[45] We might say Saul is thinking, "Be my dead son-in-law-apparent." Saul's inner speech draws himself powerful—assigning inferiors to positions; it shows his power simultaneously abridged, needing his daughter and his enemy to manage something crucial for him.

Saul consistently talks of the Philistines—whom he once fought well but not for some time now—as competent in regard to David, a role that they will never have.[46] In Saul's talk, they consistently get his hopeful credit for what they never do. He assigns them responsibility for doing what he cannot do but wants to do. Or does he?[47]

---

[43] Jobling (1998, 231) observes that there is a great gain in status to become son-in-law to the king. I think that can be so without assuming that it moves him closer to sitting on the throne. Standing near a throne is good, even if sitting on it is better. A similar point needs to be observed about the oft-supposed abdication of Jonathan in these passages (e.g., Jobling 1998, 93–99). It seems a futile gesture for one son, even an oldest, to abdicate for his whole family when there are others. Hence my stressing that the scene conveys David's being made a son, not Jonathan's resigning his crown prince position in any literal way.

[44] Nonetheless, the presentation of the topic is clearly key, as the "son-in-law to the king" expression occurs five times (Fokkelman 1986, 235).

[45] Alter observes (1981, 118), on this verse, that "As elsewhere in the Bible, attention is directed toward the use of language as a medium of manipulation." But his appraisal of Saul as "a simple character, inclined to clumsy lunges rather than deft thrusts" strikes me as reductive.

[46] Jobling (1998, ch. 10) builds a number of fantastic agendas that this maligned group fills, in the Bible and since.

[47] With a different set of reading assumptions, McCarter (1980, 316) observes that the passage may be translated, "the hand of the Philistines was on [Saul]," an option chosen by LXX B.

Though commentators tend to think Saul is unconflicted here, I am not so sure. He pushes David to putatively lethal others, either (or both) so they will snare/kill him, so that he himself will not do it. Saul may here be removing David from his own spear range so that he will not kill him, since, as we were told in 16:21, he loved him greatly. Or he may be removing him since David dodging spears marks Saul's failure as a hurler.[48] So I draw Saul's discourse as evidencing him deeply conflicted about killing David (borne out as the story winds on). So the dialogue between his spoken and silent speech is not hypocritical as much as it is torn; but it evades responsibility. Saul does not let his self join both parts of his talk.[49]

In 18:25 we get something that looks similar to inner thought, but it is not quite expressed as inner thought. At 18:25b we have a narrator comment: "But Saul thought to fell David by the hand of the Philistines." The line between direct and indirect discourse blurs (especially as we reflect that our self-talk does not necessarily proceed in polished prose); nor must we assume that the narrator's view coincides exactly with character consciousness. It is a narrator comment—not given to Saul to say himself—but he has

---

[48] An interesting suggestion was made by a student in the second Bakhtin Circle class, Uriah Kim. He pointed out a number of passages in which Saul's behaviors might be accounted for by faulty vision—moments including his odd unawareness of David's identity, his missing easy spear shots, and so forth. The observation is valuable in several ways. It marks attentive and active reader construction. The point is not, was Saul blind, but with what careful codes may he have been authored and may he be read. It helps us make explicit key assumptions that might otherwise remain faintly operative but implicit. And it assists us to connect Saul once again with the other dynasty, the Elides, whose old man was surely blind in a number of ways.

[49] For another view, see Brueggemann (1993, 228), who thinks readers are shocked at the "sudden, unexpected eruption of hostility on Saul's part." I think there are far more cilia influencing our responses than Brueggemann acknowledges. Edelman, approaching the topic from a somewhat different angle, is also of the opinion that Saul may be taking care not to kill David, may be fearful of his own rage (1991, 138–39). Her summary that Saul chooses self-preservation over his responsibility to the nation (139) seems too dichotomous an assessment. How to parse such a matter is difficult.

said something just like it, so it is not quite "not-Saul." The narrator reports it as a Saul viewpoint, which is not the same as the narrator saying it, nor the same as Saul saying it directly. The phrasing is typical of Saul—using an infinitive construct rather than
assigning an inflected verb, as well as pushing the task to others
to do—the others whom he found too much for himself and who
are themselves doing very poorly against David so far. The point
is to recognize that the narrator reports (one of) Saul's feelings
here—the one Saul can privately acknowledge only barely, which
is far from all that the narrator is drawing for us. So, in other terminology, this is not "objective" narrative reporting but approaches pseudo-objective reporting.[50]

A second speech occurs in 18:22 (double-voiced unidirectional
speech that is used pretty compatibly with its original intent): "Saul
then ordered his servants, 'Talk to David on the quiet,[51] saying,
"Look, the king is pleased with you and all his servants love you; so
now, be son-in-law to the king."''" This is easy to spot as multi-plied,
since Saul hands his servants a speech to say that encloses his own
speech—speech that he seems already to have addressed directly
once.[52] What is perhaps deviant about it is that we hear it at the
crafting stage rather than seeing it used; it clearly is used, but outside of our hearing. It is the servants' speech, in that they will speak
of the king in the third person; it is Saul's, in that he designs his own
words with himself at the center. I am classifying it as linear (and
stylized—speakers' uses are compatible) since at least on one level
Saul is using speech he already used and will use of himself in 18:25
and that is reported roughly in 18:20 (different expression). There is

---

[50] Unless I missed her equivalent of this sort of construction, the
Bakhtin nuance is of no interest to Miller and the sort of classificatory
work she is doing.

[51] Fokkelman (1986, 237) suggests we are to understand not so much
"speak in secret" as "speak discreetly," that is, without revealing the voice
of the composing king. Miscall (1983, 86) supposes that David may not
be at court, hence the need for intermediaries. Polzin's work on messengers in the Samuel narratives (1993) prompts me to search beyond the
representational for their function. As we all probably know from common experience, the more messengers the more layers for dialogue.

[52] As noted above, it is also speech that was circulating at the Goliath
contest (17:25–27).

part of Saul that is pleased with David, with some facets of David; and beyond a doubt, the servants love him (reported in 18:5 and 16, not exact wording but close). But we also know there are other dissonant factors in this speech as well, that Saul is not unconflictedly pleased with David. So it is a complex utterance, without even factoring in why Saul feels the need to proceed indirectly—perhaps since there is no verbal response from David to Saul's offer. It has to do with the scene that has preceded this one, where Saul offered David his older daughter Merab "unsuccessfully"; we can see that Saul may know he needs a better approach and may also want to put distance between himself and what was either a failure or a breach on his part (Fokkelman 1986, 238).

We may also note that though he says here, "the king is pleased with you"—he will shortly attach a condition: pleased if, pleased insofar as.... We may note also that part of Saul's shrewdness and blindness is to show David the mirror that suggests he is beloved.[53] That tactic may be effective in the short run, but will become lethal for Saul, who hates what *he* sees, looking over David's shoulder into David's mirror, reflecting back into his own mirror, as it were. It seems significant that Saul omits to mention Michal's love, which is what seems to have prompted Saul on his present trajectory.

David's response to the servants' speech (the third character speech for our consideration), which we do not witness, is a question, hurled back at those asking (masculine plural—not to Saul in the singular). It is double-voiced (varidirectional) speech, more clearly parodic, that is, used at cross-purposes with what it is quoting: at 18:23 we have, "But David said, 'Is it a trifling thing (הנקלה) in your eyes to be son-in-law to the king? For I[54] am a poor man

---

53 See Fokkelman (1986, 239–40) for a close description of how the two scenes (18:17–19 and 20–27) resemble and diverge from each other.

54 Revell reads אנכי as a status pronoun, compared to אני (both mean "I"); if true, it would align somewhat with my sense that David does not read himself as inferior; he also suggests that for a character to make a rejoinder to a superior's proposal with a first person pronoun implies astonishment and emotion, since ordinarily a response unlikely to please will be crafted by use of a third-person self-designation (1996, 288–91). Bakhtin's urgings about utterance make me simultaneously appreciative of the formal analysis offered and slightly suspicious of its authority.

and of little account/trifled with (אִישׁ־רָשׁ וְנִקְלֶה)."' Here David
quotes himself at 18:18, where he said a briefer thing, self-deprecating with less elaboration of form and content.

At first glance, the use of doubled speech (two David speeches
stuck together) might seem stylized: David uses his own speech
compatibly with his previous use. But I rather read this second as
parodic of his first utterance, primarily because of the previous
occasion where he was offered something honorific (marriage to a
princess) and then dishonored when it was removed without (narrative) ado.[55] That David's self-insult is perhaps taken at face value

---

[55] Commentators are split over the nature of David's question here (and
earlier as well). The first thing to note may be that David's "who am I ... "
rings closely to the words of those discussing rewards for a single-combat
victory against the Philistine at 17:25 (Polzin 1989, 177; Fokkelman 1986,
232); I understand Fokkelman to be implying that David's words may
remind us that he has already earned the reward Saul continues to dangle,
Polzin to sense that Saul had already promised Merab to another before
offering her to David in 18:17. Miscall (1983, 86) classifies it as perhaps a
real question, perhaps a rhetorical question; if real, it must be queried for
sincerity or insincerity. (Miscall thinks it invites Saul to construe David as
poor.) George Coats, who examined the verse (primarily its formal features)
along with other expressions of self-abasement, concludes (1970, 18) that it
is to be taken as formulaic but genuinely expressing a sense of unworthi-
ness. His suggestion that the language must be considered as court-linked
is interesting, if perhaps premature given the state of uncertainty about ref-
erential circumstances. Klein thinks it a show of humility for David (1983,
189), without explicating the nuance of "show." Stansell also thinks it best
taken at face value, though it could be ironic (1996, 57–59); Edelman usefully asks why David should want to marry into the Saul family (1991, 142).
The answer may be most uncertain, but the question is a valuable reminder
for readers to be explicit about assumptions. McCarter not only assumes but
says that to have married into the house of Saul would advance the chances
of David's gaining the northern loyalties later on (1980, 318–19); Stone dis-
agrees (1996, 130). A similar excellent question is raised (answered perhaps
less well) by Garsiel, who asks (as the story winds on) who has knowledge
of the anointing of David (1985, 110). We may also wonder who knows that
Saul has been fired. If both points are unknowable, at least our assumptions about them need to be made clear. Miller (1996, 280) reminds us that
it is narrator ideology, not putative character feelings, that are controlling
the scene; she discusses self-deprecation (271–81). Another way to put her
admonition is that we are attending primarily to language and utterance

(as the text allows us to suppose) renders a second round of the same baiting painful. So (and this is where tone would help, if we could get at it) I construe this as bitter: viz. "why are we going into this again, given what just happened?" Since Saul and by extension his servants are powerful, David's speech registers (plausibly) the sense of being trifled with here, treated slightingly; so why does he have to say it again—which he does—adding more detail?

If his self-deprecation was in fact a form that Saul ought to have acknowledged but has overridden by following through with the termination of the Merab-offer, then David has been insulted when his self-deprecation stops the plan (if that is what stopped it).[56] Fokkelman (1986, 238) thinks that David's mention of insignificant resources prompts Saul's mention of a particular service to be a brideprice.[57]

However, there is more. When we see Saul's response to the words of the servants (18:24, our fourth—given in Miller's semi-direct discourse), we can discern better what that report must have been, logically has to be. It seems to me that the servants report this speech of David back to Saul as a "yes!" Or, better, they report back "these things/words," and Saul's next move suggests that he has taken David's words as a green light rather than as a red—or perhaps a yellow (proceed but present an obstacle [expense]), except insofar as Saul does not really want a son-in-law but a dead son-in-law apparent.

---

here, not constructing character psychology or sociological custom—though if available, the latter would be invaluable. Similarly, Rosenberg's assumption (1986, 178), that it is to be assumed that a king would not engage a challenger but that an aspiring courtier would be pressed into service, makes clear to me that I am assuming the opposite. Regarding this speech of David, Fokkelman notes also that David replies to the marriage aspect but not to the military component of it (1986, 231).

[56] McCarter, obviously again working with different reading suppositions, assumes that David would see the betrothal as a chance to advance at court (1980, 317). It is a place where strategies can be compared: McCarter, here, is supposing what a likely David would plausibly think; I am trying to tease out what the words can be understood to say.

[57] Otherwise, the combination of marriage and Philistine foreskins may be incongruous, though the blend of revenge and death is not, nor sex and death.

So whatever David intends, Saul weaves David's words into his own game, apparently again taking David's claim of being a poor man at face value and setting a brideprice that is outside the usual economy. Saul is trifling with David, who, however, trifles back here, rendering his words parodic. Saul is losing even the control he may think he has, which perhaps we can see he never had.[58]

So Saul's speech here (our fifth) is also slipped in an envelope and sent to David, carefully tagged at 18:24: first, a request or a command. David has said—the servants have reported David to have said—or Saul has construed David to have said—something that moves Saul past the offer itself to the means of achieving it. If David has agreed to be the son-in-law, how is it to be managed? As was the case the first time we heard of marriage to the king's daughter, it is to be achieved by killing the uncircumcised Philistines. And it is to take revenge on the enemies of the king. This is Saul speaking of himself as king. Who is the enemy he seeks to avenge himself upon?

Reading character speech polyphonic(ally)

As a final move, I want to take the same utterance of David in 18:23 and construe it still more polyphonically, more dialogized (collapsing to some extent the gradations Bakhtin makes from Dostoevsky that are too nuanced for this narrative, I think). So, emphasizing that this graded series rises more extensively from reader choice than from formal textual criteria, what else may we construct as being argued out in David's conversation with Saul via the servants? And, where does absence come into play more than presence? Finally, in what ways can we see the characters slipping the authorial/narratorial leash here, more visibly than before? Some options:[59]

a) David's words are crafted by him to be both formally courteous and a slap in the king's face, given what happened with Merab. David, self-deprecating, also subcutaneously accuses Saul

---

[58] Pyper (1996, 200) reminds us of the potential value in characters' misreadings.

[59] A reminder is offered that I am construing language, not psychology, close though those are at this level. Also a caveat is to be noted: How court etiquette functions is always partly cultural, a point for which we lack explicit information.

of dishonoring him and thus acting dishonorably himself—and delivers this courteously accusing salvo by the hand of the king's servants, a further polite disrespecting of the king.

b) David's words, which also pick up his own lineage recitation of 17:58, remind Saul of the issue (to be worked also in ch. 20) about whether David is Jesse's son rather than having resigned that lineage in some way when kept at the palace after the Goliath episode; if the big issue between these two is "whose son," David mocks Saul here, though to the extent that Saul does *not* want David for his son, he may tease him too. (Saul's words show that he does and does not see David as a son). David may also be "quoting" the reward mentioned (by Saul's men, implicitly having issued from the king himself) at 17:25–27, which specified the reward of freedom and marriage for any who would or could slay Goliath.

c) David's words may be loophole language, his own way of sliding out of being pegged as worthy to be son-in-law to the king. In this reading, David intends his self-deprecation as an escape hatch to let him escape what Saul is planning—whatever David may sense that to be: from son-in-law ... to dead. In such a reading his נקלה/of little account may be close to truthful; so the duality is that, underneath the self-deprecation, which is not to be taken at face value, David means it, wants Saul to hear his "no" as a no.

d) Proleptically, it may suit the role David seems to select for himself later (2 Sam 7) when the prophet Nathan tells a parable about a rich man and a poor man (איש־רש). It is usual (and plausible) to see David as noninsightful when he identifies with the poor man, but it is not the only way to see his choice. Since Saul is the character in whom I am interested here, this option suggests that he, too, may have a role in Nathan's parable.

e) To construe "poor and of no account" as other than purely formal self-deprecation, we can review the anointing scene of 1 Sam 16, where David was the youngest, minding the animals, and not even thought of by his family who assemble to meet the prophet. Moreover, we heard Eliab scold David for similar qualities in 17:28. Is David rerunning those comments, quoting his family as he speaks of himself?

f) Is this David the psalmist, who talks in this humble and self-minimizing way often? Why? To what effects?

g) Is this almost-foolish David set in contest with foolish (נבל) Nabal in 1 Sam 25, where their struggle is, among other things, for the loyalty of a woman? So in that setting, in relation to that story, how do we see his moment?[60]

And finally, in the sense of being built up to by degrees, is this utterance of David bringing into some presence the absent Michal, the absent and ever-silent Merab, and Ahinoam (completely absent except for a possible naming in 14:50 as Saul's wife and in 2 Sam 3:2 as David's wife, or as the "Jezreelitess," which suggests Abigail, wife of Nabal and David as in ch. 25)?[61] The point is not what would historical Saul have done, or what historical or psychologized David have said or done, but can we, reading, catch in the language of this section any suggestion of the presence of these three women, or only their absence?

h) Of the three, Michal is the least nonpresent in the passage, since she is the object being struggled over. Saul never mentions her in terms other than as his valuable property to be exchanged as beneficially to himself as possible,[62] and his single-tonguedness about her—and the narrator's labeling of her as the daughter of Saul or subsuming her under the son-in-law term—brings her out sharply to many current readers, sensitive about the objectification of women we have experienced or witnessed. David does not mention her either except by using the term son-in-law, which implies her existence; if David is counter-bartering for his own optimal position, he objectifies Michal no less than does her father.

Under Bakhtin's dialogue with what echoes from elsewhere or what is absent, or from what we have shortly in this text, we can bring Michal's voice backward (from 1 Sam 19 and from 2 Sam 3 and 6), where she, like Merab, will be given to another man—and then reclaimed by David before being rejected again. So the narrator, assisted by a deft reader, infiltrates David's speech with discourse about Michal.[63]

---

[60] Jobling (1998, 149–58) holds the three male heroes in tension.

[61] One of the finest passages in Jobling's wonderful "commentary" is his ordering of all the women in 1 Sam (see 1998, part 3 but especially ch. 8), including those hypothetical, absent, and uncharacterized.

[62] One such payoff envisioned is to make her the equivalent of the Philistines: a snare to David (Fokkelman 1986, 235). Perhaps like them, she will rather endanger her father's interests than David's.

[63] Alter thinks (1981, 118) that Michal's love for David is unmotivated, which is to say, announced by the narrator without giving the explicit

i) Merab is less present and more silent than Michal, but not wholly absent, since her own "betrothal" narrative of 18:17–19 is locked into an embrace with this "betrothal" of Michal (Klein 1983, 186 refers us as well to 2 Sam 6). The brief exchange of Saul and David over "her" reverberates in this slightly more protracted verbal tussle they have over the second daughter; Merab is unconsulted and never emerges as subject. Nor is the narrator standing near her to offer access to her viewpoint at any place I can see. What can a reader do here? Perhaps Merab may be drawn in relation to the wife Bathsheba, or in relation to Michal—both of whose representations differ so starkly from Merab's, to some gain and loss for each. Is she drawn in relation to Leah? to Hagar?

j) Saul's wife Ahinoam is really absent, wholly absent except for being implied as her daughters are discussed, and by being listed in chapter 14. If I were drawing her into the narrative, and at the point of the marriage of her daughters, I would underline her absence perhaps with reference to Rebekah of Gen 24–27, but by now the string tying us to 18:23 is pretty thin, a filament only, but discernible.

In this last set of readings, what Bakhtin is most able to point out is the relationship between the author and the hero, and I think we must say, between the hero and the reader. The hero/character utters in ways that escape authorial control; it is impossible to envision any efficient managing of the options labeled a-j. If the Saul-David utterance of 18:23 can be read in all these ways, then at this moment, the text works polyphonically, dialogically. Insofar as a reader discerns the trace of these women, faint though it may be, construction of them may proceed, at least in terms of Bakhtin's sense of the matter.

Narrator reporting speech

As the scene winds down, the narrator takes control again, perhaps since the discourse has functioned capaciously to show charac-

---

motivation for it. Michal's response to David may not be more unmotivated than that of her father and brother, however, who also love David rather suddenly or immediately, though amid more narrative facts that can account for it. My point: the narration of her reaction is not so different from that of others. Berlin's classic work on narrative urges consideration of some relationships between the portrayals of Michal and Jonathan vis-à-vis David. Her categories may seem slightly dated, but the suggestion is a good one.

terization. David rises and goes with his men—a new grouping (his men, like Saul's daughter)—to strike twice the number of Philistines that Saul had stipulated. The dual cardinal number is not etymologically related to the adverbial "a second time" of 18:21, but the link is difficult to miss. David pays in full for not one but two items offered by their father, strikes successfully where Saul only planned to strike David against the wall—on two occasions. "And then Saul gave his daughter to David for a wife," the narrator notes.

Standing once again with Saul, the narrator comments (very similarly to 18:15) from the king's angle: Saul sees and understands (literally, knew) two things freshly and more deeply: that YHWH is with David (18:12, 14) and that *his daughter* loves David. Sight leads to insight. The double success of David with the Philistines—always in juxtaposition with Saul's matched inadequacy—makes inevitable the marriage; and then Saul witnesses what had been rumored before: that *his daughter*—note the angle of perception—Michal loves David. It is a conflicted assessment, surely made from Saul's point of view. What now, if *his daughter* loves *his* opponent? The combination of these two pieces of awareness makes Saul add to his fear of David still more; and, new consequence: Saul makes David an enemy from then on.

viii. Narrative interlude: impact of the betrothals (18:30)

The narrator offers another proleptic summary and a last observation, which Fokkelman (1986, 242) thinks sums up the whole movement from chapter 17 on: David continues more successful (שׂכל) militarily than any other against the Philistines and his reputation grows. The triple blend to be feared, the narrator continues to point out, is David's military success, signaling God's assistance, which draws others to him to approve and love him. Since David has become the enemy to Saul, Saul now has once again made God an enemy as well. The narrator is not telling us more than the characters have already revealed; it is merely an underlining and juxtaposing so that we have the skein untangled.

Part 2: Saul Begins to Lose Initiative: 19:1–24

i. What Saul wants (19:1–7)

Saul's next words are provided for us in indirect speech to his son and his servants, "to kill David." The jist is not new but only more overt and public than we have seen to date. The English translation may not give quite adequate attention to the impersonality of the expression, which is an infinitive construct, not an inflected verb.[64] Who is to kill David? The responsibility is not made explicit. Sandwiched in between the previous note on David's fame as compared with Saul's other servants, and a second note on Jonathan as finding David a pleasure,[65] we may sense in this initiative Saul's desperation, perhaps his keen if distorted awareness of realities—or his fear that *his* son and *his* servants (like *his* younger daughter) may not be quite "his" after all.

The reminder of Jonathan's feeling for David is reported by the narrator, but whose view is being expressed? Is it Saul's, so that we read his sense of conflicted or overlapping loyalties here? Jonathan loves David as a self, a brother as well as being a son? Or is it Jonathan's own understanding of the path on which he is already traveling, as he acts for both (all) of them, as he speaks to David?

Jonathan instructs David: "My father is seeking ... guard yourself; remain in hiding." "Seeking" is exactly who his father his; Jonathan echoes the narrator, characterizing, but also feeding and so constructing his father's plan or desire. Again, language is what happens here; another allegation passed on to one of the players by another without the knowledge of the third. Jonathan instructs David in his role: guard yourself, remain in hiding, concealed (סתר, חבא), from the seeker. These are the roles they are about to enact for most of the rest of their relationship, with the identity and ratio of the hiding and seeking changing toward the end. Hiding and seeking are good descriptors for David, whose sub-

---

[64] Miller (1996, 141) indicates that such speech using an infinitival complement gives us minimal access to the speaker's nuance. The vagueness or lack of answerability suits Saul's characterization well.

[65] חפץ (to delight) is part of David's character zone, as was drawn in 18:22 and elsewhere. So also are the words שׂכל (to succeed), אהב (to love), מלט (to escape/slip away), and סתר (to hide). Saul's key words, besides the שׁאל (to ask) that has characterized the story from the start, are בקשׁ (to seek) and ירא (to fear). McCarter continues to remind readers that a word like "love" is political rather than simply private (1980, 322). Garsiel (1985, 73) counts the "askings" that construct the Saul figure: nine in the Samuel birth narrative, four around the time of choosing the first king.

jectivity is guarded throughout the narrative linking him with Saul. Saul's determination is more flushed out now and is in the process of being wrested from him in this new phase of struggles between fathers and sons, kings and heirs.

Jonathan's words to his father show us his strategy and give us Saul in negative space, as it were. Jonathan's plan is to get Saul to reconsider his quest for the death of David within the hearing of David—in fact, surrounded by Saul's "two sons," one visible, the other not. Saul is also brought away from his house, where the language of intrigue and destruction are thick. Jonathan sets himself, sees and shows himself, as mediator, as advocate for David to his father, and makes Saul unknowingly give witness directly to David.

Jonathan's words to his father are doubled, in three senses. They have two intended addressees (Saul and David); they review and recount past words;[66] and they assuage and trouble simultaneously—or we can see that they have the capacity to do so. Jonathan speaks well of David, the narrator summarizes, and then we hear direct speech: "Let not the king sin against his servant David, for he has not sinned against you—for his deeds have been very good for you. He took his life in his hand when he struck the Philistine, and YHWH saved a great deliverance for all Israel; you saw it and rejoiced! So why do you sin against innocent blood— to kill David undeserving?"

The frame of the speech is that David has done nothing that Saul should be avenging. On the contrary, he has done good. Saul is in danger here, Jonathan implies, as well as David. Jonathan uses the expression טוב (good) for David, the word חטא (sin) twice for Saul. The descriptor for David is also that for the new man YHWH has chosen as king (15:28), a word that consequently rings differently for Saul than for Jonathan.

Jonathan's candor or naivete is a reproach as well as a warning, a confirmation as well as an option. And Jonathan is speaking up for both "sons" as well as for father. The example of David risking his life to fight the giant and the result God was able to accomplish are also a blend of good and bad news to

---

[66] Edelman (1991, 145–46) sets this speech of Jonathan in relation to 1 Sam 14 and 15; Polzin (1989, 175–82) redirects our attention to 14:43; 17:58; and 19:11.

Saul, we can construe from how he reacted to the earlier celebration of the deed by the rejoicing women. The utterance constructs concisely the relationship between the two. David took
his life in his hand to undertake Saul's kingly charge and, with
the help of God, succeeded. Everyone saw it and rejoiced.
Jonathan urges something we did not see—that Saul was glad.
Was Saul glad? He ought to have been, or Jonathan assumes he
must have been, says he appeared to be. Yet no sign of it has
been hinted until now.

Saul does not react visibly here to any implied or inferable
reproach in Jonathan's words. The narrator tells us what we then
hear ourselves: an oath and an asseverative: "he shall not be
killed." Saul continues to speak impersonally about death and
David.[67] The narrator ties off the scene thus: Jonathan meets with
David and tells him what he presumably heard—all these words.
He brings David to Saul and they are as previously! How were
they before? Saul will fall back into his older pattern of doubleness
and fear, hinting at the power of the undertow of Jonathan's summary of Saul's reign.

ii. Relapse (19:8–10)

The narrator performs a careful summary of how matters
stand, showing us a virtual rerun of an earlier moment (18:10–11),
though of course by being later in time, it is quite different. It is
again set off by military success of David (a great slaughter of
Philistines) and attended by the evil spirit of YHWH. The setting
is Saul's house, where the narrator points us once again to the
hands of the protagonists: Saul with his spear, David his lyre.
Though Saul does not vocalize his plan, he hurls the spear as
before and David escapes as before, but this time into the night,
suggesting that he flees out of the house, away from the scene.
The narrator confirms Saul as seeking and moves David beyond
hiding to escaping, a trajectory that will intensify in the chapters
ahead. Once is enough, apparently, this time. It is an analepsis—
we have seen it before—and a prolepsis too, since it moves the
enmity forward.

---

[67] Fokkelman notes that Saul bungles life and death continuously
(1986, 257).

iii. Michal's Choices (19:11–17)

A short scene, threaded with five direct discourse utterances, positioned by narratorial words, comprises the next unit. Michal informs David: "If you do not escape with your life tonight, tomorrow you will be killed." She picks up correctly on what the narrator has just said: Saul has sent messengers to kill David in the morning. She clearly sides with husband over father here, thwarting the one to save the other (thwarting herself to save both, thwarting them to save herself?). Her speech is a variant of Jonathan's in 19:2, but more succinct and urging escape instead of hiding, noting that the morning will bring death, not mediation and reconciliation.

Michal says to Saul's dispatched messengers (who are beginning to abound, their presence testifying both to power and failure to accomplish), "He is sick." Who is the referent? Is there more than one? The effective strategy is delay, as the messengers go back for instructions. Michal is enigmatic and opaque, her words spacious.

Saul rejoins, "Lift him on the bed to me so that he may die/to kill him." As before, the agent of the killing remains unspecified in Saul's mouth. It appears that Michal's deception with the bedclothes is discovered before the bed is brought to Saul, who instead (elliptically by the narrator) receives a report to which we hear only a sentence of response.

Saul says to Michal, "Why have you thus deceived me? You sent off my enemy, and he has made his escape." As before with Saul and his children, he draws them only in relation to his own desire to remain king. The man in question is "my enemy," not any of the other descriptors that might suit the scene from another angle. Sending is the root of this verbal exchange: Saul has sent; he accuses Michal of sending; and she will shortly attribute to David the same action. The words of Saul ring with the insight given him at the end of the betrothal passage (so 18:28), where Saul's daughter loves David. As is typical, Saul does not voice the fear but blames the other.

Michal says to Saul, "He said to me, 'Send me. Why should I kill you?'" She quotes something we did not hear (and again, English usage makes the borrowing of language clear). She may be making it up, giving truth to Saul's accusation that she has deceived him—so not with a dummy but with language. Alternatively, he may have said it. Perhaps the causative construction suggests yet another possibility: Why should I be the cause of

your dying?[68] An accusation thus emerges: Saul is drawn as potential killer of his daughter to get his enemy.

The scene, networked with dialogue, however truncated or
falsely alleged, is between husband and wife, father and daughter;
the narrator names them now Saul and Michal, not in terms of any
shared relationship (vv. 11, 12, 14, 15, 17, 18). Each of them directs
the same servant-messengers, whose views are hidden as always.
The dilemma we may sense for her is not coextensive with her
character; that is, though we recognize that she is seen earlier by
Saul as his daughter and here by the narrator as David's wife,
those relationships hardly exhaust her self, granted that the narrator, who names her independently as the scene progresses,
prompts readers to construct her larger than those two ties.

Scholarly commentary on Michal's part in the scene tends to
center on her gesture with the dummy in the bed and on the quality of her feeling for David rather than on her words, which reference neither of those two red herrings.[69] Michal's language, both in
the command to David and in the rejoinder to Saul, though cloudy,
is blunt, unnuanced, and unpadded with etiquette. As Revell (1996,
130–31) points out, Michal is the only character who does not speak
with terms of respect to the king, though it may be unwise to uni-
versalize on the basis of the only exchange to which we are privy.

What is made visible to us, I think, is Michal's perspicacity and
practicality, perhaps in contrast with her brother.[70] That the

---

[68] I have not found any support for such a translation, but I do not see
it as impossible, simply different from the usual construction.

[69] It is true that the passage recalls Gen 29–31, filled with the struggle
between husband, wife, and her father.

[70] Berlin observes carefully, if perhaps in rather dated categories, that
the siblings are drawn quite different from each other (1983, 24–25).
Edelman (1991, 147–49) discusses the scene as well, drawing Michal as
conflicted. Though one can imagine that a character could be torn in such
circumstances, I see no sign of it in her speech. For yet another view of
the episode, demonstrating the influence of reading assumptions and
strategies on interpretation, see Campbell (1989, 78–79). For a very different discussion and a good critique of Berlin, see Exum (1993, 51–60),
who shows the gender constructions of both Michal and Jonathan. Fewell
and Gunn (1993, 148–50) sketch the possibilities of reading Jonathan and
David's relationship as homosexual.

moment for adjudication is past is a reality clearer to Michal than to Jonathan. She may be communicating back to Saul that he gave her to his enemy, whom he has discovered that she loves; however, we have not heard that claim from her. Michal reads Saul's moves precisely, several times: his plan for the morning, the delay able to be extended as the servants return for consultation, the rejoinder that ends the scene when Saul makes no response. David is described passively throughout, his ticket scheduled, issued, and justified by Michal. Her "deceit" is delay, little more. She in fact makes her ploy quite open, by letting the dummy expose her choice of one person over the will of the other.

What she demonstrates is that she knows Saul better than he anticipates her, though he had sufficient knowledge to have moved differently. The strategy is more important than the details of it, reminiscent though it is of other daughters choosing self and husband over father. The more interesting thing is her last comment, which is actually a hypothetical quotation, a question directed presumably by David to her, which she now redirects to Saul. In the service of doubled speech, Michal's act and discourse may also be read as saving Saul, similar to the scenario Jonathan urges his father to avoid. To shed innocent blood is what she has prevented him from doing here, though she does not say it. Perhaps some of the blood she saves is her own.

iv. *Saul among the prophets (19:18–24)*

Though it is in some ways linked with what has preceded (Saul's recurring, ineffectual ordering of servants and sending of messengers to kill David: 19:1, 11, 14, 15, 20, 21), the passage is in other ways anomalous, not so much for content as for position of narrating. There is no inner angle here, and I take that as the point of departure. The difference in narrative technique, in position, signals the presence of a character not to be penetrated: God's spirit, which, in this story of Saul, is God's project of communication with him.[71]

That character or aspect of God-with-Saul remains opaque to the narrator, nor does Saul give access to the entity Saul-with-God.

---

[71] As my construction of the scene hints, I see no way to understand this spirit except from within the text. It obviously fits poorly within systematized reflection upon God, nor can it be equated readily with the social phenomenon of prophecy. So it must be treated epexegetically.

There is an encounter noted and minimally described, but we learn little of its nature. The narrator does not finalize God's spirit nor draw it polyphonically. What we see, we see from the outside. It is beyond the scope of this section (at least) to draw God. But how Saul constructs God is relevant (as is how Samuel does so in earlier parts of the story).

Exum (1992, 22, 28, 35) is right to suggest that the story of Saul's characterization is not able to be explained apart from God's, which includes for her God's misgivings first about kingship, then about the first king.[72] She describes God as ambivalent, even uncomfortably ambiguous, dark, and so forth. The problem I have with her line of thought is how to understand God construed apart from the techniques of representation with which we are dealing. Saul here, minimally, opposes what he understands from Samuel to be God's decision and bends his energies to resist vacating his royal post. How the dynamics of that determination work out before us (or how we participate in authoring it) is crucial for our own insight.

Exum is game to take on the evil side of God, God contending with a Saul who is more guilty than wicked, she says, and who is rejected with no forgiveness, as though God can be diagnosed apart from Saul's sense of the deity. How any of us chooses to author this authoring of God is a mirror for us, not a video that some are clever enough to glimpse. God remains inscrutable to characters, to narrator, to readers; there is no omni-science for any, biblical and scriptural genre notwithstanding.

The only direct speech in the piece comprises someone's report, "'See, David is at Naioth in Ramah'";[73] Saul's "'Where are Samuel and David?'"; an anonymous response, "'At Naioth in Ramah'"; and the enigmatic and formulaic "'Is even/also Saul among the prophets?'" (The sense that the information passes from person to person is made visible by the quotation marks.) All else is either summarized or described. Narrative technique is such that David is positioned by means of one of his key words (escape/מלט) but in a place perhaps unexpected: with Samuel, to whom he is said

---

[72] Exum writes in that chapter (1992, ch. 2) perceptively on Saul as tragic and notes a number of other studies that aim toward the same idea. I am not interested in the genre issue right here, nor in the larger issues of what is "wrong" with Saul.

[73] Fokkelman (1986, 271) notes the play on Ramah/why mock me.

to tell all that Saul has done to him. That report is not given in direct discourse; the specific content is not the draw of this short segment, though it presumably references Saul's growing animosity directed at David.[74] Saul is spoken of, then is informed of David's whereabouts, again—Naioth in Ramah, now with Samuel. Saul's combined power and powerlessness are simultaneously evoked as he sends three contingents of messengers (part of the royal [dynastic] character zone), who are overcome into "prophesying" when they arrive, with the result that Saul himself comes to accomplish his own goal.[75] Saul, once again asking (as is his primary authorial characterization) inquires about direction when he is near.[76]

The juxtaposition of Samuel and the anointed king(s) effects once again the presence of the spirit of God (10:9; 11:6; 16:13–16; 18:10; 19:9). I will stipulate here (to be developed on some other occasion) that the spirit is God's presence with Saul, positive before he has been fired and negative afterwards. That is to say, once Saul has set his own intent against that described to him as God's, the spirit contends with Saul, troubles him. It casts him into a prophetic state, whatever that may be (not the same as making him a prophet).[77] While in the spirit's grip Saul can either perform his kingship well (10:9; 11:6) or badly (other occasions). What it does to him is not clear, nor how it works; but what is shown us is that he and it are not compatible once he has been fired from reigning and David appointed and anointed in his place.

---

[74] Miscall carefully observes (1986, 128) that Samuel never speaks to David in our hearing.

[75] To "act the prophet" is not a very precise descriptor. Presumably more is involved than the communication of a pronouncement. That is, those referred to here do not become prophets but in some way resemble them.

[76] A similar technique is used in Gen 37, when Joseph is seeking his brothers prior to their removal of him from the family circle. Mimetically, the inquiring character is lost and has to ask directions; narratively, there is another function—different, I think, for each instance. In the instance of Gen 37, there is a witness (besides his brothers) to Joseph's presence and the action occurs in a place different from where the father supposes the sons to be.

[77] Polzin's hypothesis about Saul and prophecy remains unconvincing to me (see 1989, 182–86 for his sense of how the spirit functions among these characters).

The spirit is like a valence, once Samuel and David are there, representing the powerful assertion that Saul is no longer God's approved choice for king. It casts Saul wholly out of himself this time, a depiction more extreme in both narratorial expression and gesture than when he tries ineffectually to pin his successor to the wall.[78] In this case he turns on his own identity rather than David's; Saul strips off his clothes (as had Jonathan in 18:4) and lies naked. The description stresses not Saul's job but his being controlled by God's spirit like Samuel and others were wont to be. It need not be insight-provoking but rather deictic. What goes on with Saul and God's spirit all that day and night is not made clear; the episode comes to a dead end but makes no change for the better in regard to Saul's acceptance of his firing and marks no letup in his pursuit of David—to the contrary. The spirit of God is God's communication with Saul, which he is now resisting. If Saul's garments in some aspect signal kingship, though he casts them off here (Fokkelman 1986, 279–83, notes similarities between this (un)clothing and that of Saul's call), he presumably dons them again and resumes his kingly role when the spirit recedes. Part of what is being drawn of Saul over these chapters is that his increasing isolation (a result of making David his enemy) equals resistance to God, which drives him all the more. Saul is described like a man going deaf: the conversation continues around him, but he hears less and less of it and is more and more cut off, no matter how many surround him and how distinctly they talk.

Part 3: Saul Is Authored by David and Jonathan: 20:1–42

The event of chapter 20 unfolds longitudinally and in great detail.[79] The already discreet narrator backs off, especially in the

---

[78] Commentators are divided about who in this telling knows of David's anointment. I think mimetic observations like the impossibility of keeping such a thing secret are beside the point; I infer that Jonathan and Saul are not told directly that David is the successor but that each (as is evidenced by what he says) in his own way and own timing figures it out.

[79] Fokkelman gives many excellent insights and offers several charts that are visually clarifying (1986, 295–351) Edelman (1991, 153–61) has good observations of the ways in which language echoes what has been said earlier. Readers may want to consult McCarter's 6½ closely-packed pages of textual comments (1980, 335–41).

front of the story, so that in the first twenty-three verses there is little narrator work but two positionings of characters and a summary of the recommitment we saw in the first few verses of chapter 18: We are told that Jonathan cuts a covenant and loves David like himself. In this long section David and Jonathan each sketch a version of Saul, which they converge and reconcile only gradually. Each is also drawing himself and his friend, though it is not my purpose here to discuss those portraits. My interest is Saul and the art of narrating and reading him from the constructions of these two characters and eventually his own collaboration. How is Saul authored by David and Jonathan, and how does he respond?

The clearest way to move through the long narrative seems to be by taking utterances, Bakhtin's fundamental unit; here it comes to be a matter of exchanges (usually verbal). There are fourteen pairs of utterances, some very simple, others more complex: four of David (to Jonathan, who responds); two of Jonathan (to David, who responds); three of Saul (to himself and to Jonathan, who counters); and finally five apparently very one-sided ones between Jonathan and "the boy" in the field (which are actually as response-shaped as any of the others).

i. David and Jonathan: (20:1–11)

David and Jonathan start, each with his portrait of Saul. David's resembles the Saul we saw (and will see again) with Jonathan in 19:1–7: David claims that Saul senses action, guilt, or sin of David and is consequently seeking him. David questions, "What is my guilt or sin before your father that he is seeking my נֶפֶשׁ (life)?"[80] David implies that Saul is rational and just but mistaken and that he himself is unaware of his own guilt or sin, hence his claim is similar to what Jonathan maintained in 19:1–7. But the alternative, also implied, is that Saul hunts David without rational cause.

David has also authored Saul as seeking Jonathan, since their lives are intertwined (18:3).[81] That point is not made explicit by

---

[80] Craig (1994, 224) quotes approvingly research of Koch that makes the verb "sin" technical offense against one with whom one is in an institutional and communal relationship. It seems that once again words that may also be personal have larger nuances.

[81] Suggesting, confirming, that Saul saw the covenant in that scene.

David but remains implicit and clear to the reader who picks up on the doubled speech. Since the purpose is not to explore David (or Jonathan) but Saul, whether David's self-portrait is specious is not relevant; that his sketch of Saul is partly right (seeking characterizes Saul, and the life of the sons is his objective), but also off the mark is to some extent evident. Saul is reacting to many pressures, not excluding David's actions (whether guilt or sin) but not limited to them. That Saul has dismissed such concerns verbally to Jonathan in 19:1–7 does not mean he banished them, as the rest of chapter 19 has shown. These two character authorings encourage the reader to continue to reflect on her own construction of Saul.

Jonathan makes five rebuttals to David's initial three questions, his view of his father differing from David's in a number of particulars. Jonathan verbalizes Saul as confiding all his purposes and plans to his son, from great to small. That Jonathan does not know of a plan to kill David, he reasons, means it cannot be so. But toward the end of his strong denial he poses the question that moves the whole chapter forward: Why might Saul hide such a thing from his son? By asking that question, Jonathan admits the possibility that the charge may be true.

Jonathan's portrait of Saul, which he urges on David, overlooks a lot to draw this unity between them and reactivates the question of the singleness of life shared between David and Jonathan. Jonathan here must parry as well the idea of his father stalking him. Though a reader might be able to catalogue times and places where Saul has hurled a spear or urged his people to kill David or sent messengers to take him, nonetheless Jonathan is committed to the sense that such are not Saul's current thoughts. That Jonathan can overlook these moments suggests that his father may be able, driven, to do so too. So is Saul fundamentally just but mistaken? Or is he determined and duplicitous? Perhaps scattered and selective?

In 20:3–4 David responds less to Jonathan's denials than to his question. He explains away that portrait of Saul who confides in his son by suggesting that Saul is unwilling to split Jonathan's feelings by making him choose between his father and "brother." "Lest you be grieved," David explains Saul's inner process to be (hypothetical quoted direct discourse). He thus intensifies Jonathan's sense of the closeness of father and son but denies it simultaneously, draws a different conclusion from that bond than had Jonathan.

·   Whether Jonathan is at the heart of what Saul is doing remains
uncertain; whose potential grief is being offset is unclear.
Jonathan seems convinced by what David has said, abandoning his picture
of Saul who would not hide plans from a son for what David has
urged, a sketch that draws the father concerned for his son.
Jonathan consequently offers David a blank check: Whatever you
say, I will do. The phrasing is key: "What you(rself) (נפשׁ) says, I
will do for you." It begins Jonathan's direct discourse on the topic
of his bond with David (for which the narrator primed us at the
start of ch. 18).

The next lineaments of the portrait (found in 20:5–9) are supplied by David, though they shrewdly capitalize both on
Jonathan's claims to intimacy with his father's plans and on the
closeness between the two sons. He first sketches the king's table
on the morrow (a feast) and then situates himself in hiding rather
than at table. Picking up on a technique we saw with Saul in chapter 18, David hands his own words to Jonathan for him to recite
at the proper time.

David proposes a scenario that will scrutinize the issue that is
most fraught between himself and Saul: the question of sonship.
Whose son is David: Saul's or Jesse's? Whose servant: Saul's or
Jonathan's (vv. 7–8)? David is now in some ways also altering the
father-son bond shared by Saul and Jonathan. At a feast, when
David is missing from Saul's table (note that Saul's failure to
remark David's absence is not contemplated; rather, they count on
his reacting), and Saul learns he has gone to Bethlehem with
Jonathan's permission, what will be Saul's response not only to
David but to Jonathan? David calls Saul both "the king" and "your
father." He avoids referencing his own father clearly, saying rather
"his city," "the family."

David similarly crafts for Saul two utterances: either "'"Good,"'"
which will approve David's return to his father, or a wordless
anger, which will signify the opposite.[82] David again draws Saul
clearly either able to approve or to grow angry. David builds in

---

[82] Polzin queries (1989, 187–88) why the two (or either of them) should
continue to trust Saul's expressions of goodwill toward David. He thinks
(192) that Jonathan rather consistently misses the negative undertow of
persons and situations, despite David's direction that he be more duplicitous or at least suspicious.

time for Saul to watch and wonder and seems to bank on the fact that, by the second festal meal, Saul will react. David does not articulate to Jonathan what Saul might say besides "Good." David's portrait of Saul shows him seeking something between David and himself that he will not find and finding in its place the bond between David and Jonathan to which Saul has been so tardily invited. The plan implicates Jonathan, makes Jonathan the reason David is not at table, since he will have known and approved David's plan, whether Saul likes it or does not.

Again, to explore David's own articulations would take us too far afield here, but we can hear David reminding Saul that the two "sons" are one and that they deal with each other apart from him. David is also making that bond one strand thicker by his plan here. More than a test of Saul—though framed as showing what is set or established (כלה)—this is an experiment implicating Jonathan as well, and forcing that awareness onto Saul. And more than a test, it is an entrapment, whether that awareness is David's or not.

The plan envisions one of two reactions but does not push the anger into its next stage, though it spends most of its time envisioning the negative scenario. Does that scenario reveal or cause Saul's reaction? David also prescribes for Jonathan a conclusion and an implicative order: If I am to be killed, you do it; why let your father do it? A rhetorical question? Is David pretty safe in asking Jonathan to kill him? Jonathan's response is to deny the possibility.

One further point: The positive response—owned by all its speakers, "Good!" (טוב) is a loaded word in this narrative, tasting bitterly of the occasion when Saul was fired from kingship and a better man appointed in his place. Though it has been made obvious to the reader who that man is, Saul's information on the identity is less direct. The word *good* has hovered around David in the appraisal and even in the words of Jonathan about David. Is it likely that Saul will be able to use this word wholeheartedly of his protégé? I think David has drawn a feature of Saul that the king will be unlikely to manage.

In 20:10–11 the conversation moves from what will happen to how the response can be communicated. David asks that detail, prompting Jonathan to propose a change of venue. They go out to the field, the site where the rest of their planning and communication will take place.

ii. *Jonathan and David (20:12–23)*

Jonathan's initiative in 20:12–17 to move to the field makes sense mimetically in terms of their not being overheard as well as for practical purposes of rehearsing the communication of the information.[83] Jonathan here makes three complicated, condition- and oath-laden assertions: The first involves the reconnaissance and communication of each alternative Saul may take. A second voices an oath that he will send David away safely if Saul is not well-disposed toward him. The third pronounces a blessing for David with proviso for a reciprocal commitment to survivors of Jonathan's house. The detail of the king's possible anger is elaborated ominously. Jonathan's emotional reaction can scarcely be missed within this very strong utterance.

Jonathan binds David to himself and his own life to David again, recommitting them to the matters begun—granted one-sidedly and nonverbally—in 18:1–5.[84] David does not utter, but the narrator implies (by verb form) that he completes his own oath as urged by Jonathan and reminds us of the significance of what we have just heard: Jonathan loves David as himself. Whether Jonathan sketches his father as the dangerous opponent is unclear but not impossible, at least to a reader.

The next section (20:18–23) opens with Jonathan now echoing antiphonally David's speech of 20:5–8, envisioning both the king's table and the hiding David, whose position Jonathan specifies in detail, sending David as the two rehearsed but not to Bethlehem. Jonathan reiterates the particulars of the table, never quite filling in the moment of denouement, and promises information—which is the point for him, I think. He then moves on to respond more specifically to the question David proposed in 20:10: Who will communicate the bad news (presumably the difficulty would not arise if the king were to have said, "Good!")?

---

[83] Fokkelman calls the field the antipole of the court (1986, 308–309)— and a different place as well from the field in which David hid when Jonathan successfully urged reconciliation to his father; Saul's court Fokkelman names as the intersection of all the quests of this whole unit (294). Pleins suggests (1992, 34), that the field (and David's other venues) take him outside the circle of Saul's realm.

[84] David will be shown to follow through on this commitment at least externally when he deals with Jonathan's son Mephibosheth (2 Sam 9; 16; 19).

The plan he crafts seems perhaps overly complex, but for our purposes it can be classed as another doubled speech, in that it is rehearsed here for a later use and will be directed to a boy with one ostensible referent and to the hidden man with another.[85] The heft of the communication of the arrows is on the "flee danger" option, as before. That the system will break down in the event does not mean it is not sensible when set up. Is Saul well-disposed toward David or not, and what can David expect? Jonathan, with multiple oaths, promises fidelity to David and heirs. Jonathan also swears that YHWH seek out the enemies of David, which *we* know to include Saul. His own awareness of the import of his words is uncertain. Does Jonathan intend to set his father up here by oath? Jonathan aligns himself against those who see David as enemy and curses them.[86]

David has split Jonathan and Saul, has authored to Jonathan a father whom he must oppose. Notably, Jonathan does not envision what actually is about to happen, which is to say he does not explicitly acknowledge Saul as a danger to either himself or David, but the possibility reverberates in his utterance. David makes no audible response here but obeys. One implication and impact of all the planning is that it renders additional attempts at reconciliation impossible (Fokkelman 1986, 305). Saul has been made incorrigible, at least by David and Jonathan, whose oaths have asked God's participation as well. Whether such is the case is to be demonstrated.

iii. Saul and Jonathan (20:24–34)

The narrator intrudes in 20:24–26 uncharacteristically for the section, but in the usual way throughout these hundred verses, to position us for viewing, to cue us to what Saul is about to note. The time is the feast of which David and Jonathan have just spoken, and the place is the king's table. Saul is seated, Jonathan and Abner standing, David's place noticeably empty, since the narrator describes him with the language used of him recently: hiding, hid-

---

85 Fokkelman discusses the level of the communication at great length (1986, intermittently, 319–51), hiding some good insight amid a great deal of other detail.

86 Refer to Pyper (1996) and the supposition that the story of Nathan is aimed at getting an oath extracted from David.

den—David hiding from Saul or (and) David hidden as a lure for the king.[87] Saul will soon be hunting David, and/or David will be positioning himself so as to draw Saul forth in pursuit.

There is no audible utterance here, but Saul once again speaks to himself. We have been prepared to intuit the question Saul is likely to ponder in the presence of David's empty place. In fact, the answer reveals the question, querying the reason for David's absence from the table: "He chances to be unclean, surely he is unclean." The doubling of the rumination suggests the intensity of the soliloquy. Saul's construction of David as present except for a disqualifying technicality is a large and solipsistic misconstrual, as we, reading, know. Saul's portrait includes *himself, his* table, *his* men. What other possibilities Saul is foreclosing to himself are hinted at but not developed. Saul's emphatic announcement, his insecurity doubling it, crowds out other reasons for David's absence but not before they are made imaginable. The pressure to explain the absence—the slight?—is on.

The next scene (20:27–29) is one of the many doublets comprising these hundred verses. But time has moved on: It is the next day, and Saul cannot contain his speech within him any longer and poses his question to his son Jonathan—the narrator's tag again reminding us of the paternal/filial agenda. Calling David (three times, here) the son of Jesse, Saul requests, demands, to know where he is. His question now, flushed from the underbrush of his self-talk, reveals the inadequacy of his own previous effort to convince himself that it must be temporary uncleanness, since he retraces the absence of the previous day. That he is correct to doubt the excuse offered does not alter much the portrait of the king, chased by his own fears into the thicket of testing woven by David and Jonathan in vv. 5–7, 12, 18. That Saul calls David by his patronymic (dismissively in the view of most commentators) names his failure to make David his own son.

Jonathan, echoing David (v. 6) but ringing some crucial changes, starts in a sort of reporting mode: "David urgently asked to go to Bethlehem," then switching into direct discourse, he amplifies: "He said, 'Send me, please, for there is a family sacrifice for us in the city; and he has summoned me—my brother. If I have

---

[87] Using the language of the two "sons" in 20:6. The narrator is conspiring with the two.

found favor in your eyes, I would slip away (מלט), please, so I may see my brothers.'" Jonathan then drops out of his direct quoting and resumes the more indirect mode, rounding out the explanation: "For this reason he has not come to the table of the king." Jonathan's changes, whether deliberate or not, highlight some issues we already have seen to be sensitive to Saul: the father/son bond triangulating David, Saul, and Jesse as well as David, Saul, and Jonathan; the favor that David finds in the eyes of diverse appraisers; the escape of David at the hands of Michal; and now also the matter of brothers, which Saul picks up on shortly.[88] Jonathan places around Saul the scenario he and David have co-authored. Saul has preformed as anticipated, has responded as prodded to do.

In 20:30–34 we come to the heart of the whole section under discussion here, the place where Saul is most explicit about his understanding of himself (though on the Dostoevsky hero-self-consciousness scale, it may disappoint). The narrator simply confirms both what we know to expect from the previous places where Saul is thwarted in the matter of David and also what is so clearly anticipated by the two characters at 20:8, who have planned much more in terms of the angry response than the mellow one. Saul's anger, directed not unsuitably against Jonathan, slurs him and indirectly his birth.[89]

In one of his most candid reflections, Saul tells Jonathan that he knows that the son (as well as the daughter—N.B. 18:28) is choosing (בחר) Jesse's son over against his own lineage (his mother's nakedness). Avoiding, for the most part, to cite his own interest, Saul charges Jonathan with acting for David to the hurt of his own (i.e., Jonathan's) kingship. Of course, from another angle, the reference to "Jonathan's kingdom" denies the information Saul was

---

[88] Fokkelman (1986, 332–33) catches them carefully; his reading assumptions demand the question of Jonathan's intent, which in Bakhtin's mode does not arise.

[89] Fokkelman suggests the slur is not directed against Jonathan's mother per se but conveys the notion that the son is congenitally flawed (1986, 334). That may be so, though contemporary feminist theory will not so easily overlook the manner of derogation, nor will a Bakhtinian reader miss the positioning of the old conflict of sons and their parentage. For a more gender-sensitive interpretation, consult Jobling (1998, 178).

given so unequivocally by Samuel in 13:13–14 and 15:26. There is to be no kingdom for Jonathan, no matter the efforts of any.

Then, as if his blunt detailing of realities might convince his son, Saul once again demands that Jonathan send (שׁלח) David to Saul to be killed.[90] Jonathan's response to the outburst defies that fatherly expectation and echoes both his own and David's earlier language (19:4; 20:1): "Why should he be killed? What has he done?" Saul's response is to confirm the conflation of the two "sons," as he hurls the spear formerly aimed at David now at Jonathan. Saul's action belies his own verbal utterance and shows as well that Michal and Jonathan are not the only ones who have made a clear choice in regard to David.[91]

The narrator ties off the scene, having showed us the basis on which Jonathan now knows that Saul is intent on David's death. The long arc rising when we were told that Jonathan loved David as another self has descended when Jonathan also sees the spear of Saul hurling toward him. And now not one but two sons are conspicuously missing from the table, as Jonathan leaves, grieving for David, according to words of David in 20:3; the narrator, with clever ambiguity, says his father had shamed him.

Saul has stated his priority, which is to leave his son Jonathan to rule; it is a subset of his main drive, which is to remain king. Saul sets the problem in terms of Jonathan's shaming his mother and names David as the obstacle. He avoids saying that Jonathan's actions shame him and that he has been told that the obstacle to Jonathan's rule is God's preference. Even at his most forthright moment, he leaves a great deal submerged. Blaming at very least Jonathan and David, Saul refuses still to acknowledge his own role for what it is. David's life on the earth is a threat to Saul's rule as well as Jonathan's, a situation Saul has been acting on for several scenes. That his own actions have obviated his goal Saul does not acknowledge.

To throw a spear at his son is to admit, by gesture, that the quest is hopeless. Saul the king overrules Saul the father.[92] Faced

---

[90] The expression "he is a son of death," using the same filial language as Saul's epithet for his own child, means that David must die.

[91] Fokkelman (1986, 291). He also specifies that the scene, when contrasted with 19:1–7, which led to a temporary remediation of Saul's pursuit, makes reconciliation impossible (331).

by his son with the question of David's innocence, Saul hurls the spear. Jonathan's persistent tack, which is to appeal to his father for justice, shows Saul incapable of that move.

iv. Jonathan and "the boy" (20:35–42)

The last five utterances are Jonathan's, spoken both to his boy who bears his armor and to "his brother" who accepted his armor some time back. These phrasings also are double, in that they rerun language already rehearsed between Jonathan and David (vv. 20–23). Though most commentators are understandably impatient with this fake flurry of arrows shot in accordance with an earlier plan in a scene that no longer seems to call for such elaborate subterfuge, the narrator's choice to spend time on it suggests it needs scrutiny.[93] To mine it for doubled speech repays effort, though again my point is to author Saul, not these two young men. "To run" is the permission David requested in v. 6. "And the boy ran," comments the narrator, in lieu of the character's verbal response.

When in 20:37, the boy has come to the place of the arrows that Jonathan had instructed, Jonathan calls, "Is not the arrow behind you farther on?" The wording suggests the boy has turned to face his master, awaiting further cue. The other waiting figure has been instructed in 20:22: "YHWH sends you away." Saul is not demanding that Jonathan send David to him, but God is sending him away. Saul is at cross-purposes with God, pointlessly, it seems.

"Hurry, quick, don't delay" is the next command (20:38–39) observed well by the one boy, prompting the other as well. And the narrator assists us, points our vision: The one knew, the other did not.

"And Jonathan gave his weapons to the boy who was with him and said, 'Go, bring them to the city'" (20:40). A reprise of

---

92 Pleins suggests a reading of the Saul and Jonathan situation in reference to the relation of Abraham and Isaac. The strategy is helpful, though Pleins undercuts it by assuming that the narrative needs to solve the problem of how to shift dynasties from Saul to David (1992, 33). I think the dynamics are far more complex.

93 E.g., Campbell (1989, 80–83) insists that the ritual is not properly observed; Fokkelman, at the other extreme, spends pages (1986, 318–51) excavating its possible layers of signification. It is my hope to take a middle path. It is important but not endlessly mysterious.

18:4, matched there by a narratorial comment that David was successful wherever Saul sent him.

The last utterance (20:41–42) is Jonathan's alone, blending the former oaths of covenant partners with the presence of YHWH's protection and guarantee, reiterating his own words of 20:12–16, which Jonathan exacted from David too. After the narrator provides, finally, assurances of mutuality between David and Jonathan, the next "swing" verse (MT 21:1) indicates that David rose and left and Jonathan went into the city, after the boy.

Concluding Points

I do not wish to finalize Saul, especially on the basis of one hundred verses, but I do want to bring together what I think I have seen from the representation of these scenes.[94] Prior to commenting on the content, let me review the process implicit in my reading. It is my understanding and contention that DH has authored a significant work on Israel's experience of monarchy and that the figure Saul opens it meaningfully, just as Josiah and his scion in Babylon bring it to a close. Saul is not simply a king, even the first king. He also, rather, makes visible and paradigmatic the primordial flaws of monarchist rule. The section under current scrutiny shows the problem clearly.

The keyhole through which I am looking (*mise en abyme*) is 17:38–39: Saul, faced with Goliath's uttered and postured taunt that he is not able to do his royal job, accepts David's offer to do it; he clothes David in royal armor to send him against the Philistine. But David first rehearses and then refuses the gesture, going rather on his own terms to do the king's job successfully. So this brief moment exposes for me (perhaps for others) something radically true of Saul. Whether it is an insight he will appropriate remains to be seen; it surely does not happen in the chapters under present consideration.

A single moment, however diagnostic, cannot comprise the whole of a hero but may precipitate a key pattern for our viewing. For Saul, that is his refusal of responsibility layered amid his action of inviting his own replacement without acknowledging it.

---

[94] Analogously, an artist may paint a scene many times, finishing it on occasion without ever finalizing it; a performing musician does the same with a score.

David shapes Saul by both accepting and refusing the offer, wresting it from Saul's control and redesigning it as his own. This is the pattern Saul recapitulates here repeatedly, actively and passively. But this construction is not "in the text" but rises between skillful authoring and my choices, selected from the many linguistic dynamics presented within this highly artistic text and put into play under my own signature. It is my conscious choice to make focal for Saul here the problem of alterity. Not only politically but also personally Saul makes the consistent and futile effort to manage his own life, to "be" on his own, to author himself as king and in every other role that he has. The result of his refusal of relatedness is the terrible isolation that ends up attending him, in these hundred verses and as the story develops. In this aspect, too, he and the story of his rule are filled with potential insight for us, struggling with our own version of these same temptations.[95]

Recall also that the point of this exercise of reading narrative carefully is for me (others as they so choose) to gain some transformative insight.[96] Flaws notwithstanding, I hope my reading has made clear that I find Saul a very endearing figure. My resonance with his struggles is great, which is to say, his consciousness is largely compatible with what I perceive in myself. My authoring of the story, my constructing of this hero within the project of my own spirituality, can effect a growth of self-knowledge and hence possibly a transformation in me, others too, I presume.

---

[95] Ruth Coates (1998, passim but ch. 8 in particular) discusses and demonstrates the extent to which some highly classic biblical anthropology informs Bakhtin's aesthetics, ethics, spirituality and literary theory. I am bringing that spirituality to my reading, convinced of its value and appropriateness for the matter at hand. I have chosen to work with Bakhtin because of this coherence; it is not simply that I feel stuck with his framework and have to use it because I have taken up his literary theory.

[96] To read Fokkelman, who psychologizes a great deal, reinforces in my mind the sense that I am not trying to penetrate the consciousness of the biblical character but letting the representation of speech activate my consciousness. Hugh Pyper is very interesting on the psychological possibilities of father-son issues here, which he sees as complicating and complicated by the fact that it is also a kingdom being passed on. Posed differently is Robert Polzin's insight and suggestion (1989) that the first four chapters of 1 Sam comprise a parable of kingship; is the Saul story itself a parable of the national experience of monarchy?

I am (any reader may come to be) exotopic enough to see more than Saul sees but interpenetrated with him enough to be "empathetic," can both benefit from my surplus in regard to him and from "his" in regard to me. His refusal of many linkages between himself and others helps me reflect on the reality of such networks. His blindly determined destructiveness is frightening. Saul as a hero (in the Bakhtinian sense) does not function allegorically (we can see ourselves like him and so imitate or resist his patterns) but in a much more refracted way, as language works.

In addition to being given form by author and reader, characters also author themselves and each other in many decisive ways. Let me now comment briefly on each of the three sections explored above. In the first (17:55–18:30) we watch Saul primarily authoring himself; in chapter 19 the initiative slips from him to Jonathan and God's spirit; and by chapter 20 the authoring is shared out between David and Jonathan, with Saul mostly reactive.

From the end of the Goliath battle (and even sooner), Saul bends his energies totally toward the survival of his royal self and his line and gives no evidence of openness to anything else. This self-image, enhanced by Saul's view of David-as-threat and intensified by his own public failure with the Philistine, occasions him to draw himself in a particular way as a human being; it also affects his construction of everyone else, notably his son and daughter, but also God, and other people around him (named or not). He constructs himself only as a sitting king, never as moving down. In that determination the personal and political, private and public, social and individual are inextricably blended. He consequently sees others as charged with assisting him in that aspiration, enhancing his ruling self. Others-for-Saul are all related to his royal quest.

But this complex monarchical construction goes over against what the others seem to be doing, so Saul struggles to redirect them so that they are aiding him; but he fails. His self is intermeshed with them but contentiously and one-sidedly so; his authoring of himself is not respectful of them. He subsumes others into his projected self, all the while missing other aspects of them and misappropriating them to him. It is a very distorting strategy for all concerned. Saul's effort to claim David as his own is thwarted consistently by David but laterally by Jonathan, whose pact with David excludes Saul, and eventually by Michal, who appears to me to choose neither father nor husband—but surely not her father. The same dynamic can be glimpsed in regard to the celebrating women and at least potentially (later in actuality) with Saul's servants and men (in 1 Sam 21–22). But what seems clear is that Saul's single-eyed solipsism isolates him and turns others against him, first in his appraisal and then as he acts with them. As he sees the others as his opponents, so they begin to take up that role.

All this has been apparent in the carefully authored and read speech of narrator and characters. As has been said and shown, Saul's language is all transactional, in that it needs other people to finish it up with him: David to agree, servants to obey and mediate; arguably, David and the servants play him in the same way, so that he is assisting their transaction-laden language. Silence can be a great prompt to speech, hints and innuendo as well.

Saul's language links him with various persons whom he uses without any apparent conscious reflection on it or awareness of the boomerang he is making. His reliance on others does not (as the story continues) generate a healthy network of interlinkages but fears of conspiracy (e.g., ch. 22), some actual manipulations of him by those he is manipulating (e.g., 18:11–17; all of 20), and ultimately isolation and alienation.

Saul's speech shows him first struggling to clothe David as a son, son-in-law, a "royal" who will go out against Saul's enemies, the Philistines. In fact, the Philistines are in his design hoped-for allies, as they are being set up to do what Saul cannot do himself, which is to destroy David. His more natural allies, whether his officers and troops, servants, son, daughters, all become "Philistines" for him, appointed as well to eliminate David from what Saul senses lies ahead for him. So he redesigns foes as helpers, family as hostile eventually to himself. Saul's constructions are wrenched from the king's hand and reformatted, repeatedly.

Saul grabs at data and reads it as it suits him; he is a poor reader as well as an ineffective author, perhaps afflicted by (mostly[97]) myopia or dyslexia, in that he can only see a bit ahead and scrambles what he does see. And he does not see backwards, cannot

---

[97] He is amazingly prescient with his sense at 18:8 that David has almost all of it already. But he buries that moment of insight so he can battle against it.

be heard to reflect on the trail behind him. For example, if he says to David, "a second time be my son-in-law," we miss any comment from him about the first try—the same with spear thrusts; Saul seems implicitly to tear up what is behind him so it does not exist, he need not refer to it. His blindness persistently traps Saul in eventualities he does not seem to anticipate or to sense are related.

To put it succinctly: Saul uses and ex(c)-uses. There is no indication that Saul sees or can admit what he is creating by his stratagems. That is, he avoids signing his life. As a consequence of his poor eyesight, his weak insight, he becomes manipulable by others, a pattern that intensifies as the story goes on. Since a good deal of what activates him is not perceptible to him, others can blindside him, and do.

Saul's language shows him reactive, easily set off by information that comes his way; his plannings never acknowledge the roots of the issues that trouble him. Again, the narrator does little more than underline or slightly amplify his inner dynamics. No character (so far) shows Saul a mirror in which he might glimpse himself before he adjusts for the camera, and consequently be jarred into and then deepen self-knowledge. We may wish he had better friends than his people who approve David so unabashedly, than Jonathan who can only praise David to Saul, than Michal who exhibits no patience with "her father," than David who persistently trumps him, than Samuel who has abandoned him. We may wish they had a better king, leader, father, mentor.

But as has been suggested, Saul loses initiative at some point, which I have located for now at chapter 19. We may see this shift in two particular characteral authorings of Saul: by God's spirit and by Jonathan. Though very different, they provoke the same ultimate response from Saul.

God's spirit, visible throughout but perhaps most sharply in chapter 19, is decisive with Saul by the end of this section. Minimally we have seen that this spirit of God seems mediated to the kings (Saul and David) through the anointment, at God's behest, by the prophet Samuel. And once bestowed on David, we can see it turning on Saul's project of survival, activating something destructive in him. The spirit "goes off," in both senses of the word, becoming troubling to Saul and he vexatious with it.

One way to think about it is to see it as a loophole for all involved.[98] God can use it to avoid finalizing the choice of Saul as king and to give the monarchy project a new lease on life. For Saul it is the occasion to bring David to court and attends his attempts to slay him. Those around Saul, David in particular, can see that under its stress, Saul does indeed try to kill him; and thus David can counter Saul. The narrator, never giving the spirit much definition, shows Saul falling under its power; neither he nor his Samuel-and-David-seeking messengers are able to offer any direct resistance to it.

As the narrative unfolds, Saul constructs himself over against what we know he has been told God has preferred, sets himself at odds with what God can be—is—understood to want. The struggle with God's expressed preferences is a long-running issue and dominates all the episodes; the ones with other people (Samuel, Michal, Jonathan, priests, Abner, even David) are more scenic by comparison, though also more overt.

That resistance sets up a very negative dynamic, at least for a good deal of the time (presuming that Saul may do better in the end). If it may be assumed that what God prefers is the ultimate benefit of the people—i.e., if I may assume as a default position that God will prefer good rather than evil, granted the reality of conflicting goods and less-than-ideal circumstances—I assume as well that Saul's struggle against God is not healthy for Saul.

Why, beyond generalities, do I think Saul's constructing or authoring of himself is bad for his health? It can be seen in a whole host of particular situations as well as cosmically: He gets persistently caught into alibiing, blaming others, ritualizing, asking so as to shift responsibility, denying to himself and others. These are not good signs. He cannot (so far) sign his life. That assumption is verified in the realities that emerge from the struggle itself, in episode after episode. Resisting God is not good for Saul's health. He in effect makes God an enemy too, a move very hard on the health. Granted, God's preferences cannot be known in much detail, by us or by the characters on our screen. But oddly, at the end of chapter 19, Saul walks around the spirit. He

---

[98] Students in the second Bakhtin Circle class were insightful and provocative about the spirit, seeing it as a loophole (Carrie Rehak) and a chronotope (Mark Bosco), suggesting it as a limited good (Jeanne Choy Tate), an alibi for narrator and reader (Susan Sutton).

cannot resist it, but what he does seem to do is go back home and redouble his efforts at survival.

The other authoring dynamic at work in this chapter is Jonathan's. The son tries to show his father the (self-)destructiveness of his pursuit of David and the injustice of it, to draw for him the beneficence of those around the king. Interestingly enough, Jonathan is named and shown as the character capable of loving another as he loved his own self. Though comment on that characterization tends to be limited to the particular bond between Jonathan and David, at a larger angle, it takes on even deeper significance. Granted, some are easier to love than others. But a human able to love one person in this way has a leg up on the same achievement with others. And here it is a matter of a son and a father. Jonathan, telling how David took his life in his hand for the king, takes his own life in his hand as well here, speaking up to his father about the one under condemnation. And in fact Saul heeds him. But as the next scene opens, it turns out that Saul has simply walked around the words of his son as he did the pressure of the spirit. Unable to rebut, he simply disregards these strong prompts.

So chapter 20 shows David instructing the son about the father, authoring all of them in such a way that positions are greatly hardened. Saul, manipulated by the narrative his two "sons" contrive, admits some reality but pushes other realities far from him. That his rule and the survival of his line is out of the question he both sees and resists. Saul's kingship is ended, for all practical purposes. Why that is the case remains largely submerged, granted efforts of many to expatiate it. It is not, at the very least, wholly a matter of virtue or vice. Thus commentators' outrage that David's sins were worse than Saul's but that he did not get in trouble completely miss the dynamic. If the kingship of Saul is a parable about kingship in general, then to try to explicate Saul's "firing" in terms of personal dynamics will never be satisfactory. The drawing of Saul is a way of exploring and expressing something larger. Saul's story is a parable of kingship in Israel.

This long chapter has indicated some of the possibilities available by working with a few of Bakhtin's categories of types of discourse. Four other scholars, working also with Hebrew Bible texts, have made use of other facets of Bakhtin's work with many other effects. It is to the work of those four that we shall now turn.

4.
How Do Other Scholars Use Bakhtin?

"The boundaries between God's word and Moses' interpretation have been deliberately blurred to illustrate the condition of all interpretation. On the one hand it is always necessary; on the other it is finally impossible to distinguish what part of an interpretation is of the interpreter and what part of the one interpreted."

Robert Polzin, *Moses and the Deuteronomist*

This chapter will consider critically and at some length the works of four Hebrew Bible scholars who are in diverse ways utilizing aspects of Bakhtin. To identify what each is doing and how their work can be useful for our understanding of Bakhtin's thought is the object of inquiry. The primary purpose of all the studies under consideration here is to explicate biblical text; that task I will leave to them. It is my intent and hope to portray the works fairly but one-sidedly since, though they all serve multiple purposes, it is really just the Bakhtinian angle that is of interest here.

It was not so obvious whom to choose, aside from Polzin, who is in a category by himself, having spent the last ten years of his life bringing together Bakhtinian ideas and strategies and Deuteronomic prose. My selection includes those who have two pieces that draw on Bakhtin and that demonstrate the range of what is possible from his large repertoire of ideas: Kenneth Craig Jr., Carol Newsom, Ilana Pardes, and Robert Polzin.

Kenneth M. Craig Jr.

Craig's two works offer an excellent place to start. His first "Bakhtinian" book, on Jonah, makes minimal use of the Russian scholar but exposes quite usefully the points of attraction between Craig's interests and the strategies of Bakhtin, while his second work, on Esther, makes much more explicit use of Bakhtin's concept of the carnivalesque though actually stops short of utilizing it fully. Despite my critique, each study is valuable in many ways that transcend my present objectives.

Craig on Jonah

To rethink fundamentally a text one has already constructed carefully (perhaps especially a dissertation) is quite difficult; to incorporate Bakhtin's ideas demands a rerouting of thought that is very thorough. Craig's first book, *A Poetics of Jonah: Art in the Service of Ideology* (1993) remains essentially formalist, with hints of something else not fully appropriated yet.[1] As noted above, I will not discuss here the content of Jonah, which Craig does very admirably; rather, I hope to show his openness to Bakhtin's ideas, which remain, however, underutilized even at the end of the book.[2] To pick up on a point Craig himself makes in relation to the prayer of Jonah and the whole Jonah narrative: One must read the midpoint from hindsight. Therefore, knowing that Craig's work on Jonah (and on Esther) has risen from and occasioned interest in Bakhtin, I will explain why the glass he offers in his writing is both half full and half empty, the point being to assist others who may be in a similar position.

The title of the work describes Craig's fundamental question well: How are the artistic and ideological combined? What unity of effects does the author aim to present? Craig consistently demonstrates that art serves ideology, but he is actually hovering on a larger question: How (else) are the two related? He situates his project of constructing a poetics by introducing the thought of three theorists useful to him: Benjamin Hrushovski, Aristotle, and

---

[1] I myself have done what I still consider valuable pre-Bakhtin work on the Joseph story from Gen 37–50. As I was finishing my earlier book, *"What Profit for Us?" Remembering the Joseph Story* (1996), I realized that I was fundamentally dissatisfied with my wholly text-centered approach, which virtually ignored historical and readerly issues. Though seeing the deficiency, I did not feel able to shift gears. It is also true that the formalist or narratological springboard (in distinction to certain more historical ones) is one of the best preparations for appropriating the greater depth of Bakhtin.

[2] Craig names Bakhtin on a few pages but relies primarily on Boris Uspensky (who drew on Bakhtin) and on Polzin's work rather than on Bakhtin himself; his references to Bakhtin's own writings remain perfunctory and rather superficial.

Meir Sternberg. He broadens the definition of "ideology" from what is often termed "false consciousness": "I employ the word to mean a deeply held and interlocking set of religious, social, and political beliefs or attitudes about the world and how the world works." He concludes that ideology is inevitable (1993, 8). His various chapters all explicate ways in which the artistic crafting of the brief narrative helps produce its ideology. Yet, though he asserts that art and ideology are full partners, I did not find equal attention paid to the question of how ideology contributes to art. (See particularly 1993, ch. 1.) The art/ideology relation is a key Bakhtin topic, but Bakhtin's question would not be limited to how art serves ideology or to the insight that is does; rather, his thinking snakes off into the labyrinth by which art and ideology are mutually constitutive of a literary work. The production of meaning, a similarly fundamental question, is not—particularly among followers of Bakhtin—left solely or even primarily in the hands of the authorial intent but is co-constructed by many other factors.

Having sketched his central interest, Craig next lays the groundwork for one of the main components of the art and ideology partnership: attention to narratorial and to characteral language (i.e., direct discourse).[3] A key point, if I understand it correctly, is that the translator is a reader whose reading choices affect how he or she—as well as others who rely on that reading—will construe narrator and characters. Craig's comparative work on NRSV and RSV translations is highly nuanced, and he is correct to say that from such minuscule judgements authors have proceeded and readers continue to view the narrator/character bond. His point is not so much that some translations are better or worse but that various factors must be balanced in translation choices and that results will differ.

To select a few of his comparisons allows us to glimpse places where Craig shows himself Bakhtin-ready, in terms of both narrator and character speech.[4] For example, certain NRSV changes in the

---

[3] Having concluded his ch. 1 with his own translation of the book of Jonah, Craig spends his ch. 2 discussing variations between the RSV and NRSV translations.

[4] Craig offers examples of narrator speech (1993, 25–27) and analysis of direct character speech (27–28); he has other points to offer as well about translation choices, all in his ch. 2.

RSV of Jonah 1:4 highlight the role of divine agency over that of nature. Changes in 3:7, which Craig thinks more closely represent the MT, stress the king of Nineveh as source but not actual writer of orders that go out above his signature, a point that presumably enhances royal authority. And the several shifts made in the later translation at 4:1 collaborate to heighten the narrator's linking Jonah's anger to the events that have just transpired. It is not that such a connection was not implied by the RSV translation, but the join is made more explicit, tighter, in the NRSV (1993, 25–27).

Craig's comparative comments on some samples of direct discourse are similar. His discussion of what he considers genuine advances in knowledge of biblical Hebrew allows us to hear the speech of the characters differently, more accurately. So in 4:2, a new understanding of the auxiliary קדמתי (I did x at the outset— viz., fled): "I fled to Tarshish at the beginning" rather than "I made haste to flee" has an impact on our ability to construe the character's sorting of his own motives and behaviors. Moreover, the recognition that the hiphil of טוב carries the nuance of "be justified" as well as "do good" brings additional nuance to the discussion between Jonah and YHWH (4:4, 9).

Such care with the reading, whether to translate or utilize a translation, draws attention not so much to whether a given instance is right or wrong, better or worse (though that may be part of it), as to the range of alternatives available even in matters that may seem unimportant or already settled. Craig points out, rightly, that a narrator has many choices of diction, and so the path taken is worth careful attention by readers. Character speech, similarly, allows us particular access to texture. Bakhtin's sensitivities to artistic choices among narrator, various characters, and readers—as all negotiate words—are compatible with these careful observations of Craig.

Having laid careful groundwork to introduce the key players (narrator and characters, artistic author and reader), Craig goes on to describe patterns that comprise Jonah (and other relevant biblical texts as well). Relying on theorists whose interpretations are more formalist than Bakhtin (Alter, Booth, Sternberg), Craig continues to see the narrator as omniscient and reliable, intrusive or even neutral, as serving as the center of consciousness in the narrative, concepts that no longer make sense in a more developed Bakhtinian poetics.[5]

---

[5] Craig reaffirms the all-knowing and reliable narrator (1993, 127).

This important chapter discusses first the characteristics of the Jonah narrator: how he starts the story, how he allows speech, how he characterizes others (whether the ship or the deity), how he times the release of bits of information, how he changes delivery while moving from chapter 1 to 3 to 4.

Craig includes here a categorization of ways in which narrator and character speech blend: The narrator confirms the characters, the characters affirm what the narrator has said, or they share language. He also explores how characters are set in relation to each other (similar or contrasting). Finally, though conceding that a narrator may well choose to dispense all the information, Craig suggests reasons for character speech: Their perspective is limited (rather than omniscient); they may advance the plot or add scenic detail; they may reveal their own inner awareness. His conclusion is that narrator and characters have different tasks, a point he makes obvious and undeniable.

But what remains undeveloped is the question of the manner of their collaboration. Bakhtin works extensively on some features of narrator/hero interaction, a point that Craig skirts with his observation that narrator and characteral speech bleed into each other. That Jonah is a candidate for the sort of polyphonic hero Bakhtin finds in novels is doubtful, but the question is not raised— indeed cannot be while the narrator is so dominant. As suggested above, texts cannot "be" very polyphonic or dialogic until readers (attempt to) exercise those strategies upon them.

Craig next comments on the reading process, drawing our attention to the prayer(s) of the book of Jonah—first in the second chapter of the biblical book (1993, ch. 4) and then more broadly (1993, chs. 5 and 6, where he queries several details). His main point about the psalmlike prayer spoken by the prophet in some contiguity to the whale is how this particular prayer of Jonah fits or does not fit the rest of the biblical book.

Reviewing quickly but adequately the more traditional approaches to the problem, and drawing his readers' attention to the excellent verbal study of George Landes (Craig 1993, 73 and 175, n. 1) without detailing it, Craig offers his "hindsight" suggestion: that the question of "fit" between Jonah 2 and the rest of the book cannot be considered except when the part is read in relation to the whole work. That is, the matter goes far beyond asking if the style of the prayer matches the rest of the book, whether the speaker's "theology" is compatible with Jonah's, whether its provenance can be established, and so forth. Craig's insight is that *"the extended poetic prayer is part of a major pattern in the book overarching all of the action, including the crucial, final scene outside of Nineveh"* (1993, 73, emphasis original).

Making a more general suggestion about reading narratives, he explains that stories offer readers opportunities to construct frameworks for making sense of the narrative world, a process that varies from simple to complex. Information withheld prompts readers to pose questions; awareness that one's provisional interpretive structures are weak in spots occasions readers to construe so as to strengthen inherent (or apparent) instabilities and sags. Those working with narrative, Craig points out (referencing reader-response theorists), negotiate gaps, lacunae, and such indeterminacies to make sense of a narrative. So Jonah's revealing comment in 4:2 helps us identify a gap opened at 1:2: Why did Jonah resist his call? What was he dreading? Craig usefully juxtaposes, in a straightforward intertextual move, other narratives where named prophets react to their commissions: Moses, Isaiah, Jeremiah.

Craig's set of comparative factors is an excellent start but neglects the range of things that may lie outside of authorial design, namely, the web of interchanges that readers constantly select from while reading and the huge set of options available. Bakhtin's sense of the freighted history that words (let alone larger units) bring to any encounter with a reader vastly enlarges the interpretive possibilities. That such language elements contend as well as cooperate widens the set of maneuvers available to readers and decenters artistic design to some extent.

Craig's still primarily formalist mode tends to keep his screen small, though again, he does initiate sets of inquiries that are broader than those of some traditional Jonah interpreters. The multiple reports of prayer in Jonah and how they may be compared and contrasted with each other (and with other instances of biblical prayers), some issues of prose and poetry, the technical meaning of a word like swallow (בלע, at least in the small set of material that comprises biblical Hebrew), the functioning of cognate fish in ancient Near Eastern literature—all provide useful data for enterprising interpreters; but unless I mistake Craig's point, all of these are authorial clues and cues for readers to pick up on, correctly (attentively) or not. What Bakhtin's theory has to offer

Craig's work is a much greater awareness of the variety of readers who will be negotiating and ways in which their choices destabilize the capacity of the text to be neat and limited. Nothing will be lost and much gained.

A penultimate topic Craig raises, still with little explicit reference to Bakhtin, is the whole question of the inner life of the hero: how it is drawn and with what effect (1993, ch. 7). He catalogues the standard ways in which character can be drawn (action, omniscient narrator assertion, epithet, interior monologue, dialogue) and those that give access to inner life (narrator assessment, dialogue, and interior monologue—of which he will explore simply the first two). Noting that, compared to modern literature, biblical narrative gives sparse and unnuanced information about inner life, Craig nonetheless insists that, contrary to the views of some, the Hebrew Bible does indeed portray it.

He recognizes the ambivalence that attends characters. For example, he argues that Jonah must be assessed throughout the book, not simply at the end of it, and he works to make Jonah's inner life coherent from all the information, giving particular attention to the fact that an inside view withheld from the reader in chapter 1 is cleared up in chapter 4. He notes, but without further elaboration, that the narrator and characters in dialogue share vocabulary in 4:1, 4, 9a, 9b. The chapter's concluding points seem once again rather minimal: The book is more about the prophet than about the other characters; the Hebrew Bible does portray inner life; conflict can sometimes be glimpsed from the terrain of inner life; and inside views give a reader elevated access that may contribute to readerly empathy with characters.

Craig shows no interest in Bakhtin's assertion that how an author draws a hero is one of the most crucial aspects of narrative. In fairness, this notion may not be a topic that the book of Jonah can take very far. But the observation that the narrator and two characters utilize the same language might well have prompted further investigation. How does Jonah—or God—or any character slip the narrative leash? What happens when they do move a bit more independently, or when we, reading, perceive them to do so?

In his final chapter, Craig moves to converge the fruits of his study. Reminding us that the earlier chapters had worked primarily to expose the narrative artistry, itself aimed to shape audience response, he reinforces his point that the whole work is an authorial representation, mediated with various techniques but always by authorial choices. He says, "The ultimate goal of this study is to move beyond matters of technique to the communication of values and attitudes from text to reader through the medium of a story about a prophet. Herein lies the real task of this narrative poetics: to discover how individual words, phrases, and syntactic arrangements function as means of evaluation" (1993, 144).

Though sailing in this final chapter under a Bakhtin epigraph, Craig once again draws on categories of Boris Uspensky (as Polzin does at first and as I did in my own formalist study of the Joseph narrative) to talk about how a work's ideology is shaped from multiple trajectories or planes: the phraseological, the temporal-spatial, the psychological, and the ideological. He explores each of these to some extent; yet having already discussed them as techniques in the preceding chapters, his points are limited. Characters talk, are given to talk, from distinct points of view, as they perceive from distinctive angles as well. That is surely true, but is it really contested? Indicators of time and space are crucial in the narrating of the story; the narrator employs a strategy of ambiguation and complication as the narrative progresses.

Craig's concluding point, taken from Bakhtin but not really utilized well, is that there are multiple points of view. Indeed there are, but how will there not be, if there are characters and a narrator involved? Bakhtin's promise of a plurality of independent consciousnesses is apt here: How such plurality is managed, how a narrator and character—and as others add, readers—negotiate the several viewpoints is the key thing.

Bakhtin's polyphony, to which Craig alludes, is more than the fact of multiple angles; it is a technical term that suggests—rightly or wrongly—that a narrator can create a character who is a near equal to the narrator, a close-to-independent presence over whom the narrator does not choose to loom in lordly and finalizing ways. That case is neither suggested nor made for Jonah. Though Craig notes that, by the end of the narrative (Jonah 4) the judgment is angled more toward Jonah than toward foreigners, the narrator role is lessened, the dialogues move beyond their heretofore "serve and return" phase and actually become brief rallies, the characters and narrator quote each other, and the work ends with a question, still, the case for genuine polyphony remains mute if not moot.

A final point Craig offers is that the book of Jonah is not extremely didactic (or perhaps one might say "ideological" in the pejorative sense of that word). Yet, while trying to show that the ideological plane of the work is composed by the narrator and various characters, with their uneven authority (the narrator, God, and Jonah have more; the foreigners, plants, and animals have less), Craig seems too quick to rush to the conclusion that the ultimate semantic authority of the work is authorial, narrational, and divine, a conclusion buttressed with a quote from Sternberg, whose arrangement of those factors is not very Bakhtin-compatible, for all Sternberg's frequent brilliance about texts. That God is in control is the ideological home base, Craig asserts. But I wonder if that claim has become such a truism for readers of the text (Christians particularly) that it may come from readers who impose it as a given.[6] If God is in full control, one may ask, why are at least some humans so out of control? The foreigners, plants, and animals may snap back in response to divine nudges, but the same cannot be said for Jonah. Is a powerful deity visible in this story if one does not presume it when reading? As Craig's interpretation of Jonah comes to a close, he seems satisfied with the clear dichotomy between the solipsism of the human and the compassion of the divine—a conclusion not unjustified, perhaps, but a bit disappointing, at least to me.

So in this very useful study of Jonah, Craig both lays careful groundwork for a Bakhtin-linked study of a narrative and misses a number of opportunities to develop it. The best potential rises from his many acute observations about language; the greatest obstacles remain his lack of attention to the ethics and aesthetics of authoring, his insistence on narrator control, the minimal place accorded the reader, the failure to consider the significance of shared speech, and the willingness to root ideology in content rather than from angle.

---

[6] My point is that the influence of classical Christian theology, stressing the philosophically inevitable categories of God's perfection, tend to override the characterization of God in the Hebrew Bible, which is frequently far from all-knowing, all-powerful, and so forth. Those less influenced by such categories construct "Old Testament God" in slightly other terms, it seems to me.

Craig on Esther

Craig's second book, *Reading Esther: A Case for the Literary Carnivalesque* (1995), published two years after the Jonah work, shows considerably more exposure to the writings of Bakhtin and relies less on Uspensky and Polzin. Again, the point here is not to discuss or critique the work in general, or in terms of other scholarship on Esther, but to highlight its value for those interested in Bakhtin.

The primary questions developed in this study include whether the book of Esther can be considered as an example of carnivalesque (as described and developed by Bakhtin) and whether—or to what extent—it is legitimate to utilize a twentieth-century method to explicate the ancient text (1995, 12). Craig's aims, also clearly identified, are to show that such a categorization of the biblical book is fruitful and legitimate. His "real task," he identifies, is "to discover how individual words, phrases and speech unity carry ideology in the Hebrew story," including as well the aesthetic and social (1995, 29). His thesis is to show that Esther is an early example of the literary carnivalesque and to highlight not only the ideology of the text's composition but readers' constructions of it (1995, 24). The continuity with the Jonah project is thus indicated, but Craig immediately makes a move absent from his earlier work by highlighting that readers of various eras construct Esther and Vashti (and Mordecai, one assumes!) very differently, though reading "the same" text. Hence he makes the historical reader a much fuller participant in the process than he appeared to do in Jonah, where he more simply noted that readers' views vary (1995, 12).[7]

In order to advance his goals, Craig spends his second chapter situating the work of Bakhtin in general, points that are useful to know but that, for the most part, remain ancillary and undevel-

---

[7] Though it may be the case that the variance is narrower among Jonah readers than with Esther, the point remains: readers construe radically differently, and our failing to see or allow for it does not obviate it. As mentioned above, it is one of the places where contemporary Bakhtin scholars have pushed the Russian's thought. Craig also lays the foundation for multiple textual traditions of Esther as well, clarifying that the MT is not the only witness. That point, though surely true, is not the one he develops in the book.

oped in his later explication. He does stress usefully the socio-historical circumstances attending the carnivalesque and notes that Bakhtin's researches indicated that its literary forebears were Socratic dialogue and menippean satire, which come to full flower in the late Renaissance (sixteenth-century) work of Rabelais. Craig indicates that the genre, which he (after Bakhtin) names as serio-comical, has a distinctive mechanism, an alphabet of symbols by which it articulates itself. He next clarifies why Esther is a legitimate member of the serio-comic family, though Bakhtin himself had little interest in scanning biblical books for his examples.

The second part of the work is taken up with showing how features of Bakhtin's carnival genre are indeed present in the book of Esther. That is, the formal features composing the genre can be demonstrated to be prominent in the biblical book. For example, there is a fundamental tussle between official and nonofficial culture (Persian bureaucracy vs. the realm of Esther, Mordecai, and the shadowy Jewish community); multiple banquets and lavish feasts occur throughout the book; events in the public square of Susa suit the public nature of classic carnival (all points in Craig's ch. 3).

His chapter 4 points out the function of peripety in Esther, a dynamic visible in many places, ludicrous in some. The biblical book evinces an interest in the body and clothing, a comparison Craig makes perhaps less successfully: Is one full year of cosmetic therapy analogous to the sort of grotesque and earthy attention the body gets in the work of Rabelais? Clothing and other accoutrements (royal staff) feature prominently in Esther, as does the motif of crowning and decrowning. Craig's suggestion that the Rabelaisian theme of masks is matched by secrecy elements in Esther seems dubious, but again the general similarities between the late Renais-sance and the biblical literature are clearly established.

As he moves into his chapter 5, Craig discusses the parodic nature of genuine carnival, its celebration of the recognition that death and life are intricately related (the theme of pregnant death), a point that he illustrates by the threats of death and sudden reprieves into life that characterize the action of Esther. The standard and ubiquitous role of the fool is well-played by both the Persian king Xerxes and by the clueless and hateful Haman. Finally, Craig's chapter 6 picks up the festal link, though one again may wonder how a feast decreed so carefully is a sample of the genuinely carnivalesque, though the possibility of parody is present (if undeveloped by Craig). Even if the celebration of Purim, in or outside of the text, does not quite hit the standard of collective gaiety and the autonomy of the unofficial that seems to characterize genuine carnival, still its costumes and masks, mummeries, crownings, hanging in effigy and "nonreligious" character align it reasonably well with the features of the carnival as described by Bakhtin.

But, having made the formal case for Esther's suitability to be read as a carnival, Craig stops short of doing it. That is, he establishes the case that Esther can be read as a particular genre but fails to follow up with the implications. The book simply ends with the last point of similarity established. If the genre is heavily determinative, a point Bakhtin makes not only with this particular genre but others, how is that influence expressed? To put it differently, if one is convinced or at least open to the possibility that Esther's genre is not "quasi-historical" or realistic—not "novel-ish" in the classic sense of the term—but carnivalesque, how will that reader proceed? What will be different? Craig asserts repeatedly that the carnivalesque genre has a peculiar logic (1995, 12, 168). If so, how does it express itself, or better, how is it most clearly brought out? Another way to get at the same point is to query to what situation Esther is a response. If the classic carnival is the folk response to the oppression of bourgeoisie pretension, e.g., to the authority of the Holy Roman Empire and the Roman Catholic Church, then what circumstances of Esther's production or setting prompt it? How can those factors be made more prominent?

A few points can be suggested.[8] Surely at very least the slaughter at the end of the story, commenced as the threatened Jews turn on their erstwhile oppressors, becomes a very different scene from the usual treatment of it (if commentaries are any indication of its reception). Far from being an embarrassment or an anomaly, this reversal has to be the whole point of the story, the moment to which all action uproariously leads. Whatever else we may think in other compartments of our lives, that the oppressed

---

[8] Of all the Bakhtin theory (his own and that of those who have picked up and run with his ideas) I am least comfortable with the carnivalesque. I hesitate to do more than suggest possibilities in order to underscore the point that to complete a genre's formal classification is not the whole task required of an interpreter.

successfully turn on their oppressors has to be comic. As many have pointed out, reversals are susceptible of being reversed, which has its own negative humor as well. The parodic character of certain practices needs appreciation. The obsessive legality that keeps canceling out, the ultimate pointlessness of the many writing and translating processes, the celebrations that seem heedless of their constantly shifting occasions, the melodrama of the emotions of Esther (even, perhaps particularly, while at prayer) all need emphasis. Though it is possible to construe Vashti as a protofeminist heroine who draws the line at being demonstrated like a prize possession, she is probably more suitably read in carnival as a figure of fun. Similarly Mordecai, who can be seen as a Gandhi figure pioneering civil disobedience, may rather be a sort of clown himself, perhaps combining his refusal to bow with some other disrespectful gesture left to the imagination of the audience (as is Vashti's attire). If genre matters, and if Esther is a carnival, then it cannot all be so serious—even if such a construal is also possible.

The characters can be seen as burlesques of each other: Esther and Vashti—perhaps Zeresh as well; Mordecai and Haman as well as Mordecai and Xerxes, even Hegai and Xerxes. That the characters reverse positions, perhaps only temporarily, invites such comparisons. Other parodies are possible as well: the banquet room described in terms reminiscent of the hangings of the desert sanctuary, the beauty treatment offered Esther called a *ḥesed,* even the complexities that rise from unchangeable legislation.

If carnival mocks religion, it need not be restricted to Christian folk satirizing their own tradition. Irreverence is entertaining and need not imply permanent disaffection. The oddness of the moment when Esther defies the law of the scepter and the collapse of Haman across Esther's couch during the banquet may be this particular carnival's rather sedate way of hinting at the grotesque and vulgar elements of what Bakhtin called "lower bodily strata" that are so stock in Rabelais. Can those elements be completely lacking in Esther, if in fact it is under the constraints of the genre?

Finally, the whole question of the secrecy surrounding the Jewish identity of the two main characters, functioning as a sort of elephant in the living room during Esther's early reign, begs attention. How do the Jews depict themselves and how their opponents? And what is the line that separates Jew from Persian, oppressed from oppressor, violent from victim? Is such relatedness a Moebius strip rather than a line? There are surely more points to be made that will allow Craig's valuable insight—that Esther may be read as an example of carnival—to have its day.

Carol A. Newsom

Amid her many other interests, Carol Newsom has published two short pieces relevant to the present study, though unlike the works of the other scholars discussed here, they are primarily exploratory of theory rather than producing readings. But they hint at wonderful possibilities.

Newsom on theory

The first, "Bakhtin, the Bible, and Dialogic Truth," she introduces with a helpful context (1996b). A search committee at her institution, she relates, composed of biblical scholars and theologians "forced to collaborate," find each other's projects and aims opaque: theologians constantly inquiring for the center of the Hebrew Bible, biblical scholars resisting to concede such a thing; theologians seeming too reductionist, biblical scholars too diffuse and undecidable. How can productive discussion take place between these two groups: one trained to impose a general coherence about God, religious practice, the expression of it, which, as Newsom observes, almost inevitably disqualifies the irregular; and the other, now fleeing such an enterprise (1996b, 290–91).

She then adopts a Bakhtinian distinction between the monologic (decontextualized and abstract, graspable by a single consciousness) and the dialogic (contextually dependent, needing multiple strategies, and requiring at least two centers of consciousness) but also insists, appropriately to Bakhtin, that all of biblical historical-critical scholarship's many moves are insufficient to escape the monologic trap.

Moving closer to her presentation of Bakhtin's ideas, she explains that real dialogism requires a plurality of unmerged consciousnesses, not just several voices or sources; it needs to be seen as embodied in particularity, not exiled to abstraction. The dialogic requires a messy readerly construction, not something systematic, and such a work must remain open to revision, not be finalized. She recalls briefly and very helpfully by way of illustration the characterization of Dostoevsky's Raskolnikov. Raskolnikov, the reader is told, has set forth his views in a (monologic) journalistic essay. The reader never sees this essay; rather, Raskolnikov's views come to the reader only as they are discussed by characters (1996b, 293–95). Most literary works are fundamentally monologic, which is to say that the author/narrator controls the characters and voices. Work that is more polyphonic, characterized by the author's giving up control and privilege, changes the reader's job. Newsom explains: "In a monologic novel the reader is asked primarily to analyze characters, plot, circumstances. But in a polyphonic text the dialogic play of ideas is not merely a function of plot and character but is the motive of the entire work" (1996b, 297–98, drawing explicitly on Morson and Emerson 1990, 249).[9] Such readings, with their implicit recognition of literary-cultural assumptions, will be rushing away from notions of center, system, abstract summary. The question remains, of course: Is the Bible a polyphonic text— and not simply in the sense suggested by Newsom's colleague Walter Reed, who does a Bakhtin-like reading of the voices in Genesis. Does biblical narrative ever function as an intentional polyphonic text?

Newsom sketches how the book of Job is a good candidate for such a construal: written by one author, she holds, but expressly ideological and dialogic, the speakers double-voicing not only within that huge work itself but within the Bible as well. So, she says, the challenge is how to read Job with Bakhtinian strategies, how to take seriously the form of the book and the complexity of the question under discussion, which will involve the admission— even celebration—of the fact that none, not even God, are mono-logically, finalizingly correct in their assertions, but perhaps not wholly wrong either (1996b, 297–98).[10] She characterizes the work as incipient polyphony.

Further suggestions she offers as likely to respond to Bakhtin's insights, without developing them, include the voices of the Yahwist and Priestly writers, neither merged nor penned off from

---

[9] If we were to push Craig's Jonah in terms of Newsom's distinction, we might ask: What is the quality of God's deed in Jonah?

[10] Reed also approaches the narrative of Job in his book. I am grateful to Newsom for also providing for me an unpublished manuscript (1996a) making more explicit her Bakhtin-linked analysis of Job.

each other, and neither compared nor contrasted, but rather set into relationship—engaged, with whatever effect will be had. It is a suggestion Ilana Pardes will develop (though without reference to Newsom's work): How will we, reading, construe the simultaneous clash and embrace of P's assertion that humans are made in the image and likeness of God and J's narrative of the humans' effort to become like the deity?

As Newsom well notes, Bakhtin holds that dialogue engenders plot, not the reverse. What is the point under intensive discussion in Gen 1–3, she asks, and where else is such a conversation going on? She tosses out other provocative sites for investigation: the preference for order versus the constant revision of plan that characterize P and J respectively; the ongoing discussion of the patriarchal narratives on the question of the people's identity, generating a whole set of messy inquiries and experiments (1996b, 298–302).

Newsom's concluding point, quoted from Bakhtin, is a useful one: "Although Dostoevsky had a superb ability to record and reproduce actual cultural dialogues, what Bakhtin admired was something else. Dostoevsky, he says, 'brought together ideas and worldviews, which in real life were absolutely estranged and deaf to one another, and forced them to quarrel'" (1996b, 304, quoting Bakhtin, *PDP,* 91). There are lots of such quarrels in the Bible that need minimal prodding from us to get going, she notes, inviting us to engage with them in just such a symposium.

Newsom on Isaiah and Lamentations

A second (an apparently nearly simultaneous) piece (1992), "Response to Norman K. Gottwald, 'Social Class and Ideology in Isaiah 40–55,'" briefer yet but still quite helpful, engages with Gottwald the voices in Isa 40–55. Though Newsom's larger point is to critique the adequacy of Gottwald's presentation and analysis of text, ideology, history, and the absent real, all in terms of Terry Eagleton and Karl Marx, with a certain relief we will go straight to the point that suits my purposes: Are the Judahites absent from the text of Isa 40–55 (as Gottwald asserts), or are they audible, if one attends carefully—and with particular assumptions or methods? Newsom, after querying the meaning of how the absent real determines ideology, asks how Gottwald makes visible "the ideology of suffering and exilic privilege, which mystify the conditions of history that prevent the realization of the political and social order envisaged by second Isaiah" (1992, 74). That is, if I understand the place of their contention correctly, Newsom charges that Gottwald's claim to have made clear the Judahite absence may in fact fail; the voice of the Judahites is not so absent as he supposes (1992, 73–74).

If one allows the presence of double-voicing, a strategy explicated by Bakhtin, it is possible to discern the voices of the people of Judah picked up from in the book of Lamentations and reaccented, reintonated in the words of Second Isaiah. Newsom reminds readers that Gottwald himself has done extensive and helpful work on Lamentations, and she admits that she has not had time to follow up her own intuition with careful textual work. But the Zion personification, articulated in Isa 40, 49–55 (especially 51–52), allows the voices of the nonexile community to reverberate in the language of the exiles. In quoting those "at home" (assuming that the community distinction is an authorial strategy as well as a reading choice), the exilic prophet acknowledges the problem of the two communities and articulates (whether with satisfaction to all concerned or not) the exiles imagining themselves welcomed back to Zion and at least theoretically challenges Zion to envision it as well.

Newsom stresses that whether or not a common language is achieved, at very least the prophetic text is heavily inflected with exilic interests (1992, 75–78). Her quick proffering of examples draws on phraseological details (which of course arise from situation and seeing—so also depends on temporal and psychological planes of Uspensky) to notice how the stalwarts of Judah are named in Lamentations (with royal nouns: kings and princes) and in Isaiah (without such terminology: sons and daughters). It is an extremely useful point, granted undeveloped, and will link below to a place where Polzin talks about the Deuteronomist (cf. Willey, 1997).

Ilana Pardes

Pardes, an Israeli scholar (trained in doctoral studies at the University of California at Berkeley), offers a more explicitly feminist angle in her Bakhtin-aware readings. Like Craig, she works primarily with narrative, though with legal material as well; and like Craig (but unlike Newsom), she theorizes little about Bakhtin, moving simply but quite effectively to appropriate and extend his insight. Her two books, separated by an interval of eight years, give us again a pair of works by the same scholar and allow space for considering the diverse potential of Bakhtin for biblical text.

Pardes on selected biblical texts

In *Countertraditions in the Bible: A Feminist Approach* (1992), Pardes makes basic her commitment to the retrieval of past voices, difficult though that task is. She acknowledges that part of what we hear is ourselves, a charge and an insight that accord well with Bakhtin's love of dialogical and heteroglossic voices and his sense that an author and a reader are always authoring selves, whatever else may be going on as well. She brings forward the specifically heteroglot character of the text, particularly in the context of feminist criticism.

Steering so as to avoid the extremes of the depatriarchalizing project she associates with Phyllis Trible (which Pardes claims tries to eliminate the patriarchal force) and of the further reifying of that voice exemplified in the writings of Esther Fuchs (which tend to so magnify the androcentric deformation that other voices fade), Pardes also disclaims the need to rest her insights on a valorized but hypothetical matriarchal past (1992, 1–3). She aims to hear and make audible more voices, urging, "The Bible is far more of a heteroglot text than Higher Criticism would have it" (1992, 4). Conceding that the patriarchal is surely dominant, she insists that the counter feminine voices—themselves far from homogeneous—and the polytheistic, skeptical, and anticovenant voices are important to retrieve and consider. She also highlights the necessity of the reader's commitment to interdisciplinary work and to intensive and ongoing self-criticism (1992, 4–6). Pardes is refreshing to me in her bringing forward insights from many revered and sensitive readers of the past—Jewish and Israeli scholars in particular—whom I sometimes forget to consult or have dismissed as not useful to my pursuits.

Her several textual examples make clear her compatibility (a term more accurate here than dependence) with Bakhtin. Certain feminist projects share a good deal with Bakhtin, without necessarily being derived from his thought. Pardes, I sense, is a feminist who found Bakhtin helpful rather than a Bakhtin scholar who has deepened his insights in feminist projects he never imagined.

In any case, in her first example, Miriam, Pardes highlights what evidently was repressed in the narrating, clarifies which issues remain implicit, brings forward cognate stories and references (e.g., leprosy legislation), gives unusual attention to the role of the deity, and stresses how fragmentary is the information that we have (1992, 6–12). Her conclusion: "I have tried to illustrate how one can find antithetical female voices by paying attention to underexamined fragments on the margins of biblical historiography. My reading thus entails a reversal of canonical hierarchies" (1992, 11). On that particular point, she takes seriously the tremendous social authority the biblical text has accumulated with many communities but insists that no interpretation can be assumed compatible with the original encoded ideology. She hence underlines, as does Bakhtin, the importance of taking historical contexts seriously (1992, 37–38). How readers have and do read is a matter for careful and critical scrutiny, however partial the results must remain.

Her second chapter reviews and critiques feminist critics' handling of Gen 1–3, pointing out strengths and weaknesses, both healthy and disturbing aspects of what scholars have done. And in her chapter 3, she moves to extend the "Eve" set of narratives past where they usually are seen to stop (Gen 3) into Gen 4–5, which indeed allows for a fresh view of the first woman's characterization and roles.[11]

Pardes evidences no objection to taking the Yahwist and Priestly voices as distinct—hence potentially dialogic—and so sees Eve's role in shaping a genre whose subject is human propagation and naming. That Eve names is set into relationship with the moments when she is named. Pardes then locates cognate stories: the naming of children by Leah and Rachel (also in Gen) and ancient Near Eastern texts where birth goddesses name newborns. She suggests that the deed be seen as a hubris offered to God, a point she develops in dialogue with feminist scholars and representatives of the psychological, such as Rank, Freud, Roheim, Bachofen. Her point: though "the dominant thrust of the Bible is clearly patriarchal, patriarchy is continuously challenged by antithetical trends" (1992, 51). The voices are heard well enough to be critiqued, and the hierarchies urged are also continually chal-

---

[11] Pardes notes (1992, 39) that it is an essentially Christian move to draw a line with the cherubim and end Eve's functional life almost exclusively in terms of her garden existence, that is, with the "fall."

lenged. The voices P and J may each be patriarchal, but they differ from each other.

The figure of Rachel is the subject of Pardes's chapter 4, her "dream" placed in dialogue with the more commonly discussed destiny of her husband. Though perhaps not usually seen or treated as homologous, the two visions are interlinked; the dissymmetries between them can both be established and undermined. Rachel and Leah are also carefully and freshly read, suspiciously and alternatively considered. What happens, Pardes asks, when characters are not given lives long enough for transformation to occur—such as is the case with Rachel and Leah in contradistinction to their husband? The biblical text draws male heroes differently from females, she concludes (1992, 75).

With chapter 5, Pardes moves on to consider Zipporah's mysterious deed of Exod 4:24–26, raising various questions that transcend the immediate context of the action, bringing forward other narratives for dialogical exchange. Pointing out that it is standard for commentators to deal with Moses' role in the episode, she asks, rather, about Zipporah's action and sets her into conversation with the several other women of Exodus: Shiprah and Puah, Jochebed and Miriam (and she might have mentioned countless other women implied in the narrative). Pardes sees that Zipporah, from her powerless role, presents YHWH with an alternative. Thus Pardes's countertraditional reading makes Moses less of a hero (in the common meaning of the term) and sees reciprocity between the move of each character to rescue the other. Zipporah's voice also has polytheistic tones, Pardes detects, that engage the predominantly monotheistic grain of the narrative. Thus can feminine saviors be seen as well as mighty male heroes. Pardes's foray into ancient Near Eastern, Greco-Roman, and Egyptian texts (verbal and graphic) allow the repressed voices some company, which she also finds for them in rabbinic and Kabbalistic texts. That Zipporah bests YHWH seems futile in one way, since she is shortly off the scene; but a trace remains.

Pardes devotes her chapter 6 to the story of Ruth, making visible and audible Ruth's verbal engagement with other founding mothers. Central in Ruth is the bonding of two women: Ruth and Naomi love and cling to each other. There is the claim that two other women (Leah and Rachel) cobuilt the house of Israel. The two triangles—Rachel, Leah, Jacob and Ruth, Naomi, Boaz—

though not, in some sense, "the same," also evoke the triangles of Sarah, Hagar, Abraham; of Hannah, Peninnah, Elqanah; and of Demeter, Persephone, and Hades—the latter, at least, a story of male awe at female closeness. God's response is more shadowy, but Naomi's restoration of a faith relationship with God is linked by Pardes to the unconventional bond between the women. Pardes admits that not every possibility is clarified but links the doubled female subject to a critique of the "intense embodiedness" of the barren one. The doubling widens the surface of qualities, including the bitterness, which she, interpreting, accounts for in several ways (1992, 112).

In her chapter 7 she treats the voices in the Song of Songs, a book that many commentators and readers celebrate as an anti-patriarchal text. Agreeing that it deviates from the biblical andro-centric default, Pardes (while discussing its place in the canon) sets its voices over against the choir in the classical prophets whose language denigrates the female. Her gesture decenters the Song's voices to some degree.[12] She reads Shulamit's search for her lover in dialogue with Hosea's similar or analogous quest, exploring links and inversions. The male/female bond in the prophets is always hierarchical, though not in precisely the same way one finds it in Song of Songs. Nevertheless, Pardes points out the traces of patriarchal dominance that are evident in Song of Songs, relatively few though they are.[13] She observes that monotheism reduces but does not obliterate anthropomorphism ascribed to the deity; eros is part of what is retained, but it is rechanneled. In one of her rare direct mentions of Bakhtin, Pardes critiques him for apparently granting to the author so much con-trol as to obliterate the characters, hence denying the exotopy that he himself claims is necessary for genuine authoring (1992, 129). Her comment is not fully clear to me, and her very general refer-ence (Morson and Emerson, 1989) does not assist.

---

[12] She notes the centrifugal/centripetal tug of which Bakhtin writes (1992, 128–29).

[13] Pardes, perhaps because of her affinity to the psychological, likes the suggestion of recent commentators that the two search sequences may be construed as dreams; hence the female eroticism and patriarchal restric-tions on it contend in a way that is plausible. She harshly critiques Trible for missing the male threat and overseeing the female autonomy.

She sums up her work (ch. 8), as well as offering another short but rich reading (perhaps a sort of match to her Miriam study in the introduction): the brief and cryptic utterance of the character of Job's wife, who, Pardes reminds us, has more to say in extrabiblical materials.

But her main point, she reiterates, has been to work with just such broken pieces, obscure traces, remnants, fragments and to reconstruct from them and to bring to greater coherence the counter female voices, avoiding both the overidealized and the too-speculative. To find the antithetical texts is to call into the question any domineering claims by or about the others. With Bakhtin, she claims that the heteroglot voices, once included in the canon (however that process may have happened, with or without the awareness of those making the decisions), create a dialogic interplay that we need to work with. It is fair, I think, to say that where she draws most on Bakhtin is in his sensitivity to the heteroglossic, but she expands his insight in gendered categories that remained foreign to him.

Pardes on Exodus

Her second book, *The Biography of Ancient Israel: National Narratives in the Bible*, still in galley form at the time of my consultation of it, generally continues the first in regard to aims, range, and methodology.[14] There is less change of tack than characterizes the sample paired writings of Craig and Newsom or even of Polzin. Like Polzin (particularly in *David and the Deuteronomist*) and unlike Craig, Pardes seldom acknowledges Bakhtin explicitly but evidences compatibility and indeed benefit from his ideas on genre, chronotope, and particularly the dialogic in her work. Her general focus is the enunciation of the coming to be of the people Israel, the narrative of the birth of the nation. This second book, like her first, has as its larger aim the highlighting of the multi-plied strands of pentateuchal narrative (Exod in this particular case), as well as the underlining of feminist interests. She explicates biblical texts with a lucidity that both complements and compliments Bakhtin's more ponderous methodological assertions.

---

[14] For this portion of Pardes's work, I utilized both a published article (1997, for the large context) and a chapter from her then-unpublished book (Pardes 2000). I am extremely grateful for her patience in coping with my need for her manuscript before it appeared in final form.

Indeed, Pardes is quite broadly grounded in categories familiar from Bakhtin's use of them: the genre of historiography (she draws on Benedict Anderson and Erich Gruen) and its biblical counterpart (where she consults Moshe Greenberg and Sara Japhet); chronotopic issues of anthropology (she uses the work of Victor Turner and Arnold Van Gennep); and cultural poetics (she works with Stephen Greenblatt and Michael Walzer). Though she draws, as before, on the classic psychoanalytic works of Freud and Rank, she offers a modulating feminist critique to their insights as well. She brings to bear Bakhtin's sense of the carnivalesque, all the while drawing primarily on his most general dialogic (distinct from more specifically polyphonic) theory.

Her feat in the chapter under consideration here, titled "At the Foot of Mount Sinai: National Rites of Initiation," puts me in mind of a choir director who is confronted with a text written primarily for male voices, by the imposing presence of one of "the three tenors," and also by a more timid and less famous group of male and female singers. Pardes's accomplishment is to work with the disparate elements so that the tenor maintains his inevitable place but the countervoices are not overwhelmed—in fact, can be appreciated both in themselves and as a highlight to the dominant voice.

Her sensitivity to the power of dialogic language dynamics changes the performance of Exodus rather dramatically and substantially, offering the audience a good deal of freshly exposed space for imaginative reflection upon the key moment of Israel's coming of age at Sinai. She examines three moments of the process: the initial encounter between God and people (primarily at Exod 19); the interval when, in Moses and God's absence, the community make the golden calf (clearest at Exod 32); and the narratively long process of constructing the tabernacle (Exod 25–31 and 35–40).

In the first scene at Sinai (Exod 19:3–6), God's address enunciates the basis (deliverance from Egypt) for the deed now about to be accomplished, the fresh requirement of obedience, and the resulting status offered conditionally to the community: to be a peculiar treasure, a kingdom of priests, a holy nation. God's language of eagles' wings (at Exod 19:4 and Deut 32:10–11) is parental and lofty, suggesting both care and challenge as the eagle induces, even compels its young to fly. The Sinai topos suggests to Pardes not only the suckling rock from Exod 17 (and presumably Deut 32:13–14) but the steep breasts of the Song of Songs (2:8), with all the ambivalence of that site. The care with which the mountain height was to be approached evokes for Pardes the story of Icarus and Daedalus, with its analogous both tender and dangerous, filial and rebellious dynamics. Thus, and with other intertextual suggestions as well, does she sketch the articulation of these events as a story of male initiation, yet gendered in terms both male and female.

Pardes also draws out the significance of the writing of the law, suggesting as it seems to her a growth in human consciousness and a capacity of Moses, at least, to draw close to God. For the first tablets were written by God's finger and then handed into Moses' palm, while the second will be spoken by God while Moses writes, and later reads, them out. Pardes writes:

> The revelation at Mount Sinai culminates in the creation of multifarious texts. Indeed, the unique feature of the Sinaic initiation rites is the extent to which they revolve round writing. It is not art in the modern sense of the word, for God is the Author and the text is divine. Nonetheless, human hands take part in the production. Moses' contribution is indisputable, but to some extent the whole congregation participates in the translation of divine sights into texts.... Art—and writing in particular—seems to be an invaluable medium for those who wish to soar up after the Father. To write is to imitate God. (Pardes, 2000, 74-75)

Engaging James Joyce's textually composite description of Stephen Daedalus, Pardes again brings into prominence themes of father and son, of male and female lovers, of flying upward into writing and art. The blood ritual at the mountain (Exod 24) both reactivates awareness of earlier blood markings (notably Exod 12) and also marks off the moment of initiation from the process of birth.

But God's ukase and Israel's apparently matched (but actually problematic) responses at Exod 19:18 and 24:8 give way to the urge for revision. The community at Sinai's foot acts out an alternative to the demands made previously. Israel, reintonating (perhaps in parody?) at Exod 32:4 God's sovereign claim of 19:3–6, now acknowledges as saving deity the golden calf, preferring its presence to the too-detached, absent, and abstract pair vanished up on the mountain. The calf, under Pardes's gentle handling, is seen not as a total opposite of the imageless voice but rather as expressing a yearning for something more tangible and maternal. This wordless articulation is not unrelated to themes already long-present in the verbal dynamics of Exodus: so a young calf instead of a bull, an Egypt-like representation of the divine, even perhaps a grasping for the colorful and gustatory experience at least some had at Sinai's breast.[15] Pardes sees the revel around the calf as a laughter of the people, bubbling up despite official strictures, a carnivalesque reaction against YHWH's claim: too demanding, too restrictive, too exclusively verbal.

But both Moses and God respond with violence: Moses breaks the tablets, and God blazes now in wrath rather than in love. Many people are eliminated as the community splits and Levites slay others. Pardes brings an Isaian voice onto the scene (Isa 1:2) as well as the epithet "stiff-necked," which now seems to replace the three attributes promised in Exod 19:6. Initiation is not easy, nor is the transformation of a mixed multitude into a people.

But (and here is where Pardes's debt to Bakhtin is clearest) the third moment of the drama shows God (and the narrator—a pair she does not distinguish with precision) simultaneously insist upon the authority to command obedience but also give space to the need made so tangible by the episode of the golden calf. God authorizes, in massive detail, the construction of the divine dwelling place, thus giving permission to do the very thing under contention. The deity instructs the people to make an emblem of God's physical presence: beautiful, constructed of gold earrings, presided over by cherubim both winged (like the eagle) and humanoid. Pardes writes: "Much like the Golden Calf, the cherubim pose a clear violation of the prohibition against images.... The law, in other words, is more pliable than it may first seem" (2000, 86–87).

The abstract makes room for the material rather than squelching it completely. Members of the community—named artisans, wise women, princes—surge forward with wood, bracelets, rings, valuable stones, spun and dyed cloth, even mirrors. The making of the sanctuary resembles, finally, the making of the text, Pardes

---

[15] Pardes a bit later argues the case for Isis links.

suggests, its official "tenor" allowing voice to a range of counter voices and tones. The father, in a move both authoritative and reconciling, concedes the legitimacy of the youthful demand and thus secures a more gracious if not total compliance. It is a wonderful compromise but, Pardes reminds, not an easy one both from the standpoints of evidence in the text and the sort of cultural poetics that brings forth such crucial stories of national emergence. Pardes notes:

> The construction of the Tabernacle is an ars poetic [sic] moment in the text that reveals much about the biblical perception of art as it comments on the intricacies of initiation. The sacred knowledge of the community is not a fixed corpus, the invention of a select circle, but rather the product of extensive negotiations between different socioideological groups, different beliefs, and different dreams. It is the product of collective imagination and collective work. The community as a whole, here more clearly than in the preceding rites, is something of a young artist, groping for the right mode of expression. (2000, 90)

So Pardes, highlighting and tolerating the potential of the dialogic, orchestrates the medley of uneven voices to provide a novel moment of the emergence of Israel to nationhood. She concludes her chapter with a provocative question that many Bakhtin scholars would celebrate: "Sinai gives rise to a wandering shrine with a portable ark rather than a fixed temple. Does this mean that it calls into question the need for an identifying soil? Can a nation thrive without a land of its own?" (2000, 99).

Robert M. Polzin

Without any doubt Polzin is the most committed of biblical scholars to the strategies of Bakhtin. His three substantial works making use of Bakhtin to read the Deuteronomist span some thirteen years, and it is obvious that he had been studying the Russian scholar prior to 1980 (when the first book appeared) and is presumably continuing to work with the ideas currently. There has been substantial development in Polzin's appropriation of Bakhtin over the years; and so for reasons of both stability and change, as well as that he is a valuable interpreter to study carefully, he receives lengthy consideration here.

Since I referred extensively to Polzin's second book (on 1 Sam)
when presenting my own essay on the heroic Saul, I will comment
here on the first and third of Polzin's works on the biblical books
that comprise the Deuteronomistic History. Like Craig, Polzin uses
theory primarily in service of reading texts; and unlike Pardes,
whose appropriation of Bakhtin is ancillary thus far (though
intriguing), and unlike Newsom, whose sketches are preliminary
and suggestive (though right on target), Polzin's commitment is
substantial, both in terms of theory and reading (though he comments less on theory in later books than in the first).

Polzin on Deuteronomy, Joshua, and Judges
      That *Moses and the Deuteronomist* (hereafter *Moses*) appeared
in 1980 is important to remember when considering its contribution.[16] His first task, perhaps no longer necessary in quite the
same way it was in 1980, is to highlight the differences between
diachronic and synchronic study. Though bluntly distinguishing
the two approaches, he also calls for a broadening of biblical
studies to include both dimensions, a task that has come more
closely into view recently, though it remains far from easy to
accomplish. Bakhtin is very clear that each aspect is important
and models what he says by paying minute attention to texts as
well as by urging the importance of historical contexts, chronotopic considerations, social factors, and the like. His refusal to
split literary and historical is one of the reasons Bakhtin is so
important for biblical studies—Hebrew Bible in particular; he
refuses to settle for simply one dimension or the other but sees
them as inseparable, difficulties notwithstanding. (Polzin may also
resemble Bakhtin in that his historical analysis is more abstract and
sketchier than his literary analysis.)
      Polzin also stresses the situatedness of the reader (a point
implicit in Bakhtin but inferable from his theory) and points to an
analogous phenomenon in the biblical text itself: It makes a difference whether words are issuing from the lips of Moses, Joshua,
God, or the narrator. Polzin (also boldly for 1980) urged that some
of the redaction hypotheses (even the firmer-looking ones such as

---

16 The introductory remarks and studies of Deuteronomy, Joshua, and
Judges unfold in *Moses*, chs. 1, 2, 3, and 4, respectively. The final post-
script is similar in scope to ch. 1.

the suggestion of a double redaction) be placed on hold so that some other possibilities could leave the gate and attempt the course. Finally, his shrewd questions about historiography (only sharpened by scholars since the appearance of *Moses*) and his fresh approach to anomalies (e.g., gaps, dislocations, reverses, shifts, contradictions) have been fruitful. Those points stipulated, Polzin then devotes a chapter apiece to Deuteronomy, Joshua, and Judges.

His reading of Deuteronomy makes primary use of two Bakhtinian features, the first drawn from Voloshinov and Bakhtin (on reporting and reported speech) and the second from Uspensky (on the narrative planes, similar to Craig's work on Jonah). Polzin's first major insight is that to recognize the distinction between reporting speech (which comes down very roughly to narrator assertion) and reported speech (which can be loosely equated with direct discourse) exposes a fundamental dynamic in the work. Deuteronomy is composed primarily of direct discourse and, in fact, of quoted direct discourse: The speech of one character emerges from his own mouth but is also borrowed from the lips of another speaker.[17] So Moses speaks "his own" words but also quotes God, quotes himself, quotes the people, quotes hypothetical conversations, and so forth. The resulting web of intersecting voices and speech with all its borrowed coloration affects fundamentally the communication and any responsible interpretation of the book.[18]

That the Deuteronomist puts voices into layered dialogue and that Polzin adopts corresponding reading strategies to underscore and expose that technique brings to the fore many fresh insights and questions about the book itself and invites into greater complexity some long-respected truisms. For example, it is generally assumed and regularly asserted that any time God speaks, that voice is the most authoritative voice in the narrative. It is a good example of mixing "theology" with reading theory. God is a character in biblical narrative, not quite the same as God's actual presence in the universe may be, however committed believers who

---

[17] As was shown earlier, the clean split between reporting and reported speech is immediately inadequate.

[18] The word "construction" can be a convenient way to show how intrinsically joined are the authorial task of constructing a work and the reader's task of construing it.

are also Bible readers may understand it to be (see Polzin 1980, 215, n. 10 for his discussion of the point). The narrator speaks (on his own, as it were) minimally, only in some fifty-six verses in the whole of Deuteronomy, a significant and unusual datum. Consequently, Polzin urges, the authorial arrangement of speech has a braided effect. Initially it enhances Moses' authority by showing his unique privilege as single witness and hence solo communicator of the vast majority of the words God spoke at Horeb; but in fact, as Deuteronomy moves along, it becomes impossible to distinguish between speech of YHWH and speech of Moses (Bakhtin's double voicing). Simultaneously Polzin suggests that though the narrator seems very self-effacing and minimally involved, the intrusive, jejune but evidently necessary quality of his remarks uttered (e.g. 2:10–11, 20–33; 3:9, 11, 13–14) and the particular junction of the narrator's needing to vouch for Moses serve to diminish Moses in favor of the Deuteronomist (see Polzin's summary, 1980, 35–36). The quality of the utterances blurs an apparently firm edge.

The preponderance of reported speech has an impact on all levels of authoring and reading, as Polzin says when concluding:

> It is possible to drive home one truth by shouting out its denial.... The Deuteronomist composes a powerful testament to the unique prophet, Moses, in such a way that the more authority he invests in his hero, the more he will take to himself in the following books of the history.... He portrays Moses as promulgating a lawcode that so tightly weaves together God's word and man's that each is finally indistinguishable from the other. The necessity for subsequent interpretation of Moses' word is secured by its prior merging with God's word. The boundaries between God's word and Moses' interpretation have been deliberately blurred to illustrate the condition of all interpretation. On the one hand it is always necessary; on the other it is finally impossible to distinguish what part of an interpretation is of the interpreter and what part of the one interpreted. (1980, 205)

Polzin's second major Bakhtinian insight about Deuteronomy rises from the question of what Uspensky calls a work's ultimate semantic authority: Wherein lies the basic ideology, the root of the evaluative viewpoint of Deuteronomy? Is it to be found in the "reliable" narrator speech, or is it in the words of a particular character such as God or Moses? Polzin shows rather that it must be sought rather in the intersection of the voices, in the hidden dialogue that goes on silently, almost imperceptibly and yet insistently throughout the work, shifting in intensity from major section to section. The ultimate semantic authority is thus not simply the content of the narrative or the weight of some speaker but rises from the dialogue shared out among all the players (including the reader). The book's key assertions are collaborative—dialogical—in many ways, with certain claims set continuously over against each other as the book goes on.

Polzin singles out for consideration several of these fundamental debates that run persistently throughout the work: Is Moses unique or much like everyone else? Is Israel distinctively elect or quite similar to the nations? Is Moses going to be supplemented by others of comparable stature (for example, the narrating "Deuteronomist" himself), or is he fundamentally irreplaceable? Does God act primarily in terms of retributive justice or rather in terms of graceful gift? Is the law as communicated by Moses complete and unchangeable, or does the very manner of its enunciation make inevitable further interpretation as time goes on?

These questions, like support beams in a physical structure, carry fundamental stress in Deuteronomy and are argued constantly throughout. How each is resolved (to shift metaphor to a musical image) is not to be discerned apart from the discriminating ear of the reader. Polzin claims in summary:

> [T]he book of Deuteronomy is a statement against the transparency, immediacy, and univalency of the Word. Moses performs the central interpretive task of the book—he goes to the heart of the matter—not when he quotes God's ten words directly in chapter 5, but when he promulgates God's further words in chapters 12–26 in such a way that (his) word and (God's) Word are indistinguishable.... God's utterances are no longer transparent, direct, and univalent. (1980, 206)

> The style of the lawcode obliterates this apparent immediacy and establishes the main hermeneutical perspective of the book: subsequent revisionary interpretation is necessary not in order to recover the original word of God—for the narrative makes clear this is impossible—but because Moses himself establishes the precedent by immediately *applying* God's further commands

even as he is transmitting them to the people. (1980, 206, emphasis original)

How each of these voices is positioned to see and speak—itself a matter partly of time and place—constitutes the construction of Deuteronomy's ideological assertions.

There are many other points made and subtle architectonics suggested in Polzin's very dense book: how the subunits of the book cohere (Deut 1-4, 5–26, 28–34); from what temporal angle the voices are pitched; the putative psychological angle of the Deuteronomist's audience; the construction of the truth-speaking prophets and those whose words do not come true, as well as the consequences for prophet and people who alter the words communicated. If Polzin is to be critiqued in this groundbreaking work, it would be because he does not make sufficiently clear to the neophyte quite how the trail winds through the forest of Bakhtin and Deuteronomy; it is easy for a Polzin reader to become discouraged and return to camp, piqued in both senses of the term. Polzin does not always clearly define his terms (e.g., reported and reporting speech) or sufficiently explain his concepts (e.g., the planes—1980, 44 notwithstanding); he moves too quickly to talk in terms of them. I myself, having read, taught, and relished the book repeatedly over the past twenty years, and even with increasing confidence in the methodology Polzin is using, feel uncertain as I go to make a summary of his points. To some extent it is the healthy caution of the person attempting to reduce a very detailed argument to its logical skeleton; but the problem runs deeper as well and is regrettable.

When Polzin moves on to a consideration of Joshua, the argumentation continues to be dense and very intricate; it is, perhaps, his most difficult writing. I will offer three points that he establishes with the help of Bakhtinian strategies, reminding the reader that these summaries elide much crucial detail. When drawing together this section of the Deuteronomic History at the end of *Moses,* Polzin offers this comment:

[T]he Book of Joshua presents us with a sustained meditation on what it means to interpret "the book of the law." Appropriation of the law through constant reinterpretation and occupation of the land through continual struggle are themes woven together so inextricably in the book that each is an interpretant for the other.

The distance between the divine word and the human interpretation, in the case both of law and of land, is the general theme of the entire book. Utterly to be rejected in the Deuteronomist's retelling of the Israelite occupation of the land are simplistic statements of fulfillment by man of God's law and by God of his own promises ... which [assertions] are deeply ironic in the literary context in which the Deuteronomist places them (1980, 208).

This main agenda item that Polzin singles out continues readily from work on Deuteronomy. Though remarking that reporting and reported speech accumulate very differently in Joshua than they do in Deuteronomy, nonetheless the constant intersection of voices continues to structure the main viewpoint of the book. In Josh 1, for example—a chapter in which nothing happens but talk[19]— the words of Moses in Deuteronomy, of God (brought forward from Horeb), of Joshua, and of the narrator all reverberate in each other's talk, picking up authority from each other as they do so. Polzin alerts us to tiny details and shifts that arise as the characters take on each other's speech. Though the basic viewpoint of the DH narration has shifted with the departure of Moses, still there is radical continuity between Deuteronomy and Joshua, communicated as "new" speakers take up "old" lines. Though the books following Deuteronomy will have some different issues to sort from those of Deuteronomy, the general framework for the settling of the land will be that supplied from the lawbook.

A second point Polzin is able to hone from observing the interplay of language (whether reported or reporting speech) also continues a major issue of Deuteronomy: Are we to construe that Joshua fulfilled all the commands—just as God and Moses articulated—or not? The narrator summarizes in Josh 11:23 that yes, he did, but the discourse of characters and narrator that intervenes between the commitment to exact obedience (so clear in ch. 1) and the summary of it (Josh 11) belies the assertion in many ways. In fact, though Deut 13:1 warns against adding or subtracting from the words of Moses/YHWH, Joshua in fact must do so constantly, and does, with no narrative disapproval articulated cleanly.

---

[19] He discusses the language of Josh 1 (1980, 75–80). Without citing Bakhtin directly, Polzin is able to align this section of Joshua to Dostoevsky novels, where conversation is the main event.

Polzin illustrates this contention by laying out carefully the planes of composition that comprise the story of Rahab and the Israelites (1980, 85–91).[20] Among other points, he shows that their encounter brings into dialogue the question of who is Israel and who is alien. Rahab's confident statements of trust in the reputation of YHWH are the words that ought have issued from the lips of the Israelites who experienced such deeds; and the sketch of timid men who must resort to spying—even hiding amid the flax—would seem more at home in the characterization of those facing YHWH's people on their way into the land. But Rahab sees and talks like an Israelite, while the spies articulate the vision angle of Canaanites.

Polzin concludes that the story of Rahab is the story of Israel, told from the angle of an "outsider." She articulates the core problem of Joshua in terms reminiscent of Deuteronomy: Some Canaanites end up surviving in the land, not because they are deserving but because Israel is faithless. Polzin points to the shifts that occur when characters "play" each other's roles: Rahab becomes Israel, Israel becomes the Canaanites, and the spies become YHWH. It is an amazing shift accomplished by attending to the time and place and consequent angle of vision from which the phraseology is constructed. Once again the point is made that Israel and the nations are not so different and that God—certain rhetoric notwithstanding—is permissively merciful. The word of God is handled by interpretation. And Joshua closely resembles Moses.

The discernment of strategy behind (or able to be utilized while negotiating) the text, undergirded by the assumption that such doubledness is artistic rather than redactional, has the impact of bringing out the texture of the legal language that so fills the DH, rescuing it from its usual characterization as flat, mechanistic, obvious, and rigid. It is a major step ahead in reading not only Joshua but biblical text in general. If language is not utterly unambiguous but constructed by voices that overlap and intersect variously rather than coinciding, then meaning is much richer and the approach to it different than often imagined or assumed. To put that same point a bit more specifically: The ambiguation of the

---

[20] Cf. his discussion of the episode at Ai and the treaty with the Gibeonites.

language saves insiders and outsiders, deity and readers from falling victim to the relentlessness of the ban.

A third example, selected from other possibilities, involves as well the question of who is Israel and who are the other but narrows now to the tribes themselves (1980, 134–41). Polzin, reminding us that the Hebrews (עברי) become who they are by crossing (עבר) into the land, directs us to the place where the East Jordan tribes (Reuben, Gad, and half of Manasseh) cross back over the river. Once they have recrossed and constructed an altar, their status dissolves into ambiguity. They are neither full insiders nor clear outsiders, a point made repeatedly from the ambiguity of the place and the time of narration (imprecision in the direction of the crossing, lack of clear time referent for "today"/"this day"), by the phraseology of the character discourse (mixing of "you" and "us"), and by the narrator's decisions of reference (uncertainty regarding inclusion or exclusion from "the entire community" and "all the Israelites").

In the section of *Moses* that treats the book of Judges, Polzin again draws forth fresh and key points, reading compatibly with Uspensky and Bakhtin. Working with Judges' short and enigmatic narratives, it is difficult to avoid the impression that they can be read intensively in terms of Bakhtin's ideas, a process Polzin can scarcely start seriously in the few pages he has to spend. But his observations whet the appetite and suggest pathways that remain to be taken. He comments briefly on each of the major units (introductions and periods of the major judges), epitomizing his particular comments with the observation that the book of Judges is a reflection on why Israel continues to exist, i.e. why the whole project did not end with the events of infidelity narrated in these very episodes that so undercut the reliability of ideologies, however inevitable those ideologies may be (1980, 161–62). He works with basically the same "Uspensky" compositional elements that have interested him heretofore; I will indicate some sense of the gain he gets from reading four episodes.

The first material Polzin meets, of course, is the doubled, or "dialogizable," introductory sections (1:1–2:5 and 2:6–3:6) that serve as preface to the book. By setting these two units into conversation not only with each other but with the viewpoint expressed in Joshua prior to the death of that hero, Polzin moves beyond the usual redactional question (though conceding that editing has played a hand here) to another pair of queries: Why is "the same" information presented in multiple contiguous units, differing not only in temporal orientation but in psychological angle as well, and what is the advantage of reading it that way? That is, how does the manner of representation intensify insight into the question of Israel's failure to take the given land, and with no unambiguous attribution of that failure to Joshua?

Polzin asserts that the first recital (1:1–2:5) of the tribes' temporal (and spatial) dislocation is more external to the characters involved—God included—proceeding synchronically with the events related; thus there is a small ascent of hope that the taking of the land may go well. The second narrative (2:6–3:6), though managing the same information, penetrates character awareness more deeply and is angled panchronically, so that the problem of idolatrous behavior is clearer. It also circles back to the situation at the death of Joshua: Why did Joshua fail to take the land, obedient as his generation seems to have been? The certainty of the formula is problematized in both cases; there is no predictive certainty about process from viewing results.

The conclusion he reaches, articulated at the end of the whole study on Judges, fits well here:

> As with the Samson story of Judges 15, the Deuteronomist once again uses his characters' and his narrator's efforts at securing the success of their own enterprises as the starting point for a meditation upon the limitations of explanatory and predictive ideologies. There is no pattern to be perceived in all these exertions. However much they strive, these characters and their narrator sometimes succeed, sometimes not. Ultimately the Deuteronomist is calling attention to the narrator himself and asks his readers to apply the same evaluative criteria to that narrator as to the characters he introduces. The narrator, like one of his characters, might repeat so as to be better understood; yet sometimes these repetitions obscure rather than clarify. The narrator, like one of his chief characters, may shift his point of view; yet the change in perspective may not incite insight but vertigo. As with the characters so with their narrator: success or failure appears mysteriously where it will. (1980, 199–200)

There is no straightforward pattern, no reliable formula. The compositional technique, elucidated and amplified by a Bakhtinian reader like Polzin, makes visible the ambiguity.

Polzin shows the story of Ehud exemplary in several similar ways (1980, 156–61). Its matrix reasserts continual disobedience (3:7, 12), though the narrative itself implies the sort of temporary success that characterizes the deeds of the early judges. Commenting on it, Polzin highlights the polyvalence of the phraseology: Characters miscue because they understand reported speech in one way rather than in another, e.g., the "word" brought to the king by Ehud, the confident assertion by his courtiers that the doors to his chamber are locked for the relief of Ehud. Spatial ambiguity abounds as well. It is impossible to locate the story on one side of the Jordan River or on the other, hence making ambivalent the notion of crossing (עבר), that verbal signifier that looms so important in these stories of entering/leaving and crossing/transgressing. The temporal plane is variable as well. The narrator speeds more quickly and panchronically at the edges of the short scene, slowing down to jog alongside the characters as the scene in the upper chamber unfolds. And in noting the psychological plane (in Uspensky's sense of the angle of perceiving), Polzin characterizes Ehud as typical of the judge who does not see well, a profile that will recur in this book (e.g., Samson) and culminate in the figure of Eli in 1 Sam 1–4.

Polzin's appraisal of the material on the judge Deborah is more astonishing for what it does not engage, perhaps, than for points offered. He notes, helpfully, that the whole account is suffused with a certain obscurity introduced by the narrator's refusal to share knowledge from a wider angle. That is, the narrator's persistent synchronic telling (only occasionally retrospective) has the effect of throwing the characters and reader off consistently.[21]

---

[21] Polzin continues, even in his recent work, to use the term "omniscient" for the narrator, as here (1980, 164). He commented in a private communication, however, that Bakhtin's theory, once fully engaged, makes somewhat moot the question of the reliability or omniscience of the narrator, handing it over, as it were, to the skill of the reader "that is, how perceptive she is in seeing that, and to what extent, not just characters but even the narrator must in principle be speaking in double-voiced language at any time in the text. So every time we read the compositionally marked speech of the narrator, we might find the unmarked voice of this or that character in it, and every time we read the compositionally marked speech of a character, we might find the unmarked voice of the (reliable) narrator in it. So the reliability or not of the narrator becomes practically an unreliable factor in the reading process if as often happens

Reporting and reported speech accompany each other oddly and nonconcurrently, twisting to provide the unexpected. The narrator angle careens back and forth: It first spans what is more unlimited but then frames more narrowly with clinically appraising reported speech. The pair of positions again conspires to construct an ideology of slippage among layers of the narrative text. The combined instability of the three planes (temporal-spatial, psychological, phraseological), the equivocation, and the indirection combine well to suggest this odd story of God's merciful dealings with a people more intent on doing what is right in their own eyes.

The more poetic language of Judg 5, consisting almost wholly of reported speech to explicate the feat of Deborah, seems a wonderful text to be set into dialogical relation with the story of Judg 4. But Polzin does not take up that charge here, perhaps since it is more a Bakhtin than an Uspensky interest, and in this volume on Moses, the focus remains more on the latter than the former.

The comments about Micah and the Danites (Judg 17–18) plumb the same features with pretty much the same result (1980, 195–200). How, Polzin asks and begins to articulate, is the narrative of chapter 17 related to that of 18—indeed to the final episode(s) concluding the book of Judges (19–21)? Judges 17 functions to provide background, its planes of psychology, temporality, and phraseology primarily retrospective, while those angles shift to the synchronic in chapter 18. In this narrative reported and reporting speech accompany each other closely, even seeming to repeat unnecessarily. But closer observation discloses that the main characters are positioned from various angles and their utterances are often flawed and misleading. The characters exude a confidence that the narrator shows to be misplaced: The "thing" Micah makes is named differently by various people; his statement of confidence in the rightness of his position in 17:13 is dangerously slippery. Other contentious language—i.e., words whose meanings are multiple, rich, and contradictory—allow the narrative to be Delphically ambiguous in its assertions. So Micah, inquiring for the Danites, informs them that they may be assured/נכח of their path. But, Polzin reminds us, נכח may imply agreeable ... or disagreeable (the root ranges from suggesting "opposite" to "in front of," making the

---

the narrator is speaking 'someone else's language,' not 'one's own language'" (Private communication, dated February 9, 1999).

prayer intrinsically ambivalent), depending on the angle of vision; the people of Laish are characterized as בֹּטֵחַ. Is that confident . . . or unsuspecting? The Hebrew word carries the range of meaning. They are also labeled שֹׁקֵט—peaceful or idle? Again, there is room for both possibilities (Polzin 1980, 198–99). The Deuteronomist, Polzin reminds us (a point he has been developing since the section on Deuteronomy) has been making a similar point at the ideological level: It is a fateful choice to be taken in by the apparent exactitude of the language.

A last word here on Polzin's *Moses,* especially in view of my exposure to his subsequent work on the books of Samuel, is to wish for him a larger and finer set of tools for analysis. It strikes me, rereading these brief pieces of commentary, that they remain inchoate in terms of Bakhtin's ideas. Polzin has begun a sketchbook of keen observations that need further development and reapplication to larger surfaces in order to be seen at their best. As is apparent from its recent popularity in scholarship, the book of Judges is replete with enigmatic characteristics that will repay literary methodology richly. Polzin has a keen sense of where some of the nuances of discourse lodge and needs simply a wider repertoire of techniques to expose them more lucidly.

Polzin on 2 Samuel

Polzin's third book, *David and the Deuteronomist* (1993, hereafter *David*), is in many ways quite different from his first volume on Moses. His prefatory words to the third volume indicate an intent to minimize discussion of methodology in favor of reading. My task, consequently, is the reverse: I will make more explicit the nature of his reliance on Bakhtin without attempting to reargue or restate fully the particular readings he has done. And rather than make any attempt to cover all the territory included in Polzin's book on 2 Samuel, I will concentrate on the analysis of his first chapter, which explicates 2 Sam 1, reaching forward only as necessary to develop a few additional points.[22]

---

[22] One of the most challenging things for Bakhtin scholars to learn to do, to accomplish to do, is to unify what can seem like techniques, to synthesize the particular aspects of his thought from their separate strategic uses. Polzin's appropriating of Bakhtin is quite deep, and his synthesis is not easy to disentangle without diminishing it. But to name the particular

To put Polzin's achievement in *David* succinctly: He has picked up on the multiple ways in which Bakhtin—and much more Bakhtin now than Uspensky—has taught us to anticipate and engage dialogue in literary texts and has used that core insight and its related strategies to read the narratives of 2 Samuel. To name the varieties of Bakhtin's dialogism engaged and developed by Polzin and to highlight our mutual gain from reading with these particular strategies is my plan. The advance beyond and contrast with *Moses* will be clear. I will instance twelve points.

First, Polzin's fundamental and clearest assertion, and so a good place to enter his analysis, is the suggestion that the Amalekite of 2 Sam 1 is in many ways a double of David (see 1993, 2–10). The character zones of the pair overlap considerably, thus demonstrating the ways in which facets of each of them construct the other. That is, each is shown to be an escapee from the dangerous presence of Saul.[23] Each is dressed in mourning—the messenger first, who is then imitated by the one receiving the news. Each is a sojourner in an alien group. Each is characterized as having taken a token from the old king, then using it to presumed advantage.

In addition to these motifs, character discourse shows the two figures linked. David's insistent questioning of the Amalekite—as he arrives, disheveled, from the battle of Gilboa—as to his identity reminds us of the several earlier queries of identity addressed to or about David (1 Sam 17:55–58; 19:22; 20:27; 22:7–8). The suggestion that David and the Amalekite, though obviously very different in some ways, are versions of each other allows for a much richer consideration of the question of David's responsibility for the fate of Saul, a question dear to the heart of the Deuteronomist.

Second, once alerted to the strange coherence of the two men, who stand dealing across the corpse of the fallen Saul, the reported speech of David also takes on fresh significance. For example, David, recently involved in a fracas where he needed to give a judgment about the distribution of spoils after battle, indicated by aphorism that to serve at a distance (i.e., to guard

---

techniques, as well as to indicate the gain of what Polzin has seen with them, can be illuminating.

[23] Polzin (1993, 4) reminds us that Amalekites have just escaped from David as well as this individual from Saul.

the camp) counted the same as fighting the battle, so far as spoils were concerned (1 Sam 30:24). Suddenly David's own language of judgment, though uttered in another set of circumstances, rings apt in this encounter between the one man claiming on-site responsibility for killing the king in battle and "his double" remaining at a distance, ostensibly uninvolved. Similarly, once we consider David and the Amalekite as twins of a sort, sharing some responsibility for the death of the old king, David's apparently unequivocal and capital condemnation of the Amalekite for regicide boomerangs as well.

However, such a recontextualization of David's language shows us another dynamic, this time one that draws him as Saul's double. This is perhaps my point rather than Polzin's—though I did not see it until I read his sketch: As Saul has been consistently characterized as having invited his own destruction, having set up the very trap into which he will fall, now David begins to do the same. It is not a feature that has attended David as yet, and so the possibility that we are seeing the self-destructiveness of not just this king or that but of the institution per se recommends itself compellingly, at least to me. The king is the primary architect of his own fate, and not of his alone, of course. So David here, twice, pronounces judgment on himself in a key situation: his participation in the death of his predecessor, a subject of great interest to the narrator from the moment the two of them became locked in relationship.

Third, another layer Polzin detects in the Amalekite/David homology is the position the narrator takes up with regards to each of them. An apparently reliable and omniscient narrator has made unambiguous that Saul, in the last speech of his narrative life, having failed in his final request to have someone help him evade responsibility, needs at last to be answerable for it himself. Such a report casts into immediate disrepute the Amalekite who claims that *he* helped Saul end his kingship. What purpose is served by introducing so false a character, ancient and classic foe though Amalekites are to Israelites?

Polzin shows that among the gains rising from the doubled account of Saul's death (1 Sam 31 and 2 Sam 1) is the expansion of the quest beyond facticity (how Saul actually died, or the likely authorial origins of the two accounts) to the larger question of language as a way of establishing meaning. That is, the *discussion* of how Saul died, not the plot action, is the primary thing. The narrator builds additionally here on a past platform of language implicating David in Saul's death (without ever letting it actually happen).thus David has been sketched as both involved and not involved, guilty and innocent (1 Sam 24; 26; and, surreally, 25). The same narrator, bringing us the Amalekite with his too obviously false story in 2 Sam 1, seems to be setting the foreigner up as a liar.

Contrastively, the narrator's external angle continues to draw David opaque, his knowledge, motives, and responses impossible to read with clarity. Though the lying Amalekite is presumably clear to us, we are not cued clearly as to whether David reads him as false or not. If David executes a regicide, that is one thing; if he kills a man for claiming to have killed the king while knowing it to be false, that is quite another. Once again the authorial construction can imply David as guilty over the death of Saul—ambiguously, somewhat in the manner of his double. It is skilled writing and skilled reading on Polzin's part, and a substantial challenge for ourselves as well.

Fourth, the manner of composition also challenges us, Polzin urges, to attend to the larger construction of the Deuteronomist's narrative, even to biblical text in general. Sketching quickly the possibility that the Amalekite also resembles, stands in for the Deuteronomist—the narrating voice who finishes off Saul and turns next to David, who brings news that is both good and bad—Polzin says:

> The Deuteronomist, then, fashions a continuing message about the evils of kingship, but also includes the response that such a message might engender within an audience schooled to exalt the everlasting throne of David. In a fitting climax to this opening scene of the history of David's rule, David stands over a corpse that represents both himself and his biographer and utters an ironic curse: "Your blood be upon your own head; for your own mouth has testified against you, saying 'I have slain the LORD's anointed'" (2 Sam 1:16). (1993, 10)

Considered authoritative by many centuries of its readers (granted, in a variety of ways), it can and also needs to be recognized as internally persuasive (Bakhtinian terminology), compelling because of the manner and depth from which it is able to address us. Though Bakhtin did not fully anticipate the kind of readings proposed in *David,* his categories are useful nonetheless. Moving beyond these points that rise from and encourage our capacity to see two superficially disparate characters intermeshed in multiple ways compositionally and at a deper level, such insight rising from reading characterizations dialogically, Polzin alerts us to other helpful strategies of Bakhtin as well. A fifth point he makes is about genre (1993, 11, but see also 1989, chs. 1–2). Polzin alludes rather quickly to an insight well-developed in *Samuel and the Deuteronomist* (1989, chs. 1–2; hereafter *Samuel*): The narratives of Samuel's birth and the capture of the ark resemble more closely the genre parable than realistic historiography. The action comprising this initial scene of 2 Samuel—David moving quickly in responses to the news he has received—continues a similar logic. The monarchy, lethal and vicious, falls upon those who would threaten it. That is, the violence of the monarchy turns on its enemies and also consumes itself.

This doubly destructive behavior has already been enacted by its sitting dynasties: Eli and his greedy sons, down to his survivor begging for a morsel of food (1 Sam 2:36); Saul, murdering Elides and bringing his own offspring down as well, to be survived ultimately by only the lame and powerless Mephibosheth (1 Sam 22; 2 Sam 9; 16; 19); and David, executioner here and often in the narrative ahead, succeeded also by his own fratricidal scion Solomon and the many royals sons after him, including the final king named who also receives his food on sufferance (1 Kgs 2–2 Kgs 25). The king, Polzin suggests, and the monarchy, turn violently against those who threaten them—to the detriment of all.

Sixth, Polzin also details, with clear discussion of the importance of genre, that the lament of David for Saul and Jonathan (2 Sam 1:19–27) is not merely his own personal eulogy for them but articulates as well a fuller prophetic and poetic lament for Israel, fallen under the disaster of kings. Again drawing on the capacity of doubled speech to resound powerfully, Polzin shows that the language of David's poem echoes, or resonates, particular language of Isaiah, Jeremiah, Ezekiel (1993, 15–20). That is, the speech of the character and the narrator (so of David and the Deuteronomist) are saturated with the language of prophets who mourn various destructive behaviors of monarchic Israel. The

impact of the hybrid speech may on one level intensify the sad-
ness of its referents; or it turns ironic in the case of David—
monarch par excellence—as he shares speech with harsh critics of
the kingship and its inherent evils (1993, 12, 18, give us the term
"speech interference" for this phenomenon).

The main ideological communication of the whole DH, as
Polzin repeatedly asserts, using the language of Bakhtin—the
place from which the most unified viewpoint emerges struc-
turally—critiques the monarchy and those who offer misplaced
and inappropriate adulation in high places. So David's lament of
slaughter in the high places renders into conversation a number
of themes.

Seventh, though again without making specific reference to the
Bakhtinian concept of chronotope, Polzin implies, here and in his
earlier work on 1 Samuel, that the location "high up" is a particular
chronotope for dynastic sons, of which kings are the preeminent
type. He has repeatedly underlined in *Samuel* the Deuteronomist's
penchant for showing that those high up come plummeting down.
The motif occurs in the song of Hannah—to include the fall of the
mighty and the ascent of the lowly (who are presumably endan-
gered once they rise up, 1 Sam 2); the emblem of Eli falling backwards off his watching perch upon hearing of the capture of the
ark, the defeat of Israel, and the death of his sons (1 Sam 4); the
ominous qualification of Israel's first king, who rises head and
shoulders above all the people (1 Sam 9); the towering Goliath,
looming over even tall Saul until he is brought low enough for a
boy to cut his head from his body (1 Sam 17); Saul's headlong collapse when he hears from the raised-up Samuel the news of his
own defeat and the death of himself and his own sons as immi-
nent (1 Sam 28). This recurring blend of time-space that Bakhtin
names chronotopic is shown ultimately unstable. It is impossible
to remain high up for very long; height is not a position to be
smugly enjoyed. A small detail, perhaps, but an insistent and consistent one in this story of the lethal monarchy.

Eighth, that contention about the danger of high places leads
to another way in which Polzin relies on Bakhtin: the understanding that language—even individual words—carry considerable
"awareness" or memory of all the places they have lived (1993,
14–25). A word like "high places," used in David's lament in a particular sense to refer to the events on Mount Gilboa, retains, picks

up, and puts into contestation all the other nuances that expression has, Deuteronomic, biblical, even wider. Polzin reminds us how charged that word becomes within the scope of the Deuteronomist (initially positive or hopeful [Deut 32:13, 1 Sam 9:19] but turning predominantly negative from 1 Kgs on); in prophetic discourse the high places present Israel (or Israel's leaders) with a major temptation that eventually brings them down as well. Hence the use of "high places" here moves into dialogue with every other instance where the word occurs, inviting us to see such places as the repeatedly restaged site of the destruction of Israel's glory.

Polzin exposes similar pathways branching off from the text's use of the word צבי (gazelle, host, glory), the nuances of שוב (return), the references to blood and fat. With their multiple semantic links to cult and war, death and pollution, glory and defilement—such speech interference (the constant tangling of related or oddly crossing realms) permits, invites pursuit, if the reader is willing. An observation that the word "shield" functions more often metaphorically for YHWH than literally as a weapon of war makes additionally poignant the description of the shield of Saul lying neglected and begrimed at the site where Israel's glory perished.

Ninth, Polzin offers a related point about the highly repetitive use of words like אחרי (after/afterwards) in 2 Sam 2, which can easily pass unnoticed because it is such a functional word; but a skilled commentator, noticing that the word occurs fifteen times in a single chapter, suggests that the word carries additional weight in this narrative that concerns succession. His similar point about the ubiquity of brothers and of the word אחים (brothers), which is to the nonmimetic, highly stylized character of the discourse so fraught with fratricide (1993, 29–31, 47–49).

Three other examples drawn from material outside of 2 Sam 1 allow Polzin to suggest additional benefits of his Bakhtin-assisted readings. These instances include his consideration of the ideological communication regarding the promise of perpetuity to the Davidic house, the manner in which an apparently misplaced narrative about Saul's grandson actually shows a careful architectonics, and the technique of *mise en abyme,* which gives Polzin the opportunity to comment on author, hero, text, and reader. Again I will highlight the use of Bakhtin rather than struggle to reduce carefully argued points.

Tenth, Polzin raises the issue of how the Deuteronomist ideology of "house" constructs the material in 2 Sam 5–7 (and, of
course, elsewhere as well; 1993, ch. 3). He suggests that the whole
range of referents on house, starting from physical domicile, kin,
and heirs, moving to palace, and finally including temple and
nation, is "under construction" every time the topic is raised in the
text, which occurs repeatedly. He claims, "If the History relates the
ultimate tragedy of a nation that made room for David's house, it
also raises serious questions about that nation's building of God's
temple" (1993, 55). As is so often the case, the dialogical arrangement both praises and undercuts. Various voices urge that God
will build for David a secure house (e.g., 2 Sam 7:10) and assert
simultaneously that foreigners are the ones responsible for the
erecting the house (e.g., 2 Sam 5:11–13), a damning claim.
Similarly, though God makes the promise of a house at the start
of the long narrative, the final section of the history ends with the
description of the conflagration engulfing every great house (2 Kgs
25:9) to note that the house of the last survivor is a Babylonian
enclosure (2 Kgs 25:27).

A similar dialogue rages to shape the promises to David,
which are "forever" (eight times in 2 Sam 7), recalling a similar
promise extended to the house of Eli (1 Sam 2:30) but then
revoked (1993, 71–87). The key communication on the topic,
which is shared among the discourse of the deity, the king, the
prophet, and the narrator, divides into a messenger scene as well.
In such a way the narrator opens up all the fissures and rifts
(Polzin demonstrates four levels) that characterize the blend of
reporting and reported speech and that lead inevitably and unend-
ingly to analysis and interpretation not only by characters but by
readers as well.

Thus, without again invoking the concepts of authoritarian
dogmatism and critical traditionalism or authoritative versus
internally persuasive speech, Polzin shows us how to read the
text so as to nuance the apparent clarity of the permanence. He
demonstrates as well that the apparent stability of the royal
house, a fact that presumably pertained during the exilic experience, juxtaposed with the absence of the house of God, brings
into prominence another juxtaposition that deconstructs the eter-
nal solidity of the monarchy. Forever becomes a horror instead
of a joy.

Eleventh, another point Polzin develops at some length aris-es from Bakhtin's sense of architectonics, approached here in relation to placement of material within the overall DH. Noting, as is indisputable, that commentators on the story of David's reign have tended to find the story of Jonathan's son Mephibosheth disordered and clumsily appended to other mate-rial, Polzin undertakes to show the skilled placement of the material and to draw insight from attention to its position in the overall structure (1993, 94–108). His claim: "There are some hints of architectonic order within and among these apparently hap-hazard and scattered references to Mephibosheth's affairs, and I will indicate ... how 2 Sam 9 functions as the hub of a well con-structed story that has a number of definable levels to it" (1993, 95; see further 1993, 94–108).

As before, this baring of the use Polzin makes of Bakhtin is intended as no substitute for reading his careful detail. One way of summarizing his point and hinting at its richness it to suggest that the episode involving Mephibosheth in 2 Sam 9 is coherent from a variety of angles. For example, it catches a trajectory about the fate of "dynastic sons." The vector starts at 1 Sam 2:27–36, describing the fate of the last of Eli's house, who is prophetically portrayed by the nameless man of God to end his life prostrate, petitioning for food and position. The arc culminates with a refer-ence at 2 Kgs 25:29 to Jehoiachin, the last of David's crowned sons, reduced to a similar position. In the midst of this long path stands Mephibosheth, last of his line, also rendered a petitioner at another man's table.

A similar transversal extends the theme of David's commit-ment to the heirs of Jonathan (and Saul). We hear that topic raised in 1 Sam 19:14–17 and 20:42. But prior to David's insistent ques-tions of concern for Saulide scions, which open 2 Sam 9, we see the house of Saul diminish by four on Mount Gilboa (1 Sam 31) and watch the last son murdered in his bed (2 Sam 4). So, espe-cially with our insight (developed by Polzin) that David's com-plicity in the death of Saul is not easily dismissed from our minds, we may find David late or suspect when he inquires if there can yet be someone left of the house of Saul (2 Sam 9:1–4). We, read-ing, have already learned of the young man Mephibosheth in 2 Sam 4:4 (after the death of Ishbosheth), and we will watch David on three other occasions reduce safety for the Saulides: 2 Sam 16;

19; 21.[24] The point made visible and effective at the place where such lines cross is that Mephibosheth's position at the center of several narrative arrangements is far from haphazard; by disentangling the patterns we can see more deeply into the story of dynastic sons.

Twelfth, the last technique I wish to highlight from Polzin's study of 2 Samuel is actually one of which he speaks frequently in both studies on the books of Samuel, which Bakhtin did not name explicitly: the *mise en abyme*. Since I commented on the concept when using it myself to read the story of Saul, there is no need to repeat theory here. Polzin's developed illustration, however, is important to draw out. The concept is utterly dialogical, called by Polzin the "play-within-the-play." A *mise en abyme* is an authorial move that repositions certain elements frequently and pointedly enough so that they provide readerly cues as to thematic relationships among elements that might otherwise seem unlinked (or unlinkable).[25] The specific point he offers here, which is not easy to follow but worth the effort, illustrates the strategy well.

An abstract statement of it would be that a certain dynamic visible among the characters refracts the relationship between the author and presumed authorial audience (and all readers). Specifically here, Polzin argues that the nested representation in the narrative world functions as a narrator's cue to an exilic audience about the monarchic traditions. Thus Joab's conversation with David about Abner and the concomitant reaction of all Israel

---

[24] It is a truism to note that 2 Sam 21-24 do not fit tightly into the plan of the book where they occur. In one way, that is correct; chronologically they are not clearly articulated to their matrix. But in other ways, as Polzin notes, they fit well. The relevant episode here is that, when others endanger the survivors of Saul, David acts tardily to protect them (1993, 99–101). He develops a related point about the particular language of "serve/worship" and "make obeisance" that appear throughout the narrative and cluster in the material involving Mephibosheth, suggesting that obeisance (9:1–3) to a monarch partakes in the sort of idolatry that begins to be sketched as Israel chooses a king (1 Sam 8:8).

[25] Polzin discusses this item in *David* (1993, 37–47), stating that a text like the present one (he is talking specifically of 2 Sam 1–2 but constantly references the wider Saul-David narrative as well) is called "readerly," since it makes its pointing so overt and obvious.

(2 Sam 3) is both a miniaturized model of the storyline of which it is a part and also recapitulates something in the diegetic world. The context for the chapter (and the key verses) is the fratricidal struggle between the house of Saul and that of David, where the strength is shifting inexorably toward David. As that trend becomes clear, Saul's former henchman Abner approaches David with what seems to be the makings of a deal, to which David responds with conditions of his own. David's lieutenant Joab, absent from the scene for the Abnerian overture, cautions David about it, interpreting that Abner, ostensibly offering negotiation, is actually seeking to discern the nature of David's comings and goings, which comprise all of David's plans, thoughts, motives, and so forth.

What I understand Polzin to be offering here is a series of readers reading: Joab reads Abner reading David, but the narrator also draws Joab reading Abner reading David but misses David reading Abner, which is (as before) left to the reader. The narrator also sketches "the people" reading David by the episode's end. Readers, who of course are complex multiple, may briefly be swept into two piles here: the presumed exilic audience of the Deuteronomist and any of us with text in hand. Polzin draws our eye most specifically to 3:25 and 3:36–37 so we can participate in this "nested play."

He reminds us that the big question is who (in this chapter which is permeated with "an air of seduction") is successfully deceiving whom. The language of representation is hybrid (in Bakhtin's sense), concerned with the "comings and goings" of all—a motif that occurs forty-two times in 2 Sam 3, Polzin counts. That expression, used for what Joab says Abner is trying to discern when dealing with David, includes David's plans, thoughts, and motivations, specifically but not exclusively to bring Israel and Judah together under his rule. Joab, speaking in 3:25, by stressing what David "knows," actually implies pretty clearly that he does *not* know of Abner's deceit, has not recognized it prior to Joab's returning to point it out.

Polzin's interest is in our seeing how the scene has been constructed (or can be construed). He suggests that David, as always, is rendered by the narrator in such a way that we get no clear inside view. (Polzin does not comment on Joab's characterization much here.) Abner, Polzin senses, emerges from the

hands of the Deuteronomic author an undecidable character, difficult to get a grip on, enigmatic, artificial, nonmimetic, stylized,
and difficult to read as a "self." Hence Joab's abrupt about-face
(from Saul's side to David's) is difficult to account for satisfacto-
rily.[26] Abner dies of his effort to read correctly, and the
Deuteronomist takes some pains to exonerate David from
responsibility for that particular death. And as the chapter concludes, the narrator summarizes (3:36–37) that the people
approve David and accept as genuine his expression of angry
sorrow at the death of Abner and are pleased with it, as with all
of David's actions.

Polzin's insight here, not unlinked to others he has offered
elsewhere, is that the narrator's summary, though ostensibly clear,
is doubly intonated with an uncritical appraisal by the people—
reading this action of David in line with all their previous and
habitual evaluations—and with narratorial disapproval of their
naive knowing, borrowed from Joab's ironic "you know" in 3:26,
which underlines that the one to whom he addresses that expression does not know at all.

Two other links are made here, if I am reading accurately.
Polzin says, "Joab's characterization of Abner is a perfect description for the reader, who constantly desires to find out what David
is doing and what are his comings and goings, so as to understand
why all his enemies are being so conveniently and violently
removed from his path as he approaches the throne of Israel"
(1993, 39). Abner dies of poor reading—whether his primary
errors were in the text of David or Joab is not engaged by Polzin
or explicitly by the narrator. That David is a powerful persuader is
not difficult to see, so David may be deceiving Abner as much as
Abner is deceiving David. The peoples' reading, Abner-like, hints
at being similarly lethal.

That David is innocent of one particular killing is far from
being the whole issue in the matter of the violence of monarchy,
of dynastic sons. The risk of taking royal deeds uncritically, of

---

[26] Abner's artificiality is heightened as the narrator uses him to report
the words of YHWH to David regarding power given to David (2 Sam
3:10, 18). Why is such a character a mouthpiece for the deity? Besides
quoting God, Abner also asks a good question in 2:26, one that is central
to the Deuteronomist.

evaluating them as before, is a warning Polzin hears emerging from the authorial Deuteronomist, who grates together these two voices to unmask certain assertions, as we have seen on numerous occasions before. And perhaps from a slightly wider point of view, the skilled composition serves as a cue to all readers to parse the voices and not buy readily into a nonreaderly appropriation of biblical text. Polzin's work with these and other narratives, though sketchy (especially toward the end of 2 Sam) as is inevitable for several reasons, shows not only a grasp of Bakhtin's thought but a capacity to integrate it, to synthesize it and use it skillfully. He is, in my view, the mentor of others aiming to work with Bakhtin.

The diverse work of the four scholars here, plus my efforts in chapter 3, as well as the efforts of several others at work in the Bakhtin and biblical canons, testifies to the possibilities available from joining the Russian's thought with biblical text.

Conclusion
Where Can We Go with Bakhtin?

"The demands of the industry—the desire for a *Bakhtin* between two covers—need not undermine a sense of the diversity of his thinking as long as that sense is not presented as somehow completing (or 'consummating' as Bakhtin implies) the given author."

Peter Hitchcock, "The Bakhtin Centre"

After these many words, it is time to come to a close, if surely not to finalize. This last chapter represents both a distillation of explicit positions taken and some more intuitive reflections. In every case, they represent points for testing and further conversation both by biblical and Bakhtin scholars in other fields. I will limit myself to five points.

First, my conscious motive when starting this work was to provide a useful point of entry for other scholars, to provide the "article" I myself had missed when struggling (lazily) to appropriate Bakhtin's insights. What I learned, of course, is that I needed to do this work for myself and so have more modest and realistic confidence in its value for others. As has been asserted above in several ways, the thought of one person does not come prefabricated and ready-made for the projects of another. Each of us must struggle for her or his own understanding. I have on occasion presented my work on Bakhtin for students interested and eager to make headway; yet there is always a discernible change of gears, an intensification of their energy, when they realize that—if sufficiently interested—they must do it for themselves and set my "architectonics" aside.

Similarly, after reading Ruth Coates, I feel the need to revise my own constellation of points radically before trying to use Bakhtin again. I suspect this experience of needing to rethink is related to my pleasure in re-reading Robert Polzin's works and understanding them afresh, also to my awe when reexamining Carol Newsom's papers and seeing how much more she has

packed in than I had first or formerly gotten. Happily, it is also verified when I rework with a biblical text I felt I had "done" well and
find that I have many new insights. I do not bring forth this point
to enlighten those who do not already sense it but as a validation
of an experience I suspect many have had repeatedly. I did not
make a "ritual" disclaimer that others are not to blame for the flaws
in my scholarship when I thanked those who helped me. The
study I have done since this book went into production leaves me
all too aware of some of its inadequacy.

Second, I puzzle over the amount of thought that, it would
now appear, Bakhtin got wrong. He seems not to have imagined
in any substantial way that his theories might be useful for Holy
Writ, whose nature was for him so qualitatively different from
other texts. He also cast into a wholly separate pile the Homeric
epics, as though they also could not be read in continuity with his
theories. He gives little evidence of sensing lyric poetry to be
amenable to such reading. And yet in all three cases, his instincts
have been proven untrue, his insights about language having over-
taken his apprehensions about these genres. Biblical text—
whether considered as Scripture or not—is vastly illuminated by
Bakhtin's ideas, as epic may be read fruitfully as well. I have heard
poetry rendered much more rich when the interplay of voices is
made audible, thanks to Bakhtin's insights.

Similarly, Bakhtin's work on the carnivalesque is under new
scrutiny, with some suspecting he may not have seen its roots
clearly enough. His neologisms cause many to stumble—some out
of irritation and frustration at being able to crack them, others
deceived by the ease with which they may be utilized piecemeal.
Bakhtin's work on the history of genres and on the relationship of
some pieces of literature to others has not lasted well, nor have
some of his points about historiography. Perhaps most embarrass-
ingly today, he seems utterly ignorant of the vast difference that
gender makes in the construction of reality, close though that
insight might have been for one alert as he was to shifts among
class, caste, and ethnic experience. Such a list!

And yet, as Elie Wiesel is fond of saying, and yet—Bakhtin's
influence is vast and powerful in the intellectual world of the late
modern and postmodernist world. His work has had no small
impact even in some of these fields he seems not to have thought
of much—or thought much of! Culture studies and intertextuality

theories benefit from the insight of dialogism; feminists can make fruitful use of his Galilean universe of voices. And the neologisms can provoke clarifying and controversial confrontations. His root insight about disciplined but ubiquitous relationality opens windows all over the house. The evidence is clear from the diversity of the "Bakhtin industry."

The more pressing question is the adequacy of our use of Bakhtin, not his shortcomings. As I brought this project near its completion, I ended up pondering the space between two texts: Hirschkop's *Mikhail Bakhtin: An Aesthetic for Democracy* (1999) stands in the tradition of Clark and Holquist (1984) and Morson and Emerson (1990) in its erudite reconsideration of the whole Bakhtin corpus (including many newly available pieces) and his life as well as in its highly competent consideration of Bakhtin's relevance in a new realm; and a discussion between Robert Barsky and Michael Holquist (1990) that serves as a preface to a collection of significantly diverse essays on Bakhtin's applicability in many places. Barsky and Holquist discuss the question of valid and valuable readings of Bakhtin, leaving spacious borders for that project; it is possible to envision Hirschkop joining their conversation with a much different view of what is needed and legitimate in Bakhtin studies (1999, vii–x). As Bakhtin studies mature, there will be less scholarship to introduce his work, apply his ideas to new realms, and critique various elements of his theory; what is likely to emerge more strongly is work making more clear the sociohistorical and intellectual contexts that produced Bakhtin, a place in which I see relatively little room for nonexperts. Those of us continuing to utilize his thought for the fresh reading of familiar texts need to stay in active relationship to the field of Bakhtin studies as it grows in various ways if our reliance on Bakhtin is to remain responsible.

Third, in the course that was my "second Bakhtin Circle," a little revolt erupted sometime around the third week of the semester. There had been enough reading of theory, not to say utilization of it on texts, for one of the biblical studies doctoral students (joined by her two peers) to announce that *she* had no need for a theorist to do everything, to provide for *her* "the method." It was, and is, a good comment. And it gave me a new question and a fresh insight into myself.

The student who made the claim was nearing the end of her first year in a doctoral program and, by her own admission, had virtually no biblical exposure before coming to seminary to work on her Master of Divinity degree (which was a fresh acquisition). I, on the other hand, having become dubious about the still primarily historical-critical and theological methods of my own early graduate studies (which occurred in the 1970s), had veered off that path into the broader humanities and arts, where I have been happily struggling ever since. Part of the reason Bakhtin appeals to me is that, though there is nothing neat or closed about his thought, all the track is of the same gauge. After thirty years of bumping along within many systems, hopping on and off trains with all my belongings too often, I may not "need" but surely appreciate a coherent "system." It is open enough to allow for all the complexity I can cope with but does not seem prone to dead ends.

Apropos of coherence, I must also be honest enough to admit that it matters to me what kind of a human being Bakhtin was. I have no need for a guru or a saint, but I want to learn from someone whose life tested his or her ideas and whose wisdom is refracted from familiarity with the key human struggles that populate literature and life. But here I was instructed again by the comment of another.

I was eating lunch in a pub with premier Bakhtin scholar David Shepherd, who was courteously asking me about my other academic interests, having finished his comments on my Bakhtin work. That prior critique had included a caveat lest I take some of the more hagiographical biographical assertions about Bakhtin too seriously (notably, the "survivor" business). I was explaining to him a point expressed earlier in this work, that I was eager to offer sophisticated readers alternatives to literalistic biblical interpretation. As we were discussing further the benefit I thought Bakhtin could afford biblical studies, one of my points was that biblical studies had, in my view, relied too much on a sort of hidden fundamentalism where most things were assumed to be factually true. I clarified that I was not talking about rank fundamentalism but something vaguely akin to it, where the root presumption is that if not true, not important. That equation did not, I argued, always appear visibly or to be urged explicitly, and yet it was usually the default position. Bakhtin, I claimed, was an alternative to such grounding.

Shepherd perceptively circled back with me: "That was my point about hagiography," he said gently. Bakhtin need not be quite such a saint (as painted in some of the biographical material) for his thoughts to be helpful. Good point. Hirschkop (1999, ch. 3 and passim) draws detailed attention to the fictionalized biography Bakhtin seems to have enjoyed while also stressing Bakhtin's vastly inadequate presentation of the many scholars on whom his work heavily relies. I am reminded of recent scoldings of Martin Luther King Jr. for his youthful plagiarisms (if that is the word) as well as for some of his other failings. In view of the much larger ethical projects, such critique seems petty—not wrong, but disproportionate. And yet, it continues to help me to see Bakhtin's theory grounded somewhat in his life. One's life and lifework can be fruitfully linked. The struggles with "the other" are, I think, the primary moral challenge for human beings. To choose a similar example: Nelson Mandela writes well on the practice of nonviolence, but his ideas gain strength from the fact that somehow he emerged from prison after twenty-nine years and acted with strong compassion and generosity rather than with retaliation. Similarly, that Bakhtin can produce optimistic material about human interrelatedness amid the most dire of personal and social circumstances is bracing for me.

Fourth, to study and work with Bakhtin provides a tremendous boost for the interdisciplinary and collaborative study that seems likely to characterize the next phase of academic life. If, as suggested earlier, one of the key challenges for biblical studies is to coordinate much better the integration of historical and literary methods and data, then I suspect that less and less can individuals working alone manage the project. As information becomes available from and for so many more sectors, not to mention when the idea of mastering or controlling knowledge fades as a goal, scholars will have to work collaboratively and will presumably find it exhilarating in ways that solitary work—for all its joys—is not. More minds, more situated selves, will make for richer insight and better syntheses, I think.

It is already my experience that courses using Bakhtin can broaden and instruct the interests of biblical students by engaging new questions and novel fields of study through the common language of this theorist. That is a gain, in my view, for everyone. My early work with Bakhtin has revealed how many different facets of human learning are working with his thought; in fact, the students with whom I have enjoyed reading Bakhtin are working on projects as diverse as (North) American westerns and Polish poetry. The more biblically based projects include the hymns of the book of Revelation, the art generated from Gen 22, and the likely circumstances constructing the accounts of the death of Josiah. When I move to work with the rest of the story of Saul, how will I engage the question of origins of Israel, the impact of a change in the modes of production, questions of historiography, implications of reading with the genre constraints of parable, the subtleties in the presentation of such an antihero as Saul without massive help from others, without genuine collaboration?

Related to that point is the range of method and insight exposed in the fourth chapter of this book, with the work of simply four Hebrew Bible scholars rather cursorily examined. That these scholars are working in different ways from each other and that each has changed considerably between the first and second attempts to use Bakhtin is instructive. As Craig and Pardes explore the carnival genre, as Newsom works in theory, history, and with the voices in Isaiah and in Job, as Polzin works with the angled speakers in narrative, there still remains much more to do. Other Old Testament scholars working explicitly with Bakhtin include Judith Fentress-Williams (1 Samuel), Karen Gale (Genesis), Francisco Garcia-Treto (1 Kings, Amos), Harold Fisch, Herbert Levine, and Carleen Mandolfo (Psalms), Hugh Pyper (DH), Nanette Stahl (law), Seth Sykes (Haggai and Zechariah), Hugh White (Genesis), and Patricia Tull Willey (Isaiah). New Testament scholars who allude to Bakhtin when discussing the gospels are Paul Anderson and David McCracken. I look forward to hearing of others.

The question remains: At what level and with how much scope will Bakhtin be useful? Barsky and Holquist (1990, 4–5, 12–14) sort the use of Bakhtin to read Emily Dickinson's poetry and lament the absence in their volume of much interest in Bakhtin and religion. While maintaining that there is a place for an essay on Bakhtin and Dickinson, Holquist suggests that the Russian's thought is probably best characterized as providing a skeleton key for opening the door to a set of conclusions that would otherwise have remained closed. "What is important," Holquist remarks, "is not that this author is using Bakhtin, but that this author has somehow perceived something in Bakhtin that has let her do what is not ordinarily done in Dickinsonian scholarship" (1990, 5). It is my sense that Bakhtin is more than a skeleton key for biblical studies, but that the Russian Orthodox Christianity that embeds his thought will in fact remain off limits to most of us. Felch and Contino provide some fresh access to Bakhtin and religion in general.

Fifth and finally, I think that to work creatively with this set of seminal insights from Bakhtin can change the way in which we read the Bible and consequently the way the Bible is read, which has the potential to alter the way Scripture is understood. Without implying that he is the only theorist to offer new optics, let me simply speak of him here. If language works as Bakhtin says that it does, any reading that is totalitarian, absolute, or fundamentalistic in any sense is on the ropes. When any of us is looking for what is reliable, life-giving, and faithful to tradition, it will not be via the path of literalism, however well-disguised that feature be.

It matters who is reading. A responsible reader will need to sign her interpretation with her life in some way. This supposition is far from implying that only "believers" can appropriate biblical narrative, but it does assert that the particular choices we make as readers and when reading must be seen as part of what we produce. To make such a claim is not to say that it will be relativistic, that any "answer" will be able to be generated out of any text or for any problem—far from it. But reading will be vastly different than has been much reading of at least the Old Testament to date. Reading unfolds in relation to circumstances of production and reception; readers will be increasingly aware of selecting certain paths and thereby deferring many others. The notion of "the message" and ways of narrowing down to "the meaning" will diminish. Readers will become more explicit about protocols with which we are reading and about situations that give rise to insight.

Similarly, to decenter the narrator with all of the attendant claims about God—in fact to assist God to join a full chorus of polyphonic and other voices—will change the sound of the music. Terrible statements—statements of dread—about God are not infrequent in the Bible, and there are alternatives to the many dominating readings of these that we have done. To speak in many ways of the rich experience of being human, with each other, as we struggle simultaneously with the wonderful challenge of talking about God, calls for all the creativity we can muster. Bakhtin can well help us to get to where so many of us may want to go.

Bibliography

Adlam, Carol. 1997. Ethics of Difference: Bakhtin's Early Writings and Feminist Theories. Pages 142–59 in *Face to Face: Bakhtin in Russia and the West*. Edited by C. Adlam et al. Sheffield: Sheffield Academic Press.

Alter, Robert. 1981. *The Art of Biblical Narrative*. New York: Basic Books.

Amit, Yairah. 1992. "The Glory of Israel Does Not Deceive or Change His Mind": On the Reliability of Narrator and Speakers in Biblical Narrative. *Prooftexts* 12:201–12.

Anderson, Paul N. 1996. *The Christology of the Fourth Gospel: Its Unity and Disunity in the Light of John 6*. Tübingen: J. C. B. Mohr.

Bach, Alice. 1997. *Women, Seduction, and Betrayal in Biblical Narrative*. Cambridge: Cambridge University Press.

Bagby, Lewis. 1982. Mikhail Bakhtin's Discourse Typologies: Theoretical and Practical Considerations. *Slavic Review* 41:35–58.

Bakhtin, Mikhail. 1973 (1929). *Marxism and the Philosophy of Language*. With V. N. Voloshinov. Translated by L. Matejka and I. R. Titunik. Cambridge: Harvard University Press.

———. 1976 (1929). *Freudianism: A Marxist Critique*. With V. N. Voloshinov. Translated by I. R. Titunik. New York: Academic Press.

———. 1978 (1928). *The Formal Method in Literary Scholarship: A Critical Introduction to Sociological Poetics*. With P. N. Medvedev. Translated by A. J. Wehrle. Baltimore: Johns Hopkins University Press.

———. 1981. *The Dialogic Imagination: Four Essays*. Edited by M. Holquist. Translated by C. Emerson and M. Holquist. Austin: University of Texas Press, 1981.

———. 1984 (1929, 1963). *Problems of Dostoevsky's Poetics*. Edited and translated by C. Emerson. Minneapolis: University of Minnesota Press.

———. 1984 (1940). *Rabelais and His World*. Translated by H. Iswolsky. Bloomington: Indiana University Press.

———. 1986. *Speech Genres and Other Late Essays*. Edited by C. Emerson and M. Holquist. Translated by V. W. McGee. Austin: University of Texas Press.

———. 1990. *Art and Answerability: Early Philosophical Essays by M. M. Bakhtin*. Edited by M. Holquist and V. Liapunov. Translation and notes by V. Liapunov; supplement translated by K. Brostrom. Austin: University of Texas Press.

———. 1993 (1920). *Toward a Philosophy of the Act*. Edited by V. Liapunov and M. Holquist. Translation and notes by V. Liapunov. Austin: University of Texas Press.

Bauer, Dale M., and Susan Jaret McKinstry, eds. 1991. *Feminism, Bakhtin, and the Dialogic*. Albany: State University of New York.

Berlin, Adele. 1983. *Poetics and Interpretation of Biblical Narrative*. Sheffield: Almond Press.

Bezeczky, Gabor. 1994. Contending Voices in Bakhtin. *Comparative Literature* 46:321–45.

Bialostosky, Don. 1983. Bakhtin Versus Chatman on Narrative: The Habilitation of the Hero. *Revue de l'Université d'Ottawa/ University of Ottawa Quarterly* 53:109–16.

Bocharov, Sergey. 1994. Conversations with Bakhtin. Translated by V. Liapunov and S. Blackwell. Introduction by V. Liapunov. *Publications of the Modern Language Association of America* 109:1009–24.

Bonetskaia, Natal'ia. 1998. Bakhtin's Aesthetics as a Logic of Form. Pages 83–94 in *The Contexts of Bakhtin: Philosophy, Authorship, Aesthetics*. Edited by D. Shepherd. Amsterdam: Harwood.

Bové, Carol M. 1983. The Text As Dialogue in Bakhtin and Kristeva. *Revue de l'Université d'Ottawa/University of Ottawa Quarterly* 53:117–24.

Brueggemann, Walter. 1990. Sport of Nature. *Cumberland Seminarian* 28:9–25.

———. 1993. Narrative Coherence and Theological Intentionality in 1 Samuel 18. *Catholic Biblical Quarterly* 55:225–43.

Burkitt, Ian. 1998. The Death and Rebirth of the Author: The Bakhtin Circle and Bourdieu on Individuality, Language and Revolution. Pages 163–80 in *Bakhtin and the Human Sciences: No Last Words.* Edited by M. M. Bell and M. Gardiner. London: Sage.

Campbell, Antony R. 1989. The Reported Story: Midway between Oral Performance and Literary Art. *Semeia* 46:77–85.

Cartwright, Michael G. 1992. The Uses of Scripture in Christian Ethics—After Bakhtin. *The Annual of the Society of Christian Ethics* 263–76.

Cavanagh, Clare. 1993. Pseudo-revolution in Poetic Language: Julia Kristeva and the Russian Avant-garde. *Slavic Review* 52:283–97.

Clark, Katerina, and Michael Holquist. 1984. *Mikhail Bakhtin.* Cambridge: Harvard University Press.

Coates, Ruth. 1998. *Christianity in Bakhtin: God and the Exiled Author.* Cambridge: Cambridge University Press.

Coats, George W. 1970. Self-Abasement and Insult Formulas. *Journal of Biblical Literature* 89:14–26.

Craig, Kenneth M., Jr. 1993. *A Poetics of Jonah: Art in the Service of Ideology.* Columbia: University of South Carolina Press.

———. 1994. Rhetorical Aspects of Questions Answered with Silence in 1 Samuel 14:37 and 28:6. *Catholic Biblical Quarterly* 56:221–39.

———. 1995. *Reading Esther: A Case for the Literary Carnivalesque.* Louisville: Westminster John Knox.

Crawford, Robert. 1994. *Identifying Poets: Self and Territory in Twentieth-Century Poetry.* Edinburgh: University of Edinburgh Press.

Dällenbach, Lucien. 1989. *The Mirror in the Text*. Translated by J. Whiteley, with E. Hughes. Cambridge: Polity.

Danow, D. K. 1991. *The Thought of Mikhail Bakhtin: From Word to Culture*. New York: St. Martin's.

Diaz-Diocaretz, Myriam. 1989. Bakhtin, Discourse, and Feminist Ethics. *Critical Studies* 1:121–39.

Edelman, Diana V. 1991. *King Saul in the Historiography of Judah*. Sheffield: Sheffield Academic Press.

————. 1996. Saul ben Kish in History and Tradition. Pages 142–59 in *The Origins of the Ancient Israelite State*. Edited by V. Fritz and P. R. Davies. Sheffield: Sheffield Academic Press.

Emerson, Caryl. 1983. Translating Bakhtin: Does His Theory of Discourse Contain a Theory of Translation? *Revue de l'Université d'Ottawa/University of Ottawa Quarterly* 53:23–33.

————. 1988 Problems with Baxtin's Poetics. *Slavic and East European Journal* 32:503–25.

————. 1990. Russian Orthodoxy and the Early Bakhtin. *Religion and Literature* 22:109–31.

————. 1995. Introduction: Dialogue on Every Corner, Bakhtin in Every Class. Pages 1–30, 191–95 in *Bakhtin in Contexts: Across Disciplines*. Edited by A. Mandelker. Evanston, Ill.: Northwestern University Press.

————. 1996. Keeping the Self Intact During the Culture Wars: A Centennial Essay for Mikhail Bakhtin. *New Literary History* 27:107–26.

————. 1997. *The First Hundred Years of Mikhail Bakhtin*. Princeton: Princeton University Press.

Erdinast-Vulcan, Daphna. 1997. Borderlines and Contraband: Bakhtin on the Question of Subject. *Poetics Today* 18:251–69.

Exum, J. Cheryl. 1992. *Tragedy and Biblical Narrative: Arrows of the Almighty*. Cambridge: Cambridge University Press.

————. 1993. *Fragmented Women: Feminist (Sub)versions of Biblical Narratives*. Sheffield: Sheffield Academic Press.

Falconer, Rachel. 1997a. Introduction. Pages 23–41 in *Face to Face: Bakhtin in Russia and the West*. Edited by C. Adlam et al. Sheffield: Sheffield Academic Press.

———. 1997b. Bakhtin and the Epic Chronotope. Pages 254–72 in *Face to Face: Bakhtin in Russia and the West*. Edited by C. Adlam et al. Sheffield: Sheffield Academic Press.

Felch, Susan, and Paul J. Contino, eds. Forthcoming. *Bakhtin and Religion: A Feeling for Faith*. Evanston, Ill.: Northwestern University Press.

Felson-Rubin, Nancy. 1993. Bakhtinian Alterity, Homeric Rapport. *Arethusa* 26:159–70.

Fentress-Williams, Judith. 1999. "What Has Happened to the Son of Kish?" A Dialogic Reading of the Saul Narrative in 1 Samuel. Ph.D. dissertation. Yale University.

Fewell, Danna Nolan, and David M. Gunn. 1993. *Gender, Power, and Promise: The Subject of the Bible's First Story*. Nashville: Abingdon.

Fisch, Harold. 1988. *Poetry with a Purpose: Biblical Poetics and Interpretation*. Bloomington: Indiana University Press.

———. 1998. *New Stories for Old: Biblical Patterns in the Novel*. New York: St. Martin's.

Fokkelman, Jan P. 1986. *Narrative Art and Poetry in the Books of Samuel. Vol. 2: The Crossing Fates*. Assen: Van Gorcum.

Frank, Joseph. 1990. *Through the Russian Prism: Essays on Literature and Culture*. Princeton: Princeton University Press.

Freise, Matthias. 1997. After the Expulsion of the Author: Bakhtin As an Answer to Poststructuralism. Pages 131–41 in *Face to Face: Bakhtin in Russia and the West*. Edited by C. Adlam et al. Sheffield: Sheffield Academic Press.

Gale, Karen. 1998 "Pursuing Polyphony: Tracing Character Construction(s) in Genesis 29-35 and 'The Handmaid's Tale.'" Master's Thesis, Graduate Theological Union.

Garcia-Treto, Francisco O. 1992. The Fall of the House: A Carnivalesque Reading of 2 Kings 9 and 10. Pages 153-71 in

Reading between Texts: Intertextuality and the Hebrew Bible.
Edited by D. N. Fewell. Louisville: Westminster John Knox.

—————. 1993. A Reader-Response Approach to Prophetic Conflict:
The Case of Amos 7:7-10. Pages 114–24 in *The New Literary
Criticism and the Hebrew Bible.* Edited by J. C. Exum and
D. J. A. Clines. Valley Forge: Trinity.

Gardiner, Michael. 1992. *The Dialogics of Critique: M. M. Bakhtin
and the Theory of Ideology.* London: Routledge.

Garsiel, Moshe. 1985. *The First Book of Samuel: A Literary Study of
Comparative Structures, Analogies and Parallels.* Jerusalem:
Revivim.

Green, Barbara. 1996. *"What Profit for Us?" Remembering the Joseph
Story.* Lanham, Md.: University Press of America.

Halley, Jeffrey A. 1989. Bakhtin and the Sociology of Culture:
Polyphony in the Interaction of Object and Audience. *Critical
Studies* 1:163–79.

Haynes, Deborah J. 1995. *Bakhtin and the Visual Arts.* Cambridge:
Cambridge University Press.

Hirschkop, Ken. 1989. Dialogism As a Challenge to Literary
Criticism. Pages 19–35 in *Discontinuous Discourses in Modern
Russian Literature.* Edited by C. Kelly, M. Makin and D.
Shepherd. London: Macmillan.

—————. 1990. Heteroglossia and Civil Society: Bakhtin's Public
Square and the Politics of Modernity. *Studies in the Literary
Imagination* 23:65–75.

—————. 1998a. Bakhtin Myths, or Why We All Need Alibis. *South
Atlantic Quarterly* 97:579–99.

—————. 1998b. Is Dialogism for Real? Pages 183–95 in *The Contexts
of Bakhtin: Philosophy, Authorship, Aesthetics.* Edited by D.
Shepherd. Amsterdam: Harwood.

—————. 1999. *Mikhail Bakhtin: An Aesthetic for Democracy.*
Oxford: Oxford University Press.

Hitchcock, Peter. 1991. Exotopy and Feminist Critique. *Critical
Studies* 3–4:196–209.

————. 1993. *Dialogics of the Oppressed*. Minneapolis: University of Minnesota Press.

————. 1998. The Bakhtin Centre and the State of the Archive: An Interview with David Shepherd. *South Atlantic Quarterly* 97:753–72.

Hohne, Karen, and Wussow, Helen, eds. 1994. *A Dialogue of Voices: Feminist Literary Theory and Bakhtin*. Minnesota: University of Minnesota Press.

Holquist, Michael. 1981. The Politics of Representation. Pages 163–83 in *Allegory and Representation*. Edited by S. J. Greenblatt. Baltimore: Johns Hopkins University Press.

————. 1984. Introduction. *Studies in Twentieth Century Literature* 9:7–12.

————. 1989. Bakhtin and the Body. *Critical Studies* 1:19–42.

————. 1990. *Dialogism: Bakhtin and His World*. London: Routledge.

Jobling, David. 1998. *1 Samuel*. Collegeville, Minn.: Michael Glazier/ Liturgical.

Kehde, Suzanne. 1991. Voices from the Margin: Bag Ladies and Others. Pages 25–38 in *Feminism, Bakhtin and the Dialogic*. Edited by D. M. Bauer and S. J. McKinstry. Albany: State University of New York.

Klein, Ralph W. 1983. *1 Samuel*. Waco, Tex.: Word Books.

Lähteenmäki, Mika. 1998. On Meaning and Understanding: A Dialogical Approach. *Dialogism* 1:74–91.

Levine, Herbert. 1992. The Dialogic Discourse of Psalms. Pages 145–61 in *Hermeneutics, the Bible and Literary Criticism*. Edited by A. Loades and M. McLain. New York: St. Martin's.

Lodge, David. 1990. *After Bakhtin: Essays on Fiction and Criticism*. London: Routledge.

Makhlin, Vitalii. 1997. Face to Face: Bakhtin's Programme and the Architectonics of Being-as-Event in the Twentieth Century. Pages 45–53 in *Face to Face: Bakhtin in Russia and the West*. Edited by C. Adlam et al. Sheffield: Sheffield Academic Press.

Mandolfo, Carleen. 2000. The Dialogue between Faith and Experience. The Didactic Voice in Psalms of Lament. Ph.D. dissertation. Emory University.

McCarter, P. Kyle. 1980. *1 Samuel: A New Translation with Introduction and Commentary.* Garden City, N.Y.: Doubleday.

McCracken, David. 1993. Character in the Boundary: Bakhtin's Interdividuality in Biblical Narratives. *Semeia* 63:29–42.

————. 1994. *The Scandal of the Gospels: Jesus, Story, and Offense.* New York: Oxford University Press.

Mihailovic, Alexandar. 1997. *Corporeal Words: Mikhail Bakhtin's Theology of Discourse.* Evanston, Ill.: Northwestern University Press.

Miller, Cynthia. 1996. *The Representation of Speech in Biblical Hebrew Narrative: A Linguistic Analysis.* Atlanta: Scholars Press.

Miscall, Peter D. 1983. *The Workings of Old Testament Narrative.* Philadelphia: Fortress.

————. 1986. *1 Samuel: A Literary Reading.* Bloomington: Indiana University Press.

Morson, Gary Saul. 1986. The Baxtin Industry. *Slavic and East European Journal* 30:81–90.

————. 1991. Bakhtin and the Present Moment. *American Scholar* 60:201–22.

————. 1995. Prosaic Bakhtin: *Landmarks,* Anti-Intelligentialism, and the Russian Countertradition. Pages 33–78, 195–99 in *Bakhtin in Contexts: Across Disciplines.* Edited by A. Mandelker. Evanston, Ill.: Northwestern University Press.

Morson, Gary Saul, and Caryl Emerson. 1990. *Mikhail Bakhtin: Creation of a Prosaics.* Stanford: Stanford University Press.

Nielsen, Gregory. 1998. The Norms of Answerability: Bakhtin and the Fourth Postulate. Pages 214–30 in *Bakhtin and the Human Sciences: No Last Words.* Edited by M. M. Bell and M. Gardiner. London: Sage.

Newsom, Carol. 1992. Response to Norman K. Gottwald, "Social Class and Ideology in Isaiah 40-55." *Semeia* 59:73–78.

———. 1996a. The Book of Job As a Polyphonic Text. Paper presented at the Society for the Study of the Old Testament. Birmingham. January 3.

———. 1996b. Bakhtin, the Bible, and Dialogic Truth. *Journal of Religion* 76:290–306.

O'Connor, Mary. 1993. Horror, Authors, and Heroes: Gendered Subjects and Objects in Bakhtin and Kristeva. *Critical Studies* 3–4:242–58.

O'Connor, Michael. 1995. War and Rebel Chants in the Former Prophets. Pages 322–37 in *Fortunate the Eyes That See: Essays in Honor of David Noel Freedman in Celebration of His Seventieth Birthday*. Edited by A. B. Beck et al. Grand Rapids: Eerdmans.

Palmieri, Giovanni. 1998. "The Author" according to Bakhtin … and Bakhtin the Author. Pages 45–56 in *The Contexts of Bakhtin: Philosophy Authorship, Aesthetics*. Edited by D. Shepherd. Amsterdam: Harwood.

Pardes, Ilana. 1992. *Countertraditions in the Bible: A Feminist Approach*. Cambridge: Harvard University Press.

———. 1997. The Biography of Israel: Imagining the Birth of a Nation. *Comparative Literature* 49:24–41.

———. 2000. *The Biography of Ancient Israel: National Narratives in the Bible*. Berkeley: University of California Press.

Patterson, David. 1991. Bakhtin on Word and Spirit: The Religiosity of Responsibility. *Cross Currents* 41:33–51.

Pearce, Lynn. 1994. *Reading Dialogics*. London: Edward Arnold.

Perlina, Nina. 1983. Bakhtin-Medvedev-Voloshinov: An Apple of Discourse. *Revue de l'Université d'Ottawa/University of Ottawa Quarterly* 53:35–47.

Pleins, David J. 1992. Son-Slayers and Their Sons. Catholic Biblical Quarterly 54:29–38.

202   *Mikhail Bakhtin and Biblical Scholarship*

Pollock, Mary S. 1991. What is Left Out: Bakhtin, Feminism, and the Culture of Boundaries. *Critical Studies* 3–4:229–41.

Polzin, Robert. 1980. *Moses and the Deuteronomist: A Literary Study of the Deuteronomic History. Part 1: Deuteronomy, Joshua, Judges.* New York: Seabury.

―――. 1989. *Samuel and the Deuteronomist: A Literary Study of the Deuteronomic History. Part 2: 1 Samuel.* San Francisco: Harper & Row.

―――. 1993. *David and the Deuteronomist: A Literary Study of the Deuteronomic History. Part 3: 2 Samuel.* Bloomington: Indiana University Press.

Prickett, Stephen. 1986. *Words and The Word: Language, Poetics and Biblical Interpretation.* Cambridge: Cambridge University Press.

Pyper, Hugh. 1996. *David As Reader: 2 Samuel 12:1–15 and the Poetics of Fatherhood.* Leiden: E. J. Brill.

Reed, Walter. 1993. *Dialogues of the Word: The Bible As Literature according to Bakhtin.* New York: Oxford University Press.

Revell, E. J. 1996. *The Designation of the Individual: Expressive Usage in Biblical Narrative.* Kampen: Kok Pharos.

Rosenberg, Joel. 1986. *King and Kin: Political Allegory in the Hebrew Bible.* Bloomington: Indiana University Press.

Rutland, Barry. 1990. Bakhtinian Categories and the Discourse of Postmodernism. *Critical Studies* 2:123–36.

Ryklin, Mikhail. 1993. Bodies of Terror: Theses Toward a Logic of Violence. *New Literary History* 24:51–74.

Savran, George. 1988. *Telling and Retelling: Quotation in Biblical Narrative.* Bloomington: Indiana University Press.

Schneiders, Sandra M. 1991. *Beyond Patching: Faith and Feminism in the Catholic Church.* Mahwah, N.J.: Paulist.

―――. 1998. The Study of Christian Spirituality: Contours and Dynamics of a Discipline. *Christian Spirituality Bulletin* 6:1–12.

―――. 1999. *The Revelatory Text: Interpreting the New Testament As Scripture.* 2d ed. Collegeville, Minn.: Liturgical Press.

Scholz, Bernhard F. 1998. Bakhtin's Concept of "Chronotope": The Kantian Connection. Pages 141–72 in *The Contexts of Bakhtin: Philosophy, Authorship, Aesthetics*. Edited by D. Shepherd. Amsterdam: Harwood.

Shepherd, David. 1986. The Authority of Meanings and the Meanings of Authority: Some Problems in the Theory of Reading. *Poetics Today* 7:129–45.

———. 1989. Bakhtin and the Reader. Pages 91–108 in *Bakhtin and Cultural Theory*. Edited by K. Hirschkop and D. Shepherd. Manchester: Manchester University Press.

———. 1996. "Communicating with Other Worlds": Contrasting Views of Carnival in Recent Russian and Western Work on Bakhtin. *The Bakhtin Newsletter* 5:143–60.

Shumway, Suzanne. 1994. The Chronotope of the Asylum: *Jane Eyre*, Feminism, and Bakhtinian Theory. Pages 152–70 in *A Dialogue of Voices: Feminist Literary Theory and Bakhtin*. Edited by K. Hohne and H. Wussow. Minneapolis: University of Minnesota Press.

Smith, Wilfrid Cantwell. 1993. *What Is Scripture: A Comparative Approach*. Minneapolis: Fortress.

Stahl, Nanette. 1995. *Law and Liminality in the Bible*. Sheffield: Sheffield Academic Press.

Stam, Robert. 1989. *Subversive Pleasures: Bakhtin, Cultural Criticism, and Film*. Baltimore: Johns Hopkins University Press.

Stansell, Gary. 1996. Honor and Shame in the David Narratives. *Semeia* 68:55–79.

Steinglass, Matt. 1998. International Man of Mystery: The Battle over Mikhail Bakhtin. *Lingua Franca* 8:33–41.

Sternberg, Meir. 1985. *The Poetics of Biblical Narrative: Ideological Literature and the Drama of Reading*. Bloomington: Indiana University Press.

Stone, Ken. 1996. *Sex, Honor, and Power in the Deuteronomistic History*. Sheffield: Sheffield Academic Press.

Sykes, Seth. 1997. Time and Space in Haggai–Zechariah 1–8: A Bakhtinian Analysis of a Prophetic Chronicle. *Journal for the Study of the Old Testament* 76:97–124.

Thibault, Paul. 1984. Narrative Discourse As Multi-Level System of Communication: Some Theoretical Proposals Concerning Bakhtin's Dialogic Principle. *Studies in Twentieth Century Literature* 9:89–117.

Thomson, Clive. 1983. The Semiotics of M. M. Bakhtin. *Revue de l'Université d'Ottawa/University of Ottawa Quarterly* 53:11–21.

———. 1984. Bakhtin's "Theory" of Genre. *Studies in Twentieth Century Literature* 9:29–40.

Todorov, Tzvetan. 1984. *Mikhail Bakhtin: The Dialogical Principle*. Translated by W. Godzich. Minneapolis: University of Minnesota Press.

Ugolnik, Anthony. 1984. Tradition As Freedom from the Past: Eastern Orthodoxy and the Western Mind. *Journal of Ecumenical Studies* 21:278–94.

———. 1990. Textual Liturgics: Russian Orthodoxy and Recent Literary Criticism. *Religion and Literature* 22:133–54.

Venclova, Tomas 1998. The Pluralist. Review of Emerson, *The First Hundred Years of Mikhail Bakhtin*. *The New Republic* 218:25–32.

Vice, Sue. 1997a. Bakhtin and Kristeva: Grotesque Body, Abject Self. Pages 160–74 in *Face to Face: Bakhtin in Russia and the West*. Edited by C. Adlam et al. Sheffield: Sheffield Academic Press.

———. 1997b. *Introducing Bakhtin*. Manchester: Manchester University Press.

Wall, Anthony. 1984. Characters in Bakhtin's Theory. *Studies in Twentieth Century Literature* 9:41–56.

White, Allon. 1984. Bakhtin, Sociolinguistics and Deconstruction. Pages 123–46 in *The Theory of Reading*. Edited by F. Gloversmith. Sussex: Harvester.

White, Hugh C. 1991. *Narration and Discourse in the Book of Genesis*. Cambridge: Cambridge University Press.

Willey, Patricia Tull. 1997. *Remember the Former Things: The Recollection of Previous Texts in Second Isaiah*. Atlanta: Scholars Press.

Zavala, Iris M. 1988. Bakhtin Versus the Postmodern. *Sociocriticism* 4:51–69.

———. 1989. Bakhtin and the Third: Communication As Response. *Critical Studies* 1:43–63.

———. 1990. Bakhtin and Otherness: Social Heterogeneity. *Critical Studies* 2:77–89.